Healing Grief

Healing Grief

A Guide to Loss and Recovery

Barbara Ward

VERMILION
LONDON

First published in 1993 by Vermilion
an imprint of Ebury Press, Random House
20 Vauxhall Bridge Road, London SW1V 2SA

Reprinted 1994, 1995

Random House Australia (Pty) Limited
20 Alfred Street, Milsons Point, Sydney,
New South Wales 2061, Australia

Random House New Zealand Limited
18 Poland Road, Glenfield,
Auckland 10, New Zealand

Random House South Africa (Pty) Limited
PO Box 337, Bergvlei, South Africa

Random House UK Limited Reg. No. 954009

A CIP catalogue record for this book is available from the British Library

ISBN 0-09-177839-5

Set in Palatino by SX Composing Ltd, Rayleigh, Essex
Printed and bound in Great Britain by
Mackays of Chatham PLC, Chatham, Kent

For everyone who has experienced loss in their personal or professional life, and in memory of my husband John Hartley Ward, whose premature death in a car crash nine months after we were married initiated me into my stress management and 'Good Grief' work.

Acknowledgements

My thanks go to all the wonderful people who have made this book possible by their stories, expertise, and encouragement. This book could not have been written without them. Except where people have asked that their real names be used, I have changed all names of those whose stories are included here, so as to protect privacy.

I am grateful to Tessa Strickland, my commissioning editor, for giving me this opportunity to write about my life and work, which has enabled me to fill in more pieces of the jigsaw of my life, and has been a healing process in itself. Also to Jane Birdsell, for all the hard work that has put *Healing Grief* into its present form, and for thinking of the title (and to her mother, Lorna Birdsell, for being our guinea-pig reader). To Linda Shearer for her patience in typing and retyping my drafts.

I would like to thank all the people who have influenced and inspired me in the field of bereavement. Metropolitan Anthony Bloom, Dora Black, Colin Murray-Parkes and Michael Simpson were my earliest gurus. Many others have followed since and are mentioned either in the text, or in the list of recommended reading. Many clients and colleagues have generously shared their stories with me. Most of these contributors have asked to remain anonymous, so I won't single anyone out here. I hope I have thanked you all personally.

I am also indebted to all the magazines, newspapers and book publishers who have allowed me to quote excerpts. Organizations and individuals within them who have contributed their expertise and material include: BACUP; Cancer Link; The Compassionate Friends – Margaret Haywoth and Catherine Pointer and all of the members from different countries who've contributed their stories; CRUSE – Dora Black, Richard Lansdown, Pat Scowen, and Patrick Shannon of Northern Ireland CRUSE; Foundation for the Study of Infant Deaths; Helen House – Mother Frances Dominica; Kings Fund Centre for Health Service Development; National Association of Bereavement Services – Janet Haddington, Jane Warman; Mary Potter Hospice, Wellington, New Zealand – Wyn Merrick; Plymouth Reference Library; The Samaritans – Norman Keir; St Christopher's Hospice – Denise Brady; UK Families Flight 103 – Pam Dix.

Other individuals who have helped include Jim Kuykendall, clinical psychologist; Professor Caplan, Scientific Director of the Family Centre for the Study of Psychological Stress; Bill Yule, Professor of Applied Psychology at the University of London; Diana Whitmore with whom I trained in psychosynthesis, and who was my therapist; and Brentford and Isleworth Religious Society of Friends who started me on the bereavement path. Last, and not least, my friends and spiritual family for their love and support whilst writing. Many of them also contributed their stories: Chris Ayckbourn, Di Alkin, Sally Crosher, Jenny Cutcliffe, Barbara Dale, Willoughby Dampier, Maggie Dobson, Dr Uthe Ernst-Müth, Susan Jackson, Barbara, Karen and Stan Proffit, Robbie, and Rosemary Wells.

Namaskar to you all.

Contents

Introduction

Life is made of Joy and Woe
And once this we surely know
Forward through the World we go.
                    (William Blake, *Auguries of Innocence*)

This book is for everyone who, like me, has had to face loss and grief without any preparation or understanding of what was happening. You may have felt stunned and confused and sometimes unintentionally made things worse for yourself. Or perhaps you want to help a friend or relative who has suffered a serious loss. I have tried to write the sort of book that I would have liked to read years and years ago, and which would have enabled me to deal with the losses I experienced as a child and a young woman. I wish we were all taught as children about loss and how best to cope with it – instead, grief is still a taboo subject for most people.

My first encounter with death was sudden and unexpected. It left me in a state of shock for many months. I was twenty-three and my husband and I were driving home from our second honeymoon in Scotland. We had missed a turning and were driving along a busy road with miles of roadworks when a milk tanker skidded and went out of control. It crashed into our car and John was killed instantly. Many of my experiences around John's death I now recognize as textbook examples of how not to handle bereavement – I was left alone for eighteen hours after the accident; I never saw John's body; the vicar wouldn't allow me to include a poem John and I had loved in the service; my family and friends tried to keep me from being 'upset' by changing the subject when I tried to talk about what happened.

I soon discovered that tears were not acceptable: people

turned away or looked embarrassed. I learned to keep my tears, and therefore all my feelings, to myself, cutting out not only the painful memories but the good ones too. Neither I nor anyone around me understood that the feelings I was going through were normal, and that there were such things as 'stages of grief'.

I suppressed my real feelings so successfully from my awareness that it was eight years before I began to look at how loss had really affected me. I was telling a colleague in Education Welfare some of my story when she suddenly turned to me and said, 'How can you be so normal?' I was completely puzzled: until then, I had not thought of my life as being that different from other people's. A few years later a counsellor I was working with said to me, 'You know, you had a very deprived childhood.' This seemed to echo the earlier remark and unlocked the frozen memories not only of John's death but of all my earlier unacknowledged losses that had prefigured it. I realized I had been unconsciously submerging my pain for years in order to survive, and I gradually began to give myself permission to feel and release my old emotions.

Every loss will remind us of our previous unhealed losses. This makes the experience more painful, but it also gives us an opportunity to heal all our old hurts as we heal our present grief. Grief is like a butterfly cramped up in a cocoon. Once it breaks out of its confining shell it opens to the light and is transformed. I want to show in this book that pain can be transformed into a gift of love. Love is the greatest healer of all.

Reading this book on bereavement may stir painful memories, but hopefully it will help you understand more about yourself and your grief. As an anonymous poet wrote: 'Only a person who risks is free'. Your reward can be an inner healing and access to the joyful feelings that will have been suppressed along with your sadness. I hope the different perspectives, insights and strategies described by the people whose stories I have included will offer you a compassionate understanding of the effects of loss and suggest ways of transforming your experience.

While I encourage you to take the emotional risk of being willing to heal your grief, I do also advise you to respect your fears. There are many psychologically powerful activities and visualizations suggested in this book. These are fine to do alone if you are experienced in this way of working, but if all this is new to you, I suggest you do them at first with a counsellor or therapist. Please remember that to ask for help and support when you need it is a sign of maturity, *not* weakness. (There is a list of organizations that run local support groups at the back of the book.)

Living with Loss

It is one of life's laws that as soon as one door closes, another opens. But the tragedy is we look at the closed door and disregard the open one.

(André Gide)

1

Growing through grief

> There is no growth without pain and conflict and no loss that cannot lead to gain. (Lily Pincus)

To begin with, grief may seem a wholly negative experience, something you want to get through as quickly as possible; or to control so you don't become a burden on those around you. This is certainly the way Western society in general seems to see it. In fact, grieving can be a positive experience. It may be that your grief following a death or the loss of a relationship is the most emotional experience you have ever had. It may force you to realize what's really important to you in life; it may make you see those around you in a new light; and it may open you up to more love and real intimacy in your life – maybe with those you least expected to experience such things with. As my friend Jon, whose story is in Chapter 10, has said:

> There are those who say that, oddly enough, AIDS is the best thing that ever happened to them. Until they were diagnosed, they were living a life that was not nurturing them. They were unaware of the love that was all around them; they had not allowed true intimacy in their lives. It seems that when a person is confronted with the likelihood of losing life and chooses not to be victimized, then they can discover the beauty and wonder of life around them, and their own beings.

I wouldn't have chosen to lose my husband, but I feel deeply enriched by the experiences that I have had as a result of his death, and the depth of intimacy and sharing I have experienced with others in the course of my healing journey.

Our unhealed past

Most of us are carrying around unacknowledged and unre-solved losses, emotional wounds from the past. These old wounds make it more difficult for us to deal with losses that happen in the present. Unconsciously, we know we need to heal these old losses, and at the same time the part of us that thinks we must stay in control all the time wants to keep them 'safely' suppressed. The balancing act of suppression is threatened not only by a new loss in our own life, but also if we try to help a friend who is grieving. This is the reason for many *un*helpful attempts to 'help' a bereaved person. Re-marks such as, 'Pull yourself together', 'I know how you feel', 'You surely ought to be feeling better by now', 'Chin up!', 'At least you still have your health', 'You can always have another child', 'I'm sure it's all for the best', and so on, are all attempts to deflect the pain, keep successfully sup-pressing, and to paint a pleasing and 'acceptable' image of the situation.

The problem with suppression as a way of dealing with the feelings arising from loss is that it's like turning the volume of your radio down to a whisper – *all* your feelings will be suppressed, your joys as well as your sorrows, and you will feel less alive. In the long-term, such suppression is now recognized as a contributing factor in many illnesses.

Since most of us underestimate the effect loss has on our lives, it's worth looking at the now well-established link be-tween loss, stress and illness. Even desired events like marriage, starting a new job, and parenthood are stressful. A classic American study by Holmes and Rahe in 1968 (quoted in the *Journal of Human Stress* (4), 1978) rated life changes according to the amount of readjustment needed. Death and divorce scored highest, with 100 and 73 respectively. People with a combined score of more than 300 in any one year were found to have an eighty per cent chance of becoming ill in the following year.

Until recently it has been even more common to under-estimate the effects of loss on children. Several recent studies have shown that children demonstrate a high rate of be-havioural disturbance following bereavement. Their symptoms can include extreme anxiety, exaggerated re-actions to separation, clinging behaviour, excessive crying, aggression, disturbed sleep, and problems with eating and using the toilet.

Identifying your losses

The first step in healing is to realize that there is a loss to be dealt with. The death of a loved one is almost always acknowledged and grieved for, but there are many other important losses which people may skate over when they happen. Some examples, to get you thinking, are: income, home, familiar surroundings, support, independence, dignity, freedom, status, identity, confidence, memory, security, innocence, trust, companionship, religious faith, purpose in life, self-respect, sex-life. Some of the means by which losses happen are: ageing, infertility, disability, children leaving home, death, divorce, emigration, imprisonment, job redundancy and unemployment, retirement, rape, phobias, fear of death, fire, theft, accidents, violence, adoption, mental illness, drug dependency, anorexia, promotion, war, illness.

A sample of participants in a recent workshop on Good Grief that I led with my German friend Uthe reveals a variety of losses, past and present, that were affecting their lives. Jean, in her sixties, thought she had had a good life but had suddenly realized when her children left home that she had never experienced any real joy. With us, she remembered her father dying in the Second World War when she was nine. He had been due home on leave when her mother received a letter saying he was missing. 'We couldn't grieve in case he came back.' Four years later she and her mother attended a memorial service for hundreds of missing servicemen, including her dad. She was told, 'Lots of people have lost their fathers,' and her need to grieve was not recognized.

In the workshop Jean was able to get in touch with the pain of losing her father, and she realized that by shutting out the pain of his loss she had also shut out all her other feelings, including joy. At the end of the course Jean said that Uthe was the first German she had ever encountered, and that meeting her had healed the death of her father fifty years ago. Uthe burst into tears: she had carried the guilt of her fellow-Germans' wartime activities all her life. It was very moving to watch the healing that took place in that moment as they cried and hugged each other.

Andrew was gay and in his thirties. He had left (lost) his native country, New Zealand, and therefore lost family, friends, culture and background. He had also lost lovers, including one who committed suicide. Being gay had resulted in alienation from some of his family and friends, as he didn't conform to their expected way of life. During the workshop he got in touch with an earlier loss, that of being a father. He had been in a heterosexual relationship when his partner become pregnant but decided to have an abortion.

Sheila, in her fifties, was married to a senior officer in the Salvation Army and they had held a joint post of responsibility. When he retired through ill health her job went too. She was experiencing the loss of status, identity and power.

Russell was single and in his forties. He had come to increase his knowledge as a counsellor, but during the workshop he realized he also had losses that he needed to work through. He had been brought up in a close-knit community in Glasgow, where young people only left home when they married, and then generally lived nearby. He had not only left Glasgow to study, but had afterwards kept moving from one job to another, and then gone abroad. Several years later he realized he still hadn't shaken off his guilt feelings over his mother's disapproval of his move away from home.

In the different workshops I have held on loss during the last twenty years I have learned that there is no such thing as a major or minor loss. What is major to one person could be minor to another. An adult moving house, for example, may experience the change as a minor loss. A child involved in the same move may be experiencing major losses of friends, school and safely familiar surroundings.

Each time we make a change in our lives, take on a new role or let go of an old one, we experience loss. You have to lose the old in order to make room for the new. Our culture is so focused on the gains we can make in life – a new relationship, a new job, a new home, a new family – that the inevitable accompanying loss is rarely considered. We expect ourselves to adapt to any change swiftly; to 'carry on as usual'.

Common important losses include unemployment, redundancy or enforced retirement. Many young people now are experiencing the loss of their 'right to work' after leaving school. For many people such losses can result in the loss of status, money, and life direction. Equally traumatic are failures in fertility. A couple who cannot conceive may feel a loss of status and purpose. A woman who has had a hysterectomy may mourn the loss of her fertility, knowing that she can no longer conceive and bear children and that her re-productive life is over. A miscarriage or stillbirth can result in the mother feeling a failure as a woman since she can't re-produce effectively. Even when a woman or man deliberately chooses to be sterilized, there may well need to be a time of mourning for their lost fertility.

When a baby is born with a defect the parents may need to grieve for the loss of a normal baby before they can accept the handicapped one. For the child, the degree of loss may depend on the attitude of the people around; how they per-ceive it. Peter Speck in his book *Loss, Grief and Medicine* (Bailliere Tindall), says that

> if the body-image is disrupted by amputation or other sur-gery, it can lead to a grief-like reaction, which requires a period of mourning before the resulting trauma is resolved and a new, acceptable, body-image is formed. The acceptance of this by others is important.

Mastectomy often has a devastating effect on a woman's feel-ings of femininity and sexual attractiveness. In addition to the trauma of disfiguring surgery, a hospital stay, in itself, means the loss of familiar surroundings, social contacts and autonomy.

In my last job I was based in a unit for the prevention of drug abuse. Addiction to drugs can result in the extreme loss of personality. Horizons narrow and life becomes restricted, with little freedom of choice. Other losses may include loved ones, career, happiness, health, and even life itself. Once the addict has adjusted to their drug-oriented life, however, one of the difficulties of giving up drugs will be the loss of a way of life and the social contacts that go with it.

A new loss I am learning to live with more and more in my fifties is the loss of youth through ageing. I feel the same in-side, but I now wear glasses and sometimes catch a glimpse of myself in a mirror unexpectedly and see my grey hair and lines and wonder where my youth went so soon! When I was involved with pre-retirement courses, there would always be some people who refused to come as they couldn't face the fact that they would soon be regarded as too old to work.

Children and loss

No one can live long without encountering loss. Our life begins with the loss of the comfort and security of our mother's womb. Losses that happen when we are very young, before we have any perspective on life, are usually those we are most unconscious of and at the same time the ones that have the most far-reaching effects on our lives (and so are the most important ones to heal).

In order to understand loss, it is necessary to understand how we become attached to people and things. Our earliest attachments are essential for our survival. Babies need a care-taker until they are grown-up and able to care for themselves. We continue to attach ourselves to others in part because we feel we depend on them for life. For children, this dependence is absolute. As children grow older, they will develop a variety of attachments. The greater the attach-ment, the greater the potential for loss. Yet non-attachment would greatly impoverish our lives.

The very process of growing up may be seen as a loss of accustomed forms of support and attention, as well as the gaining of independence. Acquiring an education and school friends means temporary separation from parents and home. Changing from one school to another, from one class to the next, means a loss of familiar surroundings and people, despite the gains of new experiences. A new baby in the family can mean the temporary loss of attention from the mother for her other children and husband; there will also be a permanent change in status for the other siblings. Many children now have to adjust to divorce and then a new step-parent: about a third of marriages in the UK end in divorce and about two-thirds of the parents re-marry.

My job as an advisory teacher for Personal, Social and Health Education involved working with children and adults suffering from a wide range of losses. Some of these particu-larly touched me. My work involved supporting victims of child sexual abuse, which I found traumatic. Ten per cent of all children are thought to have experienced some form of sexual abuse. Such children can lose, among other things, their innocence and self-esteem, indeed their childhood itself. I well remember meeting a twenty-four-year-old un-married mother who had been sexually abused by her stepfather night and morning from the age of six to sixteen. Her meeting with me was the first time she had spoken about her experience to anyone. Such stories encouraged me to work with teachers to help create a climate where children could talk and learn more freely about previously taboo subjects and so no longer carry these burdens for years alone.

The starting-point

Over the past century death has become less and less visible in the West. People are likely to die in the hi-tech surroundings of a modern hospital; a professional firm of undertakers will take the body away, rather than friends and family laying it out at home. Longer life-expectancy means fewer people die before they are very old. It is now becoming common to live for up to fifty years without experiencing the death of anyone close to us. So when death does touch us closely, it is difficult to know how to react or what to do.

I believe learning to deal with loss is an essential part of learning to deal with life. Children are prepared for birth and marriage, so why not death and other losses? As it is, everyone's fear of experiencing 'negative' emotions such as sadness, anger and fear itself is at the root of our society's expensive dependence on drugs, its senseless violence and vandalism, and the overcrowding of our psychiatric wards. We do not realize that in shutting out 'negative' emotions we are closing ourselves to all feeling, and so shutting out the 'good' emotions too. Suppressed grief can control your life. You are likely to steer away from real intimacy with other people – such closeness could mean revealing your hidden emotional secrets. I am always moved when I run workshops by the change in people after they have shared unhappy experiences and expressed their pain. I always ask them to look around the room and see how radiant and relaxed people can look after sharing memories and pain that may have been locked in for years. If we could think of our losses as opportunities for new beginnings we could shed much of our overwhelming fear of deaths and start living fully, accepting the woes and open to the joys of life.

Beginning to heal

The easiest way to begin to heal your unresolved losses is to look back at how you learned to handle loss as a child. I always begin my workshops on grief by talking about the loss of a favourite toy, something most of us can remember. Teddy bears, in particular, are recognized as transition objects, which we use to ease our path to independence from our mother and to comfort us in times of change. The way the adults around us reacted to our loss can affect how we adapt to future losses. I remember Dora Black, a leading authority on bereavement, telling the story of her small daughter losing her teddy bear on holiday in France. Dora helped her to grieve for it and acknowledge what it represented. What a contrast to the approach many of us probably experienced, of being told, 'It's only a toy, we can soon get you a new one'.

As I began to work with unhealed grief in my own life, I realized loss began for me when I was six months old and my father left home. I never saw him again, not even in a photograph, and my mother refused to talk about him. I realized I had experienced a loss of identity because of his absence – I felt as if half of me was missing, especially since I had been told I was very like my father – and I had spent my life unconsciously searching for my missing self. I had also lost the opportunity to build healthy self-esteem – I only ever heard bad things about my father and so I unconsciously assumed I must be bad too, as I was like him.

Other childhood losses that were important to me include particular moments when I made decisions about myself – for example, when I tried (at two-and-a-half) to play with my big sister and her friends (all seven), and they laughed at me because I couldn't whistle, and ran away and left me. Later, I remember asking my mother what present I would receive if I passed the eleven-plus exam. When she replied, 'Nothing! All our family pass exams', I remember something inside me died and fear of what would happen to me if I failed took over. I did pass, but only just, and stayed in the bottom class through secondary school, whereas previously I had been regarded as exceptionally bright. It was years later before I understood my mother had been trying to encourage me.

What you can do

Write down each of your childhood losses (it can be interesting to plot them on a timeline). What did you decide about yourself/other people/life, as a result of each experience? How did you decide to cope with loss in future?

Finding the gift

Many losses are so upsetting that it is hard to recognize the opportunity they also bring with them. If there is no gain without a loss, then every loss must bring an opportunity, even if it is a hard one to accept. In one of my workshops there was a man who said he had been made redundant three times. He said it was the best thing that happened to him, after the initial shock, as he had had three different interesting careers. For myself, being given early retirement has given me the opportunity to become a freelance trainer, consultant and therapist, and to write this book.

What you can do

Write down all the losses you have experienced in the past, and opposite each loss write the qualities you think you gained from it. For example, my not knowing my father has given me empathy with other people in that situation. Constantly changing schools as a child gave me the understanding to be a successful education welfare officer, helping children and families who had difficulty with school attendance. One friend realized while doing this exercise that becoming short-sighted as a child had given her permission to see things differently from the grown-ups (who she felt kept telling her she was wrong). I heard Jilly Cooper say in an interview that when the gynaecologist told her she couldn't have children she cried all the way home and literally started writing almost straight away (happily she also later adopted two children).

  Don't try and do this assignment with a recent loss: you won't yet have perspective on it. You need to feel your grief first.

Healing childhood loss as an adult

The further back your unhealed losses took place, the longer it is likely to take for you to recognize and release all your buried grief. A large part of your personality, and the way you experience the world, will be based on your buried trauma. Most people find they get in touch with it little by little, so the changes in their perceptions are small enough for them to handle. Since our understanding of the depths of children's grief is very recent, you may have internalized your parents' and other adults' belief that the loss didn't affect you deeply. Part of the challenge in looking back will probably be to take your own feelings seriously; and to be willing to feel foolish and childlike as you re-experience your past. Since children don't have our perspective on life, emotions suppressed from childhood can loom terrifyingly – it can look as if you will be overwhelmed if you allow yourself to feel them. The key is patience: recognize that it may take years to release your old suppressed feelings; and that you are doing the best you can, just as you did when you were a child.

Derek, in his early fifties, came to one of my Good Grief workshops:

It was only after I became involved in therapy several years ago that I realized what the loss of my twin brother at birth had meant to me. As I have periodically revisited this issue, a lot of the patterns in my life begin to make more sense.

It started when I was looking at the role of fear in my life and tracking it back through school to childhood. It felt like following knots on a continuous thread, as indeed it was, each knot an experience of almost uncontrollable fear. I had reached infancy and the terror of the air-raid siren. For a moment that knot seemed to be the last, or the first, but then suddenly there it was – the big mistake! That I should never have been on my own in the first place. I was overcome with horror at this realization, hidden in my subconscious for more than forty years.

I have at times in this life felt very lonely, a stranger in a strange land. I learnt very well how to withdraw, to cut myself off from others, rather than be hurt again. I also learnt to despise weakness in others and to repress it in myself. At school it felt like teachers always wanted to sit on me and stifle me, something I must have felt at my birth as my brother followed me, a dead weight. . . . So I began life searching for that which I had lost, both in terms of companionship and in terms of peak experience.

I became divorced six years ago and was filled with terror when I first had to live on my own, realizing that I had never had to do this before, even before birth. The loneliness was more than I could bear. I understand now why I clung to my then partner in such panic. Each parting was like a death, that death again, although only later did I see the connections.

Derek recognizes that many of his positive, valuable qualities are based on his unconscious attempts throughout his life to overcome the loss of his twin. 'I have a thirst for equality and justice, for the underdog, for that which has been lost and needs to be reclaimed.'

Jane, who edited this book, has also found it has taken several years of work on herself, unpeeling layer after layer, to arrive at her present understanding of her childhood grief:

What started me on my way to healing, six years ago now, was when I suddenly began to feel slightly sick and faint all the time. (I now realize that this was the result of deeply suppressed feelings that my subconscious was trying to bring to my attention.) My doctor thought there was nothing wrong with me, but I was absolutely determined not to go on feeling like that. I went to see a homeopath, which helped a bit, and was then referred to an osteopath. He persuaded me to talk about what was going on for me emotionally. I explained I wasn't an emotional person; and that I supposed any emotional problems I might have related to when I was five and my mother had tuberculosis and went into hospital for a year at the same time as my father and brother and I moved to the other side of the country. I was full of analysis, but when the osteopath said he felt I wasn't in touch with my feelings, I had to agree. He recommended rebirthing, which is a breathing technique that helps you let go of old tensions, emotional as well as physical.

I've found that time when I was five has resurfaced again and again: it took me two years, for instance, to acknowledge I'd felt rejected by my mother. Gradually, piece by piece, I've felt the emotions I blocked at the time. I remember doing a visualization with one rebirther, where I spoke to the five-year-old me: I was shocked at how angry I was with her. I felt that if she'd handled things better, I wouldn't be screwed-up now. It made me realize how hard I was being on that part of myself that was frozen in time; that had done the best she could with a five-year-old's strength and understanding.

I thought I was pretty clear about my childhood loss when I started work on this book. I'd been working only a couple of days when the cottage I was renting caught fire and I was suddenly homeless. I didn't have time to look for a new home, so I went to stay with my parents. Once I'd lost the cottage, I realized my choices in both home and work hadn't been working, and my self-esteem and trust in myself nose-dived. I felt vulnerable and off-balance. Almost as soon as I moved in with my parents, there were a couple of TV documentaries about tuberculosis, which got Mother and I talking about her experience of it. Then, as I got back to work, I read other books on children's grief and was particularly struck by an account in *Beyond Grief* by Carol Staudacher[1] where a woman my age, whose mother died when she was five, summed up exactly how I'd felt! I realized that my feelings of being fundamentally wrong; guilty; not loving enough; insignificant; and an outsider all relate to that time. I felt overwhelmed by my feelings – as if I might be cracking up. For the first time, I told my mother how helpless I felt and how I despair of ever creating an intimate, loving relationship with a man. A large part of my block is my fear that I will be rejected and left again. Always before, I'd refused to let my mother get that close to me, for fear she would somehow betray me again. It felt good to let her cuddle and kiss me as if I was still a little girl. I thought I might lose my power, somehow, and become stuck emotionally as a child if I showed her my childish weakness, but instead I feel more at ease with her. I no longer feel the same need to hide from her. I've discovered there's a great deal more to me than I used to think: I *am* emotional; and intuitive, loving and valuable. I have many good friends all over the world. My life has become an adventure, and even though it is frustrating sometimes, I know I can't now fit back into my old 'safe' box.

What you can do

- It's best to get help to deal with deeply buried grief. There are various kinds of counselling, therapy, workshops and support groups available that will support you.
- Don't expect an instant revolution! Often, people go down

this path in order to change something in themselves, but then discover they need to accept themselves just the way they are first.

- Work on your self-esteem (see Chapter 2) at the same time.
- Read Chapter 6 and see Recommended Reading for books on childhood loss – you may recognize your own original reactions in some of these accounts.
- Don't underestimate the power of your intention to heal. Even if you don't know how to go about it, your determination will unconsciously direct you to the people, books and techniques that can help you.

Difficulties in grieving

Some of the common obstacles in the grieving process are: refusal to accept the loss; lack of practical, emotional or spiritual support; marital or family discord; mixed feelings towards the lost person; difficulties in expressing feelings; exaggerated self-control; low self-esteem; inability to attend the funeral; anxiety about money; regret over unfinished business. Once such an obstacle is recognized, it's possible to devise the necessary support and move through the grieving process.

More serious are long-term coping mechanisms which prevent real grieving and are only unhelpful in the long run. There are three common routes for avoiding grief:

Substitution

The bereaved person might swiftly remarry. Such marriages frequently fail because the grief work from the first marriage has not been done. A second option is for the person to focus all their emotional energy on their children, who may well feel smothered. Children can themselves substitute by finding a replacement 'mother' or 'father'.

Aggression

Some people can stay stuck in their anger, blaming God, the doctor, or themselves. Children may express this by fighting, or avoiding school. They can get involved in a variety of disciplinary problems, such as drug abuse or general anti-social behaviour.

Helplessness

This can involve a person getting all their friends and neighbours running around after them. The problem with being continually 'rescued' like this is that the person will never adjust to the reality of their new situation, and develop their own coping skills. Children who act out helplessness may opt out of life; they will lack curiosity, so their learning is impaired. Adults can also follow this path, becoming recluses or turning to alcohol, drugs or food for comfort.

Equally unhealthy are those people who go to the opposite extreme and, far from repressing their grief, are trapped in a state of chronic grieving.

Each of us has our own individual journey to make in healing grief. There are no set answers in the search for meaning and healing. As you begin to heal you may well feel your grief more intensely for a time. T.S. Eliot described three stages to change: ending, limbo, beginning. It takes courage to stay in limbo, to be open to your feelings and go through the pain before you build a new identity without the person or situation you have lost. But over and over again I have seen the benefits both in myself and other people when the hurt and pain are opened up to acceptance and love.

---

1 Published by Souvenir Press, 1988.

2

Helping yourself

If you walk towards the sun the shadows fall away. (Anon)

If you are grieving now – or if you are working through old griefs in order to heal yourself – it's vital to nurture yourself while you are going through such intense feelings and emotional confusion. The first essential is not to expect too much from yourself. Give yourself permission to be untogether for a while – trying to be superwoman/man will only delay or suppress your grieving.

Loneliness

This is probably one of the hardest emotions to deal with and is particularly likely to affect people who have lost their life partner due to death or separation. For the first six months after John died I felt completely cut off from everyone. I felt people were staring at me because I was on my own. John was not only my husband, but also my best friend. The danger is that loneliness can be self-perpetuating, with some people finding it more and more difficult to reach out or to accept support. An unmarried teacher who came on one of my courses said that she had asked for help twenty years earlier and been laughed at.

People will come out of loneliness in different ways. For me it was a spiritual crisis, and I came through it by making God my best friend. I know of others who've reached out to people they hear of in a similar situation, for mutual comfort. Support groups can be a great help here, or joining a society or evening class to pursue an interest. Learning to enjoy being alone is an important element in overcoming loneliness. There is a great difference between loneliness and being alone – if you're feeling lonely it doesn't matter how many people you have around you. Now, I thoroughly enjoy my own company. The important difference is choice. If I am on my own now it is because I choose to be.

Most of us get our support and emotional sustenance from one or two people. So if we lose that person, we need to extend our support network. Look around you for people who will listen to you and not get bored; let you cry; give you a hug; stay with you when you need them; will not try to cheer you up all the time; will not betray your confidence; and with whom you don't have to pretend. It may be that you will need to look to professional counsellors or support groups at first, but you may be surprised how much friendship there is available to you.

Receiving support

Many people find it difficult to ask for or receive support, particularly if their self-esteem is low. It's helpful to realize that you may be giving a gift to another person in allowing them to support you – they may feel more valuable in helping you, and enjoy the opportunity for positive action rather than having to be a helpless bystander. Asking for support, whether from friends or, via your GP, a professional counseller or therapist, does *not* mean you are inadequate. I did it myself, and I feel it is a sign of maturity.

Support groups

The rapid growth in the number of support groups available shows how essential they have become to many people's emotional recovery. They provide a great opportunity for meeting people who have had a similar experience to you, which helps with any feelings of alienation and loneliness you may have been experiencing. You will meet people who are 'further on' in their grief, which will help you to recognize that although you may not feel it at the moment, it is possible to come through. They are also good for making friends and expanding your social life – the CRUSE branch for 'widowed in mid marriage' (WIMMS) organizes social outings and also activities for children. Your local public library and Citizens' Advice Bureau will have lists of local groups; see also Useful Addresses at the back of this book.

Self-esteem

If you have lost someone you love through death, divorce or separation, your self-esteem has probably plummeted. When your self-esteem is high you feel confident, trust your judgement and know what you are capable of. When you lack self-esteem you may feel weak and helpless; be uncertain of the value of anything you do; and not trust yourself or other people's reassurances. If you don't believe in yourself, you will have no resources to deal with stressful situations – you will go under.

Self-esteem is not conceit or arrogance, but an honest appreciation of your capabilities. Building self-esteem may be difficult if you were criticized as a child and are in the habit of putting yourself down. Once you realize that this doesn't 'improve' you, you may be more willing to see what a little self-appreciation will do. Imagine encouraging a small child who is learning to walk – praise and support bring results far faster than criticism and blame. You may feel self-conscious and awkward doing some of these exercises, and it's a good idea to commit to doing the ones you choose for at least a week, no excuses allowed, to get over your initial resistance.

Suggestions for building self-esteem:

- Write a list of everything you can do, from boiling an egg on up. Buy an attractive notebook to be your 'Book of Successes'. Every night, write down at least five successes you had that day. Maybe getting out of bed was a real success – or deciding to stay there and give yourself a day off! It's good to do this for quite a while – begin by committing to do it for at least one month.
- Make a self-esteem mandala. Draw or paint a colourful wheel with segments or spokes and fill each one with something you like about yourself. Keep it somewhere private but where you will see it – inside your wardrobe, or by your bed.
- Acknowledge yourself each time you achieve something –

it's amazing how easy it is to notice all your mistakes and ignore or play down your successes. Every so often, tell yourself three things you like about yourself; and three things other people like about you.

- Practise allowing praise in. Most of us are masters of the art of rebuffing compliments. 'Oh, I found this in a jumble sale,' It's very kind of you to say so ...' Try trusting people's esteem when they acknowledge you; all you need to say is, 'Thank you'.

- Play with affirmations. These are new, positive thoughts that you choose to think in place of the old conditioning that you recognize no longer works for you. Write your current favourites on cards and stick them up where you'll see them – ones on appearance might go on your bathroom mirror; ones on money in your purse, and so on. Try statements beginning with 'I can ...', 'I know how to ...', 'I forgive myself for ...'. A good affirmation for general self-esteem is 'I love and approve of myself'. It's very powerful to say this to yourself in front of a mirror – but if you find this too much at first, just keep saying it inside your head as you go about your day. If you're feeling self-conscious with other people, extend it to 'I love and approve of myself in the presence of others' – or you could substitute one particular person, if there's a relationship you're having difficulty with. There are many books available on using affirmations for self-esteem. My favourite is *You Can Heal Your Life* by Louise Hay (Eden Grove Publications); another good one is *I Deserve Love* by Sondra Ray (Celestial Arts).

- Buy and wear clothes that make you feel good, rather than what you think you ought to have.

Practical self-support

Make sure you eat properly. It's easy not to bother if you are left to cook for just one. Do batch cooking if you have a freezer, so you've always got variety and something to offer visitors if they just drop in.

Get plenty of sleep. Sleep can be a great healer, but if you don't sleep, don't get neurotic about it. If you can't get to sleep after fifteen minutes, get up. Otherwise you will associate your bed with somewhere you don't sleep. I know many people who have done their housework or ironing in the middle of the night. Write or draw your thoughts or feelings if they keep going around in your head. Best of all, prevent a build-up by going through your day before going to bed. Think of one good thing that happened, there's always got to be *one* good thing – a cup of tea or coffee you enjoyed; someone who smiled; a job you got done – then think of all the things that have upset you or made you mad and allow the feelings to be there. When you've cleared these negative feelings, think of the next thing you are looking forward to – reading a book, or a night-time drink.

Use music to change your moods. Become aware of what sounds and visual information you're surrounding yourself with. TV programmes and song lyrics, for example, can subconsciously affect how you feel. If your favourite song is something like 'I Can't Get No Satisfaction' it could be acting like a negative sort of brainwashing! When you're feeling vulnerable, try playing relaxing or upbeat sounds.

Do some form of exercise. It can be gentle like walking, swimming, yoga or t'ai chi, or more strenuous, like aerobics or squash. It's particularly good to take some exercise if you're feeling depressed – it will get your energy moving so you don't feel so stuck.

Give yourself a treat. Often if a partner dies or leaves, a person feels there is no one to buy special things for them, or that they don't deserve treats. My relationship to myself changed dramatically after I met an American on a trip to Ireland. He kept buying things for himself at every stop. I asked, 'Don't you feel guilty buying things for yourself?' He replied, 'No. I tell myself I'm worth it.' His answer has become a favourite catchphrase of mine! I remember a colleague, whose husband had left her, saying how liberated she felt when she first bought herself a bunch of flowers. For the first few years after my husband died I would buy myself the sort of present he would have bought me – some fun clothes, or a piece of jewellery.

Treat yourself to a massage. One of the things one can miss most with the loss of a close relationship is touch. Massage can also reduce stress and tension, and be a useful aid to relaxation.

Remember the importance of keeping a balance between home, work and leisure. Following some familiar rituals can also create a relaxing rhythm and structure in your life. These can include walking the dog, reading a book on the way to work, or watching certain programmes on television. There may also be particular 'safe' places that it's good to retreat to from time to time – a particular room at home, a favourite café, or a familiar walk.

It's generally advisable to wait at least six months before making big changes after a major loss – moving house, getting involved in a new committed relationship, or changing your job, for example. You may well feel like changing everything immediately, but many people have moved quickly from an area with sad memories only to find the memories are just as strong in their new home where they have no established support-systems.

Emotional self-support

Avoid telling yourself 'I should', 'I ought', and 'I must'. That's like having a disapproving parent living inside your head, and will make you tense. Treat yourself like a grown-up instead, who has a choice about what she/he does, and suggest to yourself 'I could . . .'. Be gentle with yourself, and forgive yourself when you make mistakes.

Accept that you have indeed lost something or someone vital to you, and it or they are not going to come back. Thinking 'it should never have happened', or 'why me?' only tends to delay the time when you face up to the challenges the loss has brought with it. Acceptance is the essential first step in grieving, healing, and eventually forming your new identity.

They say you haven't got over the loss of someone you love unless they are not the first thing you think of when you wake up in the morning. So set aside time each morning and allow yourself to think of the person you have lost. I still give myself an hour's quiet time in the morning. I take my tea back to bed and read and meditate before starting the day.

Don't keep yourself busy all the time, as many people will tell you to. Your thoughts and feelings will only go into your unconscious and surface at a later date. They will then be disconnected from the event that caused them and be far harder to deal with.

When you are grieving it is often difficult to find anything good in your life. Say to yourself each morning, 'I'm open to all the good and opportunities that are available to me today'

– a little willingness will go a long way in changing your perception of your life.

Give yourself a 'transition object' – in other words, a teddy bear. Most children have a favourite soft toy or piece of material that they take to bed with them, on holiday and to hospital. If you don't still have your childhood special toy, I suggest you imagine yourself a child again, visit a toy shop and buy one your inner child likes! As a wartime child I had no soft toys. I now have over twenty, mainly bears, bought by myself and by clients for me. (I recently read of a man who has a collection of 5,000 teddy bears, which makes my collection look quite modest.)

Make a list of ten things you love to do. Put a heart next to those you have done in the last week. Try and do one thing extra for yourself each week. It could be something from your list or something new – buying yourself a bunch of flowers or going to the cinema, for example.

Healing your hurt child

At times of loss all of us tend to revert to being a hurt child. Honouring and working with your inner child can be helpful and also cathartic. If you are feeling stuck emotionally it may well be that your present experience is echoing a time as a child when you cut off; a point at which your feelings are still frozen. Try taking yourself back to the earliest time you can remember when you experienced a similar feeling – for example, loneliness, hurt, anger, sadness. Picture how you were as a child at that time. Where were you? What clothes were you wearing? What were you doing? Was anyone with you? What were the smells, tastes, sounds around you? Then picture yourself giving that child a big hug and picking her/him up and placing her in your heart and surrounding her and yourself with love and/or light. If you repeat this each time you feel stuck in an emotion you will gradually heal all the times you were hurt when you were a child. It will become easier to express your feelings as an adult and move on.

You can also hold conversations with your inner child if you're feeling stuck. You may be really confused as to why you're upset, but often a quick glimpse of your inner child, or asking them what's going on, will clarify the whole situation.

Children don't have all our rational masks – you'll probably find your child inside howling with grief or throwing a tantrum – 'I don't like this place. I want to go home *now!*' – or maybe just wanting to play instead of doing all this heavy stuff. If you'd like to do more work on getting to know and understand your inner child, I recommend *Recovery of Your Inner Child* by Lucia Capacchione (Simon & Schuster, New York).

Take time to relax

Most people think of relaxation as sitting in front of the television, or reading a book. Such activities can be enjoyable, but they can also include quite a lot of stress: your mind will still be working, and you may be even more out of touch with your body than when you're active. You're still 'doing' rather than simply 'being'. The kind of relaxation I'm recommending here is a conscious sinking into yourself; a choice of peace and awareness. Relaxation will not cure or change your problems, but it will help you to recognize when your body has tensed up, and prevent the build-up of lactic acid in your muscles, which creates fatigue. It can also help you to sleep better; reduce dependency on alcohol and drugs; prevent minor headaches and ailments; and generally enable you to adapt more easily to rapidly change.

I have suggested various relaxation techniques in the Appendix. It's good to get in the habit of deliberately relaxing each time you notice you are tense – just stop, relax your muscles, and breathe slowly for a few minutes. As you return to what you were doing, keep relaxed and slow your pace down.

Meditation can enable you to quieten busy thoughts and focus your mind. It can also contribute to mental development, to a clearer sense of identity and spiritual awareness. Like all skills, it needs practice to succeed. Meditation can include guided visualization or it can be initiated by focusing on an object such as a flower or candle, or a feeling, or a word or 'mantra'. Even if you don't learn to meditate, you may find it helpful to deepen your relaxation experience by being silent for a while. Silence allows you to be open; it encourages insight and awareness.

Self-expression

Getting your feelings out of yourself and into the world in the form of words, pictures or sounds can be a valuable part of your healing process. As you become involved with the creative process you will safely gain access to reactions and experiences you had locked away in your subconscious.

Writing

Writing can be an invaluable tool. Just as, when talking to someone, you can hear yourself say something you hadn't realized you thought, so writing down how you really felt during an experience can help both in accepting it has happened and also in showing you what is really upsetting you right now – often not what you assumed. This is valuable especially when you want to deal with past losses: you could write about them in the present tense, or as if they have only just happened, to get in touch with buried feelings.

A powerful step on from this, for some people, is to write about your experience in a poem or letter: newsletters put out by support organizations publish such material to help others who have had similar experiences. Someone who felt inspired to write in this way is Pamela Gillilan, whose husband died in 1974. She remembers, a few years later, standing on the granite steps outside the large house in which she was living and noticing a single raindrop on a leaf of the forsythia bush beside her. She was struck with great force by a terrific feeling of ephemerality, and of human transience, and she knew then with complete certainty that she was going to write. She booked herself on to an Arvon writing course for the following month. Although she has never written precisely about that particular moment of insight, she feels it is frequently there in her work, transformed perhaps into something altogether different. Since that course she has won many prizes. This poem is from her book, *That Winter*.[1]

> When you died
> I went through the rain
> Carrying my nightmare
> To register the death.

A well-groomed healthy gentleman
Safe within his office
Said – Are you the widow?

Couldn't he have said
Were you the wife?

After *That Winter* was published, many people got in touch with Pamela, including a Registrar of Births and Deaths who rang her to promise that she would never commit the unthinking verbal cruelty described in 'When You Died'.

I particularly recommend writing a journal. I always write to someone in my journal – anyone I have unfinished business with (of course, this is likely to be the person you have lost). In my case, this often means God. I write and ask for help when I feel stuck, or feel that life is unfair, or when I'm angry with Him. I always feel better within a few days, and an unexpected solution or insight will come to me.

Drawing

If you are finding it difficult to contact and express your feelings, drawing and painting are excellent ways to bypass the rational mind. This is not about displaying your artistic talent – many people have hang-ups about drawing, but this activity works fine even if you draw pin-people.

It's best to give yourself space for free-drawing – a large sheet of paper and thick felt-tip pens, crayons or paints. It can be good to put pen to paper and just see what comes. Or you can draw a feeling – anger, or sadness, for example.

A friend of mine went on a four-week art therapy course after leaving his wife. Each person was given two large sheets of paper pinned to the wall to cover, a large paint brush and lots of different coloured paints. He had never painted in his life before, but found himself covering the paper with great patches of black and other dark colours, and felt enormous relief at the end of the four weeks.

When you've finished a picture, it's good to write down in your journal how you felt as you were doing it and what it means to you. An excellent book called *The Secret World of Drawing: Healing Through Art* by Gregg M. Furth (Sigo Press, New York, 1989), gives suggestions on interpreting pictures – you may have drawn more than you realize!

Expressing sounds and feelings

This is a big step for most people brought up in the West – particularly those of North European origin. In many cultures, expressing sound is seen as natural, and there may be professional mourners to start the crying at a funeral. People who learn to get over their embarrassment and express feelings and sounds usually say they feel much better for it. One way to begin is by screaming, shouting, or making animal noises in your car as you're driving along the motorway, or a country road, so there is no fear of being overheard. I stamp my feelings out – when I'm out walking, if I need privacy – or punch a pillow. Usually I end up laughing.

Imaginary conversations are also a powerful way of getting in touch with your feelings. A popular method, first introduced by Fritz Perls in Gestalt Therapy, is to imagine a specific person, alive or dead, with whom you have unfinished business sitting opposite you. It can be helpful to place an empty chair in front of you. Start talking to the person you have chosen – tell them how you feel; then swap places and reply for the other person. Continue the dialogue until it feels complete. It's a good idea to then write about it in your journal to ground the experience. People often have unexpected insights about their relationships. You may want to keep doing this process each day until you feel at peace with the other person.

Reading and quotations

Discovering other people's experiences, philosophies, and religions will help you widen your understanding of yourself and other people. These books don't have to be heavy. One of my favourite authors is Susan Howatch. I also read the *Daily Word* religious meditations from Silent Unity in America. Its non-denominational messages go out to more than two million people.

I've also found it helpful to keep a special book in which I collect poems and quotations I like. Right at the front is my favourite, which has often kept me going: 'Life is a mystery to be lived, not a problem to be solved.' That was given me by my second dad, now in his nineties. A minister for a hospice I worked with said he kept a scrapbook of sayings and poems which he left with the patients. They often added new ones. Lady Mountbatten said she received hundreds of letters of sympathy after the terrorist attack on her family. One letter included the following old Chinese poem, which she still often reads:

> He took his candle
> And went into another room
> I cannot find.
> But I know he was here
> Because of all the happiness
> He left behind.

Personal memorabilia

When someone dies or leaves there is often a tendency either to clear everything away, or to keep everything in order to hold on to them. When my father left, the pain was so much for my mother that she got rid of everything to do with him. When my husband died, his business partner came within a fortnight and insisted on clearing out all his clothes and tools. I kept the cap he was wearing when he died and his wallet, which contained, among other things, his favourite photos of me. I also had the photographs taken on our last holiday together. For the first few months they went everywhere with me. In contrast, a friend whose wife had died suddenly after a car accident left for six months, hanging on the picture-rail of their bedroom, the clothes his wife had been deciding between on the night she died. He also left her personal things in the bathroom.

There are no rights and wrongs here: you need to choose what feels right for you. If you decide to keep everything for a while, it may help to ask a friend to be there when you finally decide to clear them out. You may decide to keep certain things in any case. Photographs are important remembrances, and making an album or scrapbook of the person's life can be an important 'letting go' process.

When you are sorting things out, don't forget the value of keepsakes to other people. In the few months before she died, my mother gave every member of the family something special of hers or her husband's. She gave me her watch; I still wear it eight years later. My sister had a brooch she had always admired. Her eldest grandson was given her husband's watch. For young children who will never know the dead person, keepsakes are particularly important.

Remembering anniversaries

Unlike birthdays and happy wedding anniversaries, most friends forget the date of death anniversaries after the first year. It's hard to say to people who've forgotten or didn't know the person, 'I'd rather not go out on Tuesday, as it was her birthday,' or, as in my case, 'I don't want to celebrate Christmas. It reminds me too poignantly of all the pain there is in the world.' Many people do not know what to do at the time of the anniversary. A father I rang recently said, 'We are approaching the first anniversary of Mike's death, and are not sure how to mark it.' Other cultures do have ceremonies, particularly for the first anniversary, and some of these are described in Chapter 16.

What you can do

You are going to be thinking about the person anyway, so make an occasion of the day:

- Go out into the country, or to a place you enjoyed together.
- Read poems or listen to music they enjoyed.
- Light a candle for them. Talk or write to them.
- Ask people who knew the person for a meal. Suggest they bring a dish to save work.
- Most importantly: be aware of the day (most people say the thought of the day is worse than the day itself), and be nice to yourself.

Keeping pets

This is a controversial suggestion. 'Helpful' relatives may turn up with a puppy or kitten for 'company' when the last thing you want is the extra stress of cleaning up messes and training it. Pets can also tie you down if you want to go and stay with friends and family. If it's your choice, though, a pet can be a real support; and stroking them is said to reduce blood pressure and be generally relaxing. A letter to the *CRUSE Chronicle* described one woman's positive experience:

> Jason came into my life a month after my husband died, and he has without doubt been a lifesaver.
>
> The walks have introduced me to many people, and the dog obedience classes are quite an experience. But I have even been grateful for the amount of work he makes, like the mopping up of puddles in the early days, and the help he gives me when I am gardening.
>
> I love it all, but I would impress on anyone thinking of becoming a dog-owner that the work side of it must be considered. Having done that, all the good points well outweigh the not-so-good points.

Reaching out

When you feel ready, helping other people can be a most rewarding and empowering experience. Hilary, whose son Jonathan was killed in a mountaineering accident, contacted someone she read about in a national paper whose son died in a similar way. They visited each other and listened to each other's story. Both felt less alone as they shared their experience. Mr Webb was eighty when his wife died; they had been inseparable. He began visiting a lady with poor eyesight opposite, and did shopping for her. He realized he was still useful, and his self-esteem improved.

Spiritual beliefs

A serious loss may make you question the meaning of life. Symptoms of such a spiritual crisis are feeling cut off or alienated from yourself or others; feeling out of touch with God/spirit/your soul/commonly held religious or cultural beliefs; unresolved anger against outside forces such as the medical services, family, friends, God; feelings of meaninglessness, hopelessness, powerlessness, intense pain; and feelings of guilt – 'it must be my fault'.

One of my clients is currently experiencing all these feelings at different times. Her nephew, who was like a son to her, recently died of anorexia. This triggered a crisis of meaning and unlocked an earlier frozen loss, the death of her father when she was eleven. The crisis was made worse because she found it difficult to express her feelings. She had been bullied between the ages of two and sixteen by her older sister, with whom she shared a room. She had had no protection from the other members of the family. Her deep negative beliefs are 'there is no support' and 'it's all my fault'. These thoughts, her deep pain, and the feeling that she is cut off from God have combined to make her feel suicidal. I felt the most helpful thing for her would be to reconnect with her own spirituality, and we have been doing the 'Wise Person' visualization described in the Appendix.

You may not have a religious background at all, or perhaps the religion you grew up with no longer has any meaning for you. There are many paths in spirituality besides organized religions. Many people find that thinking in terms of the 'life-force' – the energy in all life that causes it to grow – or a 'higher self' – the part of every person that is loving and wise – is more meaningful than talking about 'God'. It's really a matter of focusing on the love and connection between all life rather than feeling everything is separate and meaningless. Animistic traditions, ancient religions all over the world (for example, the Native American tradition), see spirit in all things – animals, minerals, plants, humans, and the elements. Jungian psychology talks about the 'collective unconscious', patterns of experience and memory common to all humankind. Each of us finds what has spiritual meaning for us – it's important to honour what feels true for you rather than what other people say you should do. You may find that an interest in the natural world, music, art, or poetry helps your search for meaning.

Religious and spiritual beliefs can help people to accept the reality of their losses and also carry them through if the losses are ongoing. It is also true, though, that over-rigid beliefs can distort our perception of loss. Even if you believe that 'death is not the end' you still need to mourn the fact that you will miss the person in this lifetime.

A minister I used to know encouraged people to be angry with God when they had a sudden or unexpected death in their family. He would urge them to go into his church on their own or with him and shout at God. Much less helpful are people who feel that such anger or lack of belief is wrong. If you take their disapproval personally, it can make your negative feelings worse and add guilt to them.

You may feel the need to explore different religions and philosophies. David is in his fifties and married with four children. Recently one of his sons died of leukaemia. David was a practising Catholic and very involved with the Church, but now feels he needs to explore other beliefs to help him make sense of what has happened. 'There must be millions of people experiencing this overwhelming pain I have experienced with the death of my son.'

What you can do

- Recognize that a spiritual crisis, or search for meaning, is a normal response to loss.
- Remember a previous crisis and the strength and resources that carried you through. Visualize yourself with those resources and that strength in your present situation.
- Do the 'Temple of Silence' and 'Wise Person' visualizations given in the Appendix as often as you need to.
- Share your feelings with others who are going through or have been through a similar experience.
- Explore different religions and philosophies. My search for meaning has taken me from Quakerism to Eastern philosophies to shamanism in order to understand and accept the unity of all life and experience.
- Try some meditation. Prayer can also be a source of strength for some people.
- Talk to a minister or representative of an appropriate faith.
- Ask God, or whoever or whatever you believe in, for help (and listen for the answer!). The Bible says, 'When you are weak is when I am strong.' I hold a constant dialogue with God. A minister suggested this to me – he said if he could give people only one idea, this would be it. God is now my best friend, with whom I share my highs and lows.

---

1 Published by Bloodaxe Poets, 1986.

3

Helping other people

Don't walk in front of me, I may not follow.
Don't walk behind me, I may not lead.
Walk beside me and just be my friend. (Camus)

In my experience, helping another person through the grieving process is simply about staying with people in their pain,
not trying to provide answers. It is about suggesting new
opportunities and choices if you feel it's appropriate, or they
are asked for, but also learning not to be hurt if your suggestions are not taken up. It's always easy for us to see what we
think or feel other people need. But unless the person you
are helping feels the same way and admits their need, there
will be no lasting benefit and often only resentment for your
interference.

Many of the things which people describe as being helpful
have little to do with giving advice, but more to do with the
qualities that the helper demonstrates. Your greatest gift will
lie in 'being' rather than 'doing'. The ability to be totally present for another person, with all your attention focused on
them, is both healing and therapeutic, but most of us find
this difficult to achieve. Until you have explored your own
losses, attitudes and feelings, you may be unable to recognize the blocks you could have to truly helping others. This
self-awareness is the first step to change. For example, if
tears weren't allowed when you were young, how are you
going to feel comfortable when someone cries? If you feel
anger is wrong, or are afraid of it, you are not going to be able
to deal with someone getting angry. If someone approaches
you with a similar loss to one you have experienced, it could
also bring up unresolved feelings for you. A doctor on one of
my workshops told us he always found it difficult dealing

with patients who had cancer because his own father had died of cancer.

I like C.S. Lewis's remark, in *A Grief Observed:* 'Death is like a big hole: you never fill it, but only build around.' I feel this applies to all types of loss, not just death. It doesn't mean you will never get over your losses, but you need to learn to embrace them before offering your help to other people, otherwise you will never be able to be totally present for others. You will be constantly wanting to relate your own story; or you will unconsciously cut yourself off because you don't want to feel your own unresolved feelings; or you will project those feelings on to the other person.

Reading this book can help you to be aware of any old losses you need to deal with, and places where you are stuck emotionally, as well – I hope – as suggesting ways to heal them. Please don't think you have to wait until you are 'healed' or 'perfect' before you can help someone – every one of us is in this process at different stages, and we can all help each other right now. Being willing to see that your old ideas and judgements may be mistaken, and to engage in the healing process for yourself as well as those you are helping, will ensure that you are the best help you can be to those around you. Most of the clients I draw to me have similar issues to mine. In my psychosynthesis training we were told to remember that we would usually be only one step ahead of our clients!

I love the feeling I have that when I am helping people I am giving back to the world some of the support I have received over the years. I know from experience that the earlier people are given permission to grieve, the less likely there are to be lasting ill effects from loss: so supporting someone is a truly valuable and effective thing to do. Passing my learning on to others, and I hope preventing some unnecessary suffering, makes me feel there has been a purpose in all I have gone through myself. I find people's willingness to trust and be open with me a great gift, and I grow myself as I help others to grow. It is vital to realize that you're engaged in a healing process yourself as you support someone else, and to make sure you yourself are also nurtured and supported.

When to help – and when not

I find it best to ask the person what they want. If they are in-decisive (which is often the case in bereavement), I might say, 'We could look at -- or -- ; which do you think would be most helpful?' Or I use the 'my brother John' technique as I'm talking to them: 'I know someone who in a similar situa-tion did . . . ' This is a way of suggesting choices to them. Don't feel you have to help everyone you meet. There are times in my life when I need space and have my own 'stuff' going on. My friend Uthe says she has to honour the times when she doesn't feel able to talk in depth with dying patients. The other person will always know if you don't really want to be with them, anyway. Avoid shoulds, oughts and musts. Do what feels comfortable for you. If you don't feel able to help right now, suggest you could in the future; or suggest someone else who might be able to. (I believe if I don't feel able to support someone, there will be someone else more appropriate for that person; and, of course, they may simply need to experience their own space for a while.) Or you may feel able to give practical support rather than emotional. Don't forget this person has coped with life before and will again: you can help them to recognize this and to build the skills they need to deal with their new situation.

How you can help

Be yourself, and treat the bereaved person as normally as possible. When a person's model of the world has been upset, the last thing they want is for people around them to treat them differently. Someone in our road whose sister had drowned herself had to go up to people and say: 'It's all right to talk about her, you know!'

Take your cue from the other person. A big mistake most people make is deciding what the bereaved person needs, rather than asking them. An elderly man told me that when his wife died, his daughter bought him a puppy for 'com-pany' without asking him first. He said trying to look after the puppy was almost worse than losing his wife. Also, his daughter wouldn't have anything to do with him as she thought he ought to be grateful, and was upset when he wasn't!

It's dangerous to make assumptions. Not everyone is sorry a person close to them has died or left them. One counsellor went to visit a newly widowed client in her sixties and said, 'You must feel very sad.' The widow replied, 'I'm glad he's gone. He was mean, bone idle, and made my life hell!'

When you arrive, it's helpful to tell people how long you can spend with them, and before parting to make a definite arrangement to visit or telephone again. In this way, people know how long they have to share their feelings. Otherwise, there is a tendency to make small talk and only come round to important matters at the end, when there often isn't time to do them justice. Bereaved people are often invited to telephone or visit friends or family 'if they feel upset'. Since most people's self-esteem will be very low at this time, it can be hard to ring someone up and say, 'I feel terrible'. If a definite meeting or telephone call is arranged, it gives the bereaved person permission to talk.

Remember, the most important losses are someone to talk to of right, and feelings of self-worth. A lovely retired man who had been a successful accountant, and who had many interests, told me he refused invitations to go out after his wife died. He said, 'People are only being kind, they don't really want me.' When we started the CRUSE Call-in Centre in Hillingdon (CRUSE was set up originally to support widows, but now provides counselling services for all bereaved people), we found people would often walk past the entrance for several weeks before they had the courage to come in. Your acceptance of a grieving person just as they are, and your willingness to listen, will go a long way towards restoring their self-esteem.

The art of listening

> If we were supposed to talk more than listen we would have been given two mouths and one ear. (Mark Twain)

When I meet a bereaved person, I generally say, 'I was sorry to hear about ---. Would you like to tell me about what happened?' I've never had anyone refuse yet. Most people are relieved to be given permission to talk. One woman said to me, 'I could talk for two years.' It's generally our own ease or lack of it which will affect our response. Shunryu Suzuki, in *Zen Mind, Beginner's Mind*,[1] suggests the ideal way to listen:

> When you listen to someone, you should give up all your pre-conceived ideas and your subjective opinions; you should just listen to him, just observe what his way is. . . . Usually when you listen to some statement, you hear it as a kind of echo of yourself. You are actually listening to your own opinion. If it agrees with your opinion you may accept it, but if it does not, you will reject it or may not even hear it . . . A mind full of preconceived ideas, subjective intentions, or habits is not open to things as they are.

Most people have the answers inside them; give the space and time to allow them to surface. I sometimes will sit with someone for up to an hour without talking. I'll just say, 'I'm here if you want to talk, but if you don't I'm happy just being with you.' Even if you are not saying anything, you are communicating a great deal all the same; and similarly, you will be picking up most of your information from the other person 'between the lines' of what they are saying. Research by Owen Hargie published in *A Handbook of Communication Skills*[2] shows that people around us are aware of what we are feeling even if we are not actually saying it: communication is 55% non-verbal, 38% in the tone of voice, and 7% actual speech.

The best guidelines on listening I have are the 'Guidelines for Befrienders' published by the Foundation for the Study of Infant Deaths:

You are *listening when . . .*

- You come quickly into my private world and let me be me.
- You really try to understand me when I do not make much sense.
- You hold back your desire to give me good advice.
- You don't take my problem from me but trust me to deal with it in my own way.
- You give me enough room to discover for myself why I feel upset, and enough time to think for myself what is best.
- You allow me the dignity of making my own decisions even though you feel I am wrong.

- You don't tell me that funny story you are just bursting to tell me.
- You allow me to make my experience one that really matters.
- You accept my gift of gratitude by telling me it is good to know I have been helped.
- You realize that the hour I take from you leaves you a bit tired and drained.
- You grasp my point of view even when it goes against your sincere convictions.
- You accept me as I am – warts and all.
- You don't offer me religious solace when you sense I'm not ready for it.
- You look at me, feel for me, and really want to know me.
- You spend a short valuable time with me and make me feel it is for ever.

You are not *listening to me when* . . .

- You do not care about me, and you cannot care about me until you know something about me to care about.
- You say you understand before you know me well enough.
- You have an answer for my problem before I have finished telling you what my problem is.
- You sense that my problem is embarrassing and you are avoiding it.
- You get excited and stimulated by what I am saying and want to jump right in before I invite your response.
- You are trying to sort out all the details and are not aware of the feelings behind the words.
- You are dying to tell me something, or want to correct me.
- You tell me about your experience which makes mine seem unimportant.
- You refuse my thanks by saying you haven't really done anything.
- You need to feel successful.
- You are disturbed by loaded words or abusive language.
- You feel critical of my grammar or accent.
- You come up with all the clever answers which have little to do with me.
- You are communicating to someone else in the room.
- You cut me off before I have finished speaking.

Encouraging people to express their feelings

Anger, tears and laughter are all a natural part of grief. If you can accept and allow a grieving person to feel whatever emotion is uppermost for them at the moment it will be invaluable in helping them to accept their own feelings. A CRUSE counsellor went on a first visit to a recent widow. In her supervision afterwards she said, 'There doesn't seem any point in going again – all she did was laugh!' We talked about how laughter can be a release of tension, as well as a sign of stress and embarrassment. On her next visit the widow was able to express other feelings, such as sadness and anger.

One of the most important things you can do is to give someone, by your attitude, permission to grieve. Family members' concern for each other can involve unhealthy collusion. A counsellor I know told me about a funeral he attended, where everyone was making polite small talk rather than talking about the dead person. He said in a loud voice, 'Why aren't you talking about her?' Whenever I go to a funeral or visit people who've been bereaved, I start the ball rolling by saying, 'Do you remember when they . . .'

Without such support, it's easy for grief to get locked inside. Betty's husband died suddenly. They had no children. Her sister arrived the day before the funeral and said, 'This is the start of the rest of your life. You are not going to grieve.' After the funeral Betty couldn't bear living on her own, so she went to stay with two elderly ladies. Every time she got upset, they said, 'Have a drink', or 'Watch TV', instead of letting her express her feelings and talk about her husband. Two years later Betty was on tranquillizers and visiting a therapist. The same thing happened to me twenty years earlier. Whenever I mentioned John's name, friends changed the subject. It felt as if they wanted to pretend he had never existed – I didn't understand they were afraid of their feelings and mine.

Often the people who are most vulnerable to suppressing their grief are those whose image is one of efficiency. A hospital theatre-sister told me that when her mother died people said, 'If anyone can cope, you can.' Two years later she broke down after trying to live up to this image. Some people never break down, and their unexpressed grief can be a cause of chronic illness. My 'second mother' (I 'adopted' her as a child) was told by her husband not to cry as she had been so 'brave' when her mother died. Forty years on, she has still never cried and suffers from arthritis, which is sometimes known as 'crystallized grief'. She also gets very sad and depressed about all the losses in the world.

If someone is suppressing their grief, there may be a way to help them physically. Watch to see what happens to their body, especially their face, when they cut off from their feelings. I often find people smiling when they are telling me incredibly sad stories. Gently pointing out what you have observed will be enough to spark a change. Once they realize what they are doing, choosing to change their physical habit can allow people to start feeling and healing. A 'stiff-upper-lip' attitude may be linked to a tense jaw that can be helped with gentle massage. You may notice that someone is in the habit of actually swallowing their feelings. One man I know said when he felt himself swallowing, he deliberately opened his mouth and breathed through it. In this way, the tears came easily. One day he found himself in tears in the super-market at nine-thirty in the morning for no apparent reason and just allowed himself to cry. He is no longer afraid of his tears, or of breaking down in public.

What to say

Most of your talking should be encouragement to the other person to talk about their loss and go over and over what has happened so they can internalize it. After the first couple of weeks, many people will expect a grieving person to be 'over it'. I feel one of the most useful functions I can serve is to warn bereaved people about this and to arrange regular times so they can talk about their loss to me. If they have no one else to talk to , I encourage them to write about it too.

Reassure them that the mixture of emotions they are feeling is normal. Often, people feel they are going mad or being silly. Many people punish themselves twice over for what has happened. First of all for the loss itself, and secondly for the feelings they don't understand and feel they shouldn't have. The minister at the church near me said he always introduced people to the 'stages of grief' (see Chapter 4) and told them what feelings to expect after the death or separation from someone close to them.

A spoken or written tribute that celebrates the special qualities of the person that has died is far more valuable than platitudes such as, 'time heals' or, 'you still have . . . ' I found the following tribute in the Inter-Varsity Club magazine particularly helpful after the death of my husband:

> John's tragic death has been a great shock to his many friends in the club who will sadly miss his warmheartedness, the stimulus of contact with his alert mind and his zest for living. John had for long been associated with IVC and had contributed much to it as Debates Organizer, Subsidiary Societies Secretary and council member, and in many other ways. But the loss extends far more widely than this, for he was a man of real talent who had much to offer to the architectural profession and to society in general.
>
> We mourn the loss of a good companion and we offer to his widow our heartfelt sympathy.

This appreciation made me feel that although his life had been short, it hadn't been wasted.

Usually you can reassure the person that they did not cause or contribute to the death or loss. This is particularly important for children in the 'magical thinking' stage (ages 3-7). If the bereaved person feels they have contributed in some way, it's important to encourage them to share their feelings early on and do some 'reality testing'.

Good advice for anyone who has suffered a loss is not to make hasty, rash decisions about jobs, relationships and moving. After a major loss, it's best to wait for at least six months, and preferably a year, if possible, before such major new choices.

Sometimes the most helpful thing is to ask the other person to help you. A fellow counsellor told me about her visits to a woman who had been widowed nearly a year before and who was too depressed to even get dressed. In desperation the counsellor said, 'I need you to do something for me.' It was the start of a dramatic change. The widow suddenly felt needed again and never looked back.

If someone is very depressed, don't be frightened to ask direct questions about suicide. You won't make the person commit suicide by asking them. In fact, for many people it is a great relief to admit their feelings. I don't know anyone who has lost someone close to them who hasn't wished they were dead too at some stage in their grieving process. If you have any fear that the person may act on their feelings (this is extremely difficult to assess, so err on the side of caution), make sure their GP knows the situation, and support them in going for professional counselling.

Don't deny or avoid any feelings that come up for you. It's a good idea to tell the person you are helping how you feel, so you can check if it's really your 'stuff' or if you're picking up their feelings. I might say, 'I feel we are not getting anywhere/we seem to be going round in circles – how do you feel?' Sometimes they feel the same, and we can look at what's going on. Other times they might just say something like, 'I was thinking about . . . ', or, 'I just needed some space for my feelings'.

Practical support

Try to arrange help with everyday tasks. Cooking meals, taking children out or to appointments or school are examples of practical help that are often welcomed. Elderly people, in particular, may find it difficult to take over their partner's role. I remember panicking about looking after a car on my own after John died, and crying my eyes out when I was faced with putting on a plug for the first time. If the person you are supporting is not used to looking after themselves – they don't know how to cook, for example – encourage them to do jobs for themselves rather than creating a new dependency. You could start by suggesting you do the job together. (Cookery classes are a great way of making new friends, incidentally, and they often include having a meal together.)

If you feel comfortable doing it, massage can be a wonderful gift to offer. A nursing officer I worked with told me she hadn't been touched by anyone but her hairdresser in the three years since her husband died, even though she belonged to a caring church and had many friends and interests. Touch can be a powerful trigger for feeling. Don't be afraid to cry or laugh with the person you're supporting. It is possible to misuse such an opportunity for intimacy – it may be that you yourself are needy for physical touch. I always ask myself first, 'Am I touching for my own benefit or theirs?'

When to encourage someone to get professional support

Lasting physical symptoms; excessive guilt; extended anger; severe depression; the threat of suicide; uncontrollable grief; no grief at all; or denying the necessity for grief are all signs that a person really needs professional help. GPs are often the best place to start; see Useful Addresses for other helping agencies.

Looking after yourself

Encourage the person you're supporting to rely on a network, not just you. Most of us enjoy being needed, but it is really important not to create a new dependency in someone who has recently experienced a serious loss. Do make sure that you nurture yourself.

Care for the caretaker

- Be gentle with yourself!
- Remind yourself that you are an enabler, not a magician. We cannot change anyone else – we can only change how we relate to them.
- Find a hermit spot. Use it daily to relax (see Appendix).
- Remember that in the light of all the pain we see, we are bound to feel helpless at times. Admit it without shame. Caring and being there are sometimes more important than doing.
- On the way home, focus on a good thing that occurred during the day, then think of all the things that upset you and allow the feelings to be there. When you feel complete, think of the next good thing you are looking forward to.
- Use your friends or a support group as a source of support, assurance and re-direction.
- Say 'I choose' rather than 'I should/ought/have to', and 'I won't' rather than 'I can't'. If you never say no, what is your 'yes' worth?
- Laugh and play. Do something creative to recharge your batteries.

How long does it take?

As a supporter, you will need patience and commitment to continue to be available when your friend needs you. The most inappropriate response I have heard to a sudden death was from a GP to a twenty-eight-year-old widow with two young children. Her husband had fallen off the scaffolding at work and died two days later without gaining consciousness. When she visited her doctor six months later he said, 'Aren't you over that yet?' as if she had something mild like measles.

The saying has it that time heals. I feel it is more that the passing of time allows the work of grief and the healing that follows to take place. For some people the period of grieving can be relatively short, while others still experience grief into the second or third year or longer. One mother bereaved some three years earlier said, 'I hate being told I should be over it now. How do you ever get over losing your child?' I say to people, 'Don't expect miracles overnight. Live your life not just one day at a time, but half an hour at a time.' After my husband's death I used to say when I woke up, 'Thank you for getting me through the night', then after my breakfast, 'Thank you for my breakfast', and so on throughout the day. It was just words to start with, but I gradually came to really feel my gratitude after the first year.

People often lose confidence when bereaved, and it's important to encourage them to get back into the mainstream of life. When I worked for CRUSE, I would encourage people to take one small step each week, for example ringing someone up, inviting someone for coffee, going swimming. I'd always make a point of asking them the next week what had happened and discussing what else they could do. In this way I hoped I would encourage them to develop their support network and not become dependent on me.

Because there is no mourning period in our culture, many people need permission to stop grieving. I might say to someone who seems stuck, 'Don't you think you've grieved for long enough? Do you think --- would want you to continue to be so unhappy?' Don't forget that all rules are made to be broken. If you feel the person you're helping has been stuck for a while, and it's getting to you, maybe your spontaneous impatience with their stuckness could be the greatest gift you could give them.

Since my whole approach to supporting people is encouraging them to stand on their own two feet, they will often decide when they no longer need my support. With friends, it's often a more evolutionary thing – our relationship will gradually turn back to a more casual interaction, where we get together for fun as well as mutual support.

A summary of do's and don'ts

Do

- let your genuine concern and caring show.
- be available to listen or to help with whatever seems needed at the time.
- say you are sorry about what happened and about their pain.
- allow them to express as much unhappiness as they are feeling at the moment and are willing to share.
- encourage them to be patient with themselves, not to expect too much of themselves and not to impose any 'shoulds' on themselves.
- allow them to talk about their loss as much and as often as they want to.
- talk about the special, endearing qualities of the person or place they've lost.
- reassure them that they did everything that they could.
- accept their behaviour no matter how odd.
- take your cue from them and be yourself.
- help them with practical problems.
- provide food and encourage sleep.

Don't

- let your sense of inadequacy keep you from reaching out.
- avoid them because you are uncomfortable (being avoided by friends adds pain to an already painful experience).
- say you know how they feel. (Unless you've experienced their loss yourself you probably don't know how they feel.)
- say 'you ought to be feeling better by now' or anything else which implies a judgement about their feelings.
- tell them what they should feel or do.
- change the subject when they mention their loss.

- avoid mentioning their loss out of fear of reminding them of their pain (they haven't forgotten it).
- try to find something positive (a moral lesson, closer family ties, etc.) about the loss.
- point out at least they have their other . . .
- say that they can always have another . . .
- suggest that they should be grateful for their . . .
- make any comments which in any way suggest that their loss was their fault (there will be enough feelings of doubt and guilt without any help from their friends).
- tell them about your own woes.
- tell them they are luckier than some.
- tell them about everyone else's misfortunes.
- tell them they'll get over it eventually.
- tell them it could have been worse.
- leave them out of your social circle.
- tell them not to worry or think about it.
- encourage them to go to the doctor for tablets.

These negative responses deny the reality of the loss and lack sensitivity to the feelings surrounding it. Many platitudes and patterns of behaviour have the best intentions, but they usually make the person giving them feel better, rather than the person to whom they are addressed!

You're bound to make mistakes as you try and help someone – none of us is perfect. If your intention is loving, trust that it's that love that will help the healing. Sometimes, amazingly, our mistakes can turn out to be the greatest help to someone, in ways we couldn't possibly predict!

1 Published by John Weatherhill Inc., US/Japan.
2 Published by Croom Helm, 1986.

The Grieving Process

Your joy is your sorrow unmasked. . . .
The deeper that sorrow carves into your being,
the more joy you can contain. . . .
When you are joyous, look deep into your
heart and you shall find it is only that which has
given you sorrow that is giving you joy.
When you are sorrowful, look again in your
heart, and you shall see that in truth you are
weeping for that which has been your delight.
(Kahlil Gibran, The Prophet)

4

To feel is to heal

Grief is a natural, normal response to the loss of something or someone we love. The sooner we learn to grieve, the sooner we can begin to enjoy the life we still have. Grieving is the process through which a person comes to terms emotionally, spiritually, physically and mentally with losses, setbacks, disappointments and death.

> Pain can be physical, emotional or spiritual – whichever aspect it starts with, it will always spread to the others, so the earlier we start dealing with the pain of loss and death, the less likely it is to affect the other aspects.
> (Laura Mitchell, International Stress Management Conference, 1987)

There aren't 'right' and 'wrong' ways to grieve; and there's certainly not a simple short-cut to the healing process. Grieving will take you through many different emotions. This chapter explores the most common of these and suggests ways to move through them. Realizing that grief has different aspects cannot stop the pain, but it can help in accepting whatever emotions come up, in simply allowing the grieving process to take its natural course. The more you allow yourself to feel it all, the more easily you will experience good feelings as well as bad.

Stages of grief

Grieving can be an emotionally chaotic and deeply upsetting process. Your old reality has collapsed and you can find yourself standing, bewildered, in limbo, with nothing to take its place. We each have a strong inner impulse to wholeness, and though you may not see your way clear now, your strong emotions may also be seen as the beginning of building your new self, your new reality.

Researchers into the grieving process invariably try to see an order in the emotional confusion. Such ways of looking at the process can be helpful to the griever, too, in making sense of what is happening. I can still remember the great sense of relief I experienced when I first learned about stages of grief. I realized for the first time that the feelings I had after my husband's death eight years before, and still had from time to time, were normal. Also that, like many people, I had been punishing myself twice over. First for what had happened, and secondly for all the overwhelming feelings I had and didn't know how to deal with. I had often felt I was going mad. All my feelings, I later discovered, are common to most people who are bereaved.

The model I use to help people understand the different feelings involved in the grieving process is:

Stages of grief

- Shock and disbelief
- Denial
- Growing awareness of feelings, including some or all of the following:
- Longing
- Anger
- Depression
- Guilt
- Anxiety
- Acceptance

These stages can apply to all forms of loss. One morning the secretary where I worked arrived very upset. She had told her husband she was leaving him, but he didn't seem to be affected in any way. I told her about the stages of grief. She later told me she watched her husband working through most of them during the next few months, and this knowledge had helped her enormously in dealing with the situation.

Other people find looking for stages of grief positively *un*-helpful. I know one sister in charge of a hospice who says she hates them. She feels supporters stand over dying or bereaved people waiting for the stages to occur, or trying to make them happen. But very often a bereaved person can only resume a normal emotional life after working through their stages. It *is* important not to get hung up on a particular order or time for the stages. People can move 'backwards' and 'forwards', and not necessarily go through all of them. In some cases, especially where there has been preparation for the loss, only a few of the stages may be experienced. To give a better idea of the variety of most people's actual experience, here is a summary of what a sample of my workshop participants felt (they had experienced a range of different losses):

Immediately

Disappointed; angry; disbelieving; resigned; mixed-up; abused; inconvenienced; sad; torn; in a panic; embarrassed; stupid; powerless; humiliated; incomplete; irritated; affronted; cold inside; clammy hands; 'Why me?'; 'I mustn't care'; 'Got to start again'; 'Things will never be the same again'; 'Will it happen again?'; 'It's my fault'.

A week later

Numb; angry; afraid; pleased; disbelieving; indifferent; empty; at a loss for words; still looking for it; missing value and purpose; 'It doesn't matter'; 'Can I live with this?'

A month later

Foolish; relieved; disappointed; frozen; frightened; bored; supersensitive; less involved; restless; untrusting; very stressed; cautious; building strategies; still telling the story; more resigned; 'I've shut it out'; 'I can see the other side'; 'I've stolen something of the person I lost'; 'There's got to be more'.

A year later

Cynical; reforming; more cautious; humorous; angry; impotent; lingering guilt; still missing it; back to commitment; 'A year has passed'; 'Still feel loss'; 'More immediate things to think about'; 'On to fresh fields and pastures new'; 'Still hoping I might find it'; 'Given up hope'; 'It's all my fault'; 'No point in telling anyone; they wouldn't understand'.

Shock and disbelief

When someone experiences a great loss, their model of the world is upset. Shock can appear as complete apathy and withdrawal, or abnormal calm. It can also take the form of physical pain or numbness. Numbness has often been described as nature's anaesthetic. It enables a bereaved person to cope with immediate jobs and needs.

It is important to be aware of the effects of shock. It can be difficult for a recipient of bad news to take information in. Professional carers now generally arrange to see a person who is in shock again at a later date to give further information. People are often more accident-prone at this time. A competent, successful businessman, whose wife had just died, went to work one morning leaving the kitchen tap on. He returned home to find his house flooded.

What to do

Patience and nurturing are the keywords here whether you've experienced a shock yourself, or are supporting someone else who has.

Denial

This generally occurs within the first fourteen days and can last minutes, hours, weeks, or forever in some cases. Bereaved people often behave as if the dead person is still there, and no loss is acknowledged. The dead person's place is still laid at meal times, for example, or a widower may make arrangements for both him and his wife to go somewhere together. An elderly neighbour of mine stayed in denial all the rest of her life. She always talked about her dead husband as if he were still alive, and carried on her life just as she had before he died.

More commonly, there will be varying levels of denial around different aspects of the loss for a certain period. Gradually, the griever will accept the full reality of what has happened. A favourite story that illustrates this turning-point came from a health visitor who told me one day that she'd done something terrible. I smiled because I knew she was too sensitive to have done any such thing. It turned out she had been calling each week to see an older man whose wife had died six months before. Although he had expressed the normal grief feelings, he had never really accepted his wife was dead and had withdrawn from his previous social contacts. He was chatting in his usual way, when he told her he was going to buy a new carpet next day.

'It's just like the one my wife chose before she died,' he said.

'Then why are you buying it?' asked the health visitor. 'Your wife's dead, and she's not coming back.'

He looked stunned for a moment, then the realization slowly dawned. 'No, she's not, is she?'

Next time the health visitor called he had got a very nice new carpet, but not the one his wife had chosen. From then on he gradually continued to try out new ways of being and doing things. I reassured the health visitor that although she felt she had been a little blunt, she had really done him a favour in moving him on through the grieving process.

On the other hand, my friend Robbie has never been able to acccept the reality of the death of her ninety-eight-year-old mother. Robbie was seventy when it happened. They had lived together as 'best pals' from when Robbie was twelve. They had shared everything: friends, holidays, even the same bedroom. Robbie's father and only brother had died within a few years of each other when she was just ado-lescent, and when she was in her thirties, the man she had hoped to marry was killed. Robbie has a great fear of losing people. Her mother had died a year or so after mine, and I suggested she became my adopted mum, so she was able to transfer some of her emotional energy to me. We have in this way helped to heal some of our past experiences by nurtur-ing and supporting each other.

Many people freeze their grief at times of loss. They may not know how to express it, or haven't the time or oppor-tunity to do so. Sue's story is typical of this pattern. She was in her early teens when her favourite grandmother and her cat died in quick succession. Her father, who she was closer to than her mother, also left home without telling her and kept little contact with her. Her brother told her she had no feelings and cut off from her. Sue's mother was involved in her own grief and didn't recognize that Sue needed to grieve too. It was more than two years before Sue even talked to her best friend about what had happened. Sue appeared 'normal' on the surface, apart from being very overweight. (Food comforts the inner child, particularly chocolate.) She married, had two children, a wide circle of friends, and a job giving other people the help she needed herself. Inwardly, she felt depressed and suicidal a large part of the time. Thirty years after her original losses, she came to a bereavement course and finally did her grieving. She found writing poetry a great help in integrating her losses.

Meg, a New Zealander, seized her opportunity when a relatively minor loss unlocked her frozen feelings:

> Four years ago I had a lump come up on my breast overnight. I went to the doctor immediately. Within two weeks I had been diagnosed as having cancer and had to have my breast and some of my lymph glands removed. I didn't grieve at the time as I was so busy supporting my family through it. [Meg is married with four sons.]
>
> A month ago, one of our sons left to live abroad for a year. I went with my family and friends to see him off at the airport. I felt sad and shed a few tears. I felt I was saying goodbye to part of myself.
>
> When I got home I felt this deep grief in my heart. It was so strong, it was deeper than tears. I felt I must stay with this feeling of sadness as fully as possible. It reminded me of when I had my breast off, too. I went into my bedroom and sat and hugged my knees for about half an hour. It felt like I was going through a tunnel. Then the grief burst and went into nothingness. I knew I had reached the bottom of my grief and the depths of my being. As well as contacting my grief at the loss of my son for a year and the loss of my breast, I also contacted the grief of losing my mother. That night I slept very deeply and woke the next day feeling so happy and light.

What to do

A certain amount of denial is nothing to be alarmed about. Your unconscious may be aware that there is too much going on in your life for you to be able to deal with it all at once. If

you are supporting someone bereaved who is persistently re-
sisting taking any opportunity to feel, I suggest:

- Lending them an appropriate book, such as *The Courage to Grieve*, by Judy Tatelbaum (Heinemann, 1981), or (for a widow with children) *Living with Loss* by Liz McNeil Taylor (Fontana, 1981), or this one!
- Encouraging them to write to the person, or about what has happened; or draw their feelings.
- Encourage them to use inner child work (see Chapter 1) to get in touch with their feelings.
- Saying something like, 'You must miss -- very much' to bring out the pain (I would only do this if I knew the re-lationship was a good one).

Don't be hard on yourself or others about denial. As Judy
Tatelbaum says,

> It takes enormous courage to face pain directly and honestly,
> to sit in the midst of such uncomfortable feelings until we
> have expressed them and finished with them. It takes courage
> to be willing to experience fully the pain and anguish of grief
> and face feelings at the time rather than postponing them.

Growing awareness

As they come out of denial into a growing awareness of their
feelings, many people feel they are abnormal. They have
never before experienced the waves of savage feelings that
surge through them, over which they temporarily have no
control. Once someone begins to feel their sadness and pain
they are on the path to healing.

Longing

The beginning of this opening up can take the form of an
urge to remember the loss repeatedly; to visit where it happened in order to make what happened real; or to try and
find a reason for it. The mind tries to make sense of the new
reality, and the heart can feel a depth of anguish and pining
for the lost person that is almost unbearable. People often

have vivid dreams of the person they have lost; or feel the person is still with them.

Anger

A grieving person can be angry with any or all of the following: the medical services; the person who has left (includes those who have died); God, for letting it happen; the person who caused the loss (accident, murder, or sometimes 'the other woman / man' in separation); and themselves. While it's not helpful to stay stuck in feelings of blame, it's important to allow yourself to feel your anger and thus allow it to move through you and be released. Anger is a strong emotion, and if you repress it you block out a great deal of energy. Also, your repressed anger will tend to come out at inappropriate times or in inappropriate ways, such as through sarcasm, or avoidance of people you're angry with. A great deal of stress is due to repressed anger. Millions of pounds are spent every year on tranquillizers, sleeping pills and anti-depressants. There is also an increasingly thriving market for relaxation classes, tapes and therapies. All of these can relieve stress, but they will have no lasting effect unless the underlying feelings of rage are healed.

Many people in our culture have grown up believing it is unacceptable to express anger. It is probably the most difficult of all emotions to deal with. Women, in particular, suffer from repressed anger. In men, anger is often seen as a sign of strength, whereas women earn their brownie points for pouring oil on troubled waters. An angry woman is more likely to be regarded as hysterical than as strong – and to see herself that way, too. It took me until my forties to acknowledge my anger. Repressed grief or anger can contribute to long-term diseases such as arthritis. Writer Gail Linderfield developed arthritis during the breakdown of her first marriage, when she was feeling resentment and anger. Through therapy she was able to own and release those feelings and today no longer has any trace of arthritis. The people I have met with arthritis have generally had repressed anger or resentment, or have not cried when they were bereaved.

Anger often masks hurt. If a client says, for example, she is angry with her husband for leaving her, I might say, 'You really miss him, don't you?' The tears will then come. One of my clients contributed the following thoughts on anger in depression:

> If rather than expressing anger, we turn it inwards, it is experienced as guilt. Guilt produces feelings of depression, incompetence, helplessness, and ultimately self-destruction.
>
> Admitting we are angry acknowledges how we feel, defuses intensity of feeling, and clarifies our perception of a situation.
>
> Forgiveness involves letting go of the anger and cancelling the charge against oneself.

There may be real things to be angry about when a loss happens. Expressing your anger, without a great deal of blame that will only put people on the defensive, can be a positive experience and even helpful to other people. Medical staff, for example, can make mistakes. If no one tells them how they feel, how can staff know not to make the same mistake twice? A friend of mine's son died of cystic fibrosis. She had looked after him and nursed him when necessary right up to his death, which took place in hospital. The doctor looking after Philip asked the nurse to take Vera out of the room for the last moments of his death, to spare her. She had wanted to be with him to the last – she had experienced seeing him in distressed circumstances on many occasions before. Several weeks after the death I persuaded her to return to the hospital to share her feelings with the medical staff, in the hope that they would never put another parent through her experience. They said they had thought they were acting in her best interests, but realized in future they needed to check with the parents first to see what their wishes were. It was a positive learning experience for the staff and allowed them to share their feelings of pain, too, at Philip's death.

Often when we are angry about something the real source of our anger lies deeper. Nicole's father died in 1959 and her divorced mother claimed she was penniless. Nicole then had a stepson at school and a sick husband. She went without to give her mother money for the next eight years. When her mother died in 1967, Nicole found she was a wealthy woman. The anger Nicole felt then helped her to release the anger and hurt of all the other emotional blackmail she had experienced from her mother throughout her life.

Suggestions for releasing anger

Most people's greatest fear of expressing their anger is that they will lose their self-control. If you have kept your anger in for a long time, however, it will generally also take a long time to come out. There are many ways to get the stuck energy of suppressed anger moving through and out of you. None of them involves hurting or blaming anyone else. It's best to give yourself a private time and space to try whichever exercises appeal most. I recommend including at least one that's really physical.

- Recognize and acknowledge your feelings, and know that it's safe to do so. Just because you are angry doesn't mean you have to hit someone or something. Identify the real cause of your anger – keep saying, 'The thing I'm *really* angry about is . . .' (complete the sentence with the very first thing that comes into your head), until you feel in touch with your true anger.
- When you have calmed down, if possible tell the person concerned how you feel. Avoid blame by phrasing what you have to say, 'When you do --- I feel angry', not, 'You make me angry'. (You are the source of your own emotions – no one else can actually *make* you feel angry.) If you are not able to speak to the person due to their absence or death, you can write to them instead.
- Shouting, screaming, or making animal noises helps. Cars are a good place to do this where nobody can hear.
- Hit cushions, bean-bags or a mattress with your fists, another cushion, or a piece of soft hosepipe. A friend of mine who's a doctor says she felt no anger when she first started doing this. Then suddenly she got in touch with an earlier experience of loss. First came the anger, and then the pain and tears behind it.
- Tear up telephone directories or thick catalogues. Blow up balloons, then jump on them and make them burst. Make some bread and as you pummel the dough, think of it as the person or situation you're angry at (this worked a treat when I taught Home Economics in a secondary school!).
- Stamp your feet as you walk along, saying, 'I'm angry about . . .'. Walk along a beach or by a river and throw stones into the water, saying what you are angry about with each one. Climb a hill and scream or shout when you get to the top.
- Get a large sheet of paper and a wide brush or thick

crayons and paint or draw your anger in any shape or colour that feels right.

- Imagine the person you are angry with. Then imagine all the awful things you can think of happening to that person (it's safe; you can't really hurt the person – this is only an exercise in imagination). I was amazed when I did this exercise with my stepfather. I imagined him in the sea with medieval torture weapons and then his eyes being gouged out by sharks. I'd no idea I had such violent feelings inside me until I did this! Afterwards, I could see him as he really was: an emotionally unstable, lonely man. I no longer felt any of what had happened between us was my fault. It's important to complete this activity each time you do it by imagining the same person on a stage or screen in front of you and seeing only good things happening to them.

- Imagine your anger is locked in a small metal box, which you have the key to. Think of as many ways as possible of releasing your anger. People at my workshops have come up with a wonderful variety of responses to this exercise. One man blew his box up with dynamite; another opened up the box gradually and let out a little rage at a time. The one I liked best was the woman who opened her box and found nothing there. So often our fear of anger is far more real than the anger itself!

Depression

This is particularly common after bereavement. It accompanies feelings of despair, emptiness, and pain for the loss. Depression often involves feelings of redundancy, low self-esteem, and disillusionment – a general lack of belief. Crying usually helps to relieve stress. Depression can be a sign of being stuck in anger or guilt. But it is also a natural stage in the letting-go process. This depression is not an illness, and people who experience it may need reassuring of that fact.

The following letter, asking CRUSE for help, vividly describes the blankness of this stage:

The death of my husband after thirty-two years of marriage has made my life totally empty. I go through the motions of working, cooking, gardening, seeing friends, worshipping at

Church – but inside I am dead. Nothing gives me any plea-sure and life has lost any meaning for me. The daily companionship of a very intelligent, witty and able man, who looked and acted like a man ten years his junior, seems to have been the only thing that gave meaning to my life. Of course, I love my son and his family deeply – but I am very aware of the dangers of encroaching on their lives and of becoming emotionally dependent on them. They have each other and I could only ever be on the periphery of their life. My mother, albeit not senile, is physically handicapped, hard of hearing and does not share any of my interests. My work is lonely and although quite challenging, often repetitive, and I do it really mainly for the money.

I cannot see any way out of my complete despair. Suicide is out of the question for religious reasons and because I would not wish to inflict this trauma on my family. Is there anything you can advise or do to help me? My state of mind seems to be getting worse every day and my best moment comes when, with two antidepressant tablets prescribed (reluctantly) by my doctor, and half a Mogadon, I drift into sleep. I sometimes wish I could dream of my husband, just to bring him nearer and to enjoy his company, if only in another existence.

In a case like this, I would encourage the griever to ex-perience her emptiness and loneliness, which is part of the letting-go process, but also to nourish herself while she is doing so (see Chapter 2 for suggestions). I would give her the opportunity to go over and over what has happened, and to talk about her life with her husband – she could also make a scrapbook of his life. I feel anti-depressants generally aren't helpful. They push feelings further inside the griever but when you stop taking them the feelings are still there, just as strong, but now disconnected from the original reasons that caused them, and so you are likely to feel emotionally con-fused. If you can't sleep, it's probably for a reason: I suggest getting up and writing about how you're feeling, and why you can't sleep. I would also encourage this woman to join a support group to share her pain with others in a similar situa-tion. At this point she needs to live her life half an hour at a time, without trying to look to the future at all. She might also find it helpful to talk to her husband, or to God, and tell him how she is feeling.

Guilt

Everyone experiences guilt to some degree at some time. It is one of the most difficult emotions to cope with. People often say after a loss, 'If only I had called the doctor/not gone out/ not worked so hard/paid more attention to them' and so on. The negligence or harm they see themselves responsible for can be real or imagined: the feelings will be as strong in either case.

Suppressed guilt can result in the idealization of the lost person, especially in the case of death. The survivor feels they could have loved the person better, particularly if the relationship was difficult. When I lived in a first-floor flat, one of my older neighbours was married for the second time, not very happily, to a man a lot older than herself with a heart condition. He frequently had to stay in hospital. She made remarks like, 'I hope he comes home in a box.' They had frequent rows and she would throw crockery over the balcony at him. After his death, she never stopped singing his praises. He suddenly turned into an ideal man who had never said or done anything out of place in his life.

In the early stages of grief, bereaved people can feel guilty about what they are feeling, and their inability to enjoy life. Later on, the opposite can happen. People can feel guilty about being happy or enjoying life without the person they have lost – 'survival guilt'. When I ask workshop participants to examine their feelings about loss, there are always responses such as, 'I'm still angry with myself'; 'I'm stupid'; 'I'm to blame'. These judgements will refer to losses that go back years, which means those people have been carrying those negative feelings all that time.

I then ask the group to close their eyes and think of something they feel guilty about either now or in the past. After a minute I ask them to open their eyes and discuss what it felt like. Most people say it's a familiar feeling that often goes back years and feels awful. I also ask them if it changes anything – if it brings the person or situation back – and they all say, 'No'.

I like what Professor Michael Simpson says about guilt: 'We all make mistakes, but I aim to make them new ones.' Guilt is generally about events that are perceived to have happened in the past, or that sometimes could happen in the future. Few people deliberately go out of their way to lose somebody or something they care about. The 'if only' of guilt is usually about us not being prepared to accept the loss.

If you are feeling guilty, I suggest you do a 'reality test'. The organizer of a course I ran in Liverpool confided that he felt guilty about not keeping in touch with his college friends. He had left college ten years earlier, was married with two young children, had a demanding job, and did voluntary work. I asked, 'Do they keep in touch with you?' He slowly grinned, realizing he had been punishing himself for nothing!

Often, guilt comes from the mistaken idea that it's wrong to let go of old relationships. I think each relationship we have is a learning experience. Once we've got the lesson we either need to deepen the relationship – explore new aspects – or move on. This doesn't mean the relationship wasn't important at the time but, like an old garment, you have outgrown it. You no longer have the same things in common: your lives have gone in different directions.

I see life as a school: we are here to complete our lessons. Once we are complete we are perfect and don't need to be here any more. Since we are all still here, we can't be perfect yet – so why feel guilty? Most of us do the best we can at the time with the knowledge and ability we have, and we need to let ourselves off the hook.

What to do

Occasionally there are real grounds for self-blame – in someone whose drunken driving caused an accident, for instance. Sometimes people suffering 'real' guilt need professional help. Prayer is powerful, if the person is open to spiritual help. Writing to the victim (whether alive or dead) is also helpful. (See also the later chapters on the death of children, handicap, and sudden death.)

Recognize that your guilt is not helping you or anyone else, and choose to let it go. One way of doing this is to imagine yourself enveloped in a black wet-suit of guilt. Now, imagine gradually peeling it off, bit by bit. To begin with, you may only be able to imagine getting a sleeve off. When you realize you have the power to remove it, rip the suit off. Most people experience a great sense of relief and wonder why they have allowed themselves to 'wear' guilt for so long.

Whenever you realize your thoughts are trapped in guilt,

say to yourself, 'I forgive myself for . . .' If you find it hard to recognize your innocence, this could be a good time to do some visualization work about your inner child (see 'Healing your hurt child' in Chapter 2). Keep focusing on the essential innocence of the child inside you, and notice how you feel in your body as you experience that innocence.

Once you have let go of your guilt and recognized your innocence, you can choose to use your experience in a practical, constructive way. Most voluntary organizations have been started by people who had feelings they needed to deal with and experiences they feel will benefit others. Do beware of acting out of old guilt though – you could find yourself trying to prove your innocence to the world, when it is you yourself who has judged yourself, and only you who need forgive yourself.

Anxiety

As the full realization of the loss begins to come through you will probably feel anxiety about the changes and new responsibilities that are taking place, and the loneliness looming ahead. In extreme cases, this can become panic, and there may be thoughts of suicide. Anxiety, or fear, is the other side of love. At times of loss it is normal to feel alone and unloved.

What you can do

I find the best remedy for anxiety is to focus on love.
- Hold your arms up and out in front of you at waist level. Imagine love in one hand and fear or anxiety in the other. Say to yourself, 'I choose love'. Bring both hands together, one on top of the other, over your heart and feel a white light shining through them and you as the fear in your heart dissolves.
- Remember a time when, as a child, you had the same feeling of fear and anxiety. Picture that child sitting in your heart surrounded by love.
- If you are feeling suicidal, don't hesitate to talk to someone. If there is no one near that you trust, phone the Samaritans. If you are concerned about a friend's suicidal

feelings, make sure their GP is informed and encourage them to seek professional counselling.

Unexpected feelings

This is not really a separate 'stage'. Sudden, maverick feelings, often positive, can occur at any time and be disturbing to both grievers and their supporters since they don't fit pictures of 'normal' grief. Many people feel a sense of relief when someone dies after a painful illness, or if a partner leaves when the relationship has been difficult. Witnessing a 'good', peaceful death can be a euphoric experience. More difficult to accept can be a 'high' after an accident or a completely unexpected, abrupt end to a relationship. This is the result of the adrenaline that automatically kicks in to get us through crises. It may take a few days for the body to be back to normal, and there may be a reactive 'low' to deal with then.

I remember an elderly aunt arriving at my husband's funeral with an enormous bunch of flowers, just as we were leaving. The funeral directors had sent her to the wrong place. My husband had a wonderful sense of humour, and I suddenly had an image of him looking down at us all and laughing. I started to laugh myself, but felt I had to pretend I was crying instead!

As a health education officer, I took part in 'stop smoking' groups. At the end of one six-week course, two participants burst into tears and told me their problem was bereavement, not smoking. I talked to them both and went home with one of them. She told me all the funny things that had happened around her partner's death. She said she hadn't felt able to laugh about them with other people. We had a good laugh together as she told me her stories.

What to do

Allow yourself to feel whatever comes up – don't judge yourself. Your emotions are chaotic and it won't help to try and restrict yourself to what you think you ought to feel.

Acceptance

This is the vital completion stage of the grieving process. It's important not to get hooked on this 'goal' and try and make it happen – you will only be suppressing your uncompleted feelings. You may find yourself going in and out of acceptance for a while – there's rarely a clear-cut boundary.

Elisabeth Kübler-Ross defines acceptance as a feeling of victory, a feeling of peace, of serenity, of positive submission to things we cannot change. The time it takes to reach this stage varies enormously, depending on how important the loss is, and how easy it is for you to go through the grieving process. In the case of bereavement, it generally begins to happen in the second year, after the death has been relived at the first anniversary, and the first Christmas, holiday, birthdays and so on have happened without the lost person. The griever can then start to relearn the world and be open to new situations with their possibilities and changes. Many people feel guilty because they are not 'over it' in a year, and the textbook says they should be. In the case of sudden death, for example, or the loss of a child, it would be absurd to expect to reach a state of acceptance in a year.

Overviews

As I said earlier, the stages of grief are simply one way of looking at the grieving process; of making sense out of the emotional chaos that is the actual experience of grief. Other people working in this field have suggested different models. You may find one of them more helpful, particularly as an overview of the process.

The whirlpool of grief

This is a recent model, suggested by Richard Wilson, Consultant Paediatrician at Kingston Hospital. It is a vivid picture of grief. Richard sees the river of life running along smoothly until it suddenly falls over the cliff-edge of loss. The waterfall of bereavement, when the river turns into individual droplets thrown out in all directions, is a state of shock, numbness and denial. Then the chaotic water hits the pool below and forms a whirlpool of grief – a state of falling apart or emotional chaos. The water can hit rocks around the pool, producing pain and physical symptoms in the griever. Or it can wash up on the opposite bank and stay stuck there in a state of severe disorganization ('all washed up') or breakdown. Eventually, the water from the whirlpool flows on through mourning and an acceptance that the loss is real to reorganization in its new channel, and loving again.

Richard is keen for counsellors to recognize that each person's experience of bereavement is individual. He feels the detailed view of stages of grief can lead to a rigid approach; and to attempts to impose a fixed 'treatment plan' on those who are grieving.

A conversation should begin with the recognition that we know nothing about this particular person until we have listened to what they have to say. Their previous experiences in life, the person they have lost, the manner of their dying and the reactions of the world are all different. . . .

In grief, there is a disorganization of life and thought and values, but most people are then able to reorganize their life in a new way. Although old emotions can always return in almost the same intensity, they do so infrequently and for much shorter periods of time.

from Richard's contribution to my *Good Grief (1)* teaching pack

The transition curve

This concept, developed by Barry Hopson and Mike Scally,[1] is particularly useful in explaining reactions to losses other than death, such as redundancy or reorganization at work. It describes the dip in self-esteem that happens between the loss of the old and the integration into a new reality. How deep the dip is, and how long the return to the previous level of self-esteem takes, depends on the seriousness of the loss and the flexibility of the person concerned.

The Chinese word for crisis carries two meanings: 'danger' and 'opportunity'. Hopson and Scally emphasize that transitions, however unwelcome, offer the prospect of growth and development. Even difficult losses such as unemployment, bereavement, or disablement, offer opportunities for personal re-evaluation, widening horizons, and developing new talents and interests.

The first three stages on the transition curve relate to various stages of grief, beginning with *immobilization* ('shock and disbelief'), then *minimization* ('denial'), and *self-doubt/depression* ('depression'). The low-point of the self-esteem curve is *acceptance/letting go*. This is not the peaceful acceptance that completes the stages of grief, but rather the step out of denial. Once the reality of the loss is accepted, the curve of self-esteem rises through *testing* (trying out new ways of being), and *search for meaning*, until at *internalization*, self-esteem has returned to the level it was at before the loss.

These last three phases describe important elements in the recovery process. Recovery from grief involves developing a new identity that allows you to function in the world without the person or way of life you have lost. *Testing* describes the process of trying out new ways of being. A favourite poster of mine shows a cat sitting on a windowsill wondering whether to jump off or not, with the words, 'Each journey starts with just one step'. As a counsellor, I encourage my grieving clients to do something new each week: ring someone up; invite someone to coffee; go out to a new place.

The *search for meaning* indicates the deeper levels of building a new identity. This can take the form of a religious, spiritual, or practical direction. Renée was in her late fifties when her husband died. They had had a rather Victorian marriage. She had stayed at home and done all the shopping and cooking for her husband. On his death she joined a travel club and was last heard of living in Canada.

The final stage of *internalization* describes a deep level of integration. One of my neighbours, whose twin brother had died a few years earlier, told me a week after John's death that once I had got over the initial pain of losing my husband, he would become a part of me. Three months after his death, I had a job interview where I had to make a five-minute speech. The week before I had been practising, but was so nervous I couldn't make anything last as long as five minutes. On the train going to Letchworth for the interview, I suddenly spotted an unusual building and decided to talk about architecture. My talk was very successful, but I felt it was John talking through me. He had been an architect and had also run a debating group. I have had similar experiences over the years, when I've had to face important decisions.

When I was considering changing careers, I heard John's voice saying, 'If you are going to take a risk, take a big one.' I did, and the change was the right one for me. He had used that phrase in a discussion we had shortly before he died. I know many other people who have had similar experiences. The have found themselves doing jobs or activities the dead person had always previously done.

Peter Marris, Professor Emeritus at the University of California, sees the search for meaning as the most essential part of the grieving process:

> To a casual observer who sees, for instance, an attractive widow with growing children, the extraordinary difficulty of [recovery from bereavement] may appear baffling. Hasn't she still a great deal to live for? Yes, but each part of it – her children, her family and friends, her career and home – has had its meaning in the context of a relationship with her husband whose loss changes everything. To discover what each can still mean to her involves an insistent searching out of that thread of continuity. She cannot repudiate a past which represents so much of what she valued and experienced and struggled to achieve, without denying her own self, but she cannot go on dwelling in that past, without distorting it and stultifying her life. She has to transform and abstract its meaning, so that it can become relevant to her future, and this is the central task of grieving.
>
> (Speech at the Second International Conference on Bereavement in Contemporary Society)

A short model to end with

If all the ideas in this chapter seem too complicated to you, I'd like to leave you with William Worden's model (he is the author of *Grief Counselling and Grief Therapy*), which is the simplest I've come across. If we don't accept that the person or situation we have lost will never come back, we can't ever move on.

- Acceptance of the reality of the loss.
- Experiencing the pain.
- Adjustment to life without the person / situation.
- Withdrawal of emotional energy from the old situation and reinvestment in the new.

And remember, grieving is an emotional experience, not a mental one. I've heard it said we are eighty per cent feelings and only twenty per cent mind; so don't worry if your feelings don't make sense to you.

---

1 See their *Life Skills* teaching programmes (Life Skills Associates, 1980).

5

Grieving parents

Consider at your own death
You only die
But you have to keep living
After the death of others. (Mascha Kale to
The Compassionate Friends in Germany)

The death of a child is the most devastating tragedy that can occur in a family. It upturns the natural order of things. We expect old people to die one day, but no parent is ready to accept the death of a child cut off by an accident or illness from all their dreams and aspirations. As Harriet Sharnoff Schiff says in *The Bereaved Parent*, 'When your parent dies you lose your past; when your child dies, you lose your future.'

Childhood is still the most common time to die in many underdeveloped countries, as it was in England until this century. Forty per cent of the population in the mid-nineteenth century were dead by the age of six, with the average age of death being nineteen. The sweeping social changes of the last century, and the general improvements in living standards – sanitation, housing, nutrition, hygiene – mean it is now the exception, rather than the rule, for children to die in the Western world. For most of us, a child's death is a shocking affront to the way we live now.

Modern medicine cannot always perform the miracles we expect. In the case of an anticipated death, there can be time for emotional preparation. But often with modern forms of treatment, death can be delayed for several years. Parents may deal with this situation by denying that death is ever going to happen, and be even more overwhelmed when the actual death does occur. I have looked at such situations in later chapters – see 'Living with handicap', 'Life-threatening conditions', and 'Dying'.

Parents who have lost a child not only have to cope with grief and, frequently, guilt, but also to find a way to accept the unnatural prospect that they have a future when their child has none. A mother whose fifteen-year-old son was killed in a road accident remembers going on holiday after his death and feeling guilty because he wasn't there. 'We had often been on holiday without him before but it just seemed wrong that he should be dead while I was still here.'

Mothers commonly want to talk the tragedy through and then to talk about it again and again. But fathers often try to repress their feelings after the initial expression of grief. Losing a child may put a great strain on the parents' relationship. If there are other children in the family, it may be particularly difficult for everyone to get their needs met at this time.

Pre- and peri-natal loss

Parents' shock, bewilderment and feelings of guilt after a stillbirth or cot death are likely to be more severe and long-lasting than after a death which is anticipated or understood. In the case of a child's last illness, however reluctant parents may have been to recognize the inevitable, there has at least been a chance to anticipate and come to terms with the separation and grief of death. It can be harder to come to terms with unexpected death, and often the parents' reactions are correspondingly extreme. Their grief is also complicated, especially in neonatal deaths, by the fact that their child was not yet an individual personality, especially if they didn't see their child. Other people may feel they have no one to mourn.

Miscarriages

It has only recently been recognized that miscarriages need to be mourned for. One woman told me that when she had a miscarriage her doctor just said to her, 'One in four people lose their babies in this way.' She wasn't supposed to be affected by it.

Because the loss can be 'invisible', it's easy for parents to get trapped in denial, and not admit how bereaved they feel. Support groups are helpful in encouraging parents to share their feelings. There are also films and books available which show the foetus at different stages of development. Looking at these can help parents acknowledge what has been lost.

Stillbirths

Many people do not understand that for parents a stillborn child is a real person, and his or her mother and father will naturally grieve for them. If the baby dies before birth, there can be an incredible sense of loss for the mother in giving birth to a dead baby. It is particularly hard for parents who have lost a baby to see other parents taking their babies home with them – instead of their anticipated joyful homecoming with the new baby, they are left with feelings of emptiness, bewilderment and pain.

Most mothers will have a sense of failure, as Bel Mooney so vividly describes in the film *The Life That's Left*.[1] She felt guilty, and kept thinking she could have looked after herself better, and that she was being punished. A father also may feel shattered, and wonder if some paternal genetic factor was responsible. Other children in the family are generally nearly as upset as their parents. They may secretly feel that in some way they were to blame. They need to be told the truth as simply as possible and to be lovingly reassured, particularly if they were jealous of the new baby.

In the last few years there has been a greater understanding of the needs of parents of babies that are stillborn. They will need to let go of all their months of preparation and their dreams of the future. They may well have prepared a special room, with drawers full of baby clothes.

I remember Bridget, a member of the Quaker Meeting I belonged to, having a stillbirth. It was her third child.

I realized when I went into labour something was wrong, but no one would talk to me about it. I spent a long time in labour and then the baby was taken away. Later, I was allowed to hold her and she looked perfect. I couldn't understand why she wasn't breathing and thought she'd wake up and be all right. I felt a failure when I went home and had no baby to show the other children, family and friends.

Bridget found looking at the dead baby's photograph and touching the layette helped in her grieving. As a result of her experiences, she joined a telephone helpline for mothers who had lost a child.

Seeing and holding the dead baby generally helps parents to accept their loss, and makes the baby easier to remember and mourn. Some parents do not wish to do this: the important thing is that they have a choice about it. Giving the child a name and having a photograph also help the grieving process. Some parents like to have a lock of hair. Most hospitals will take photographs in any case, as parents who refuse at the time often regret it later. If the stillborn baby is handicapped, it can be even more important for the parents to see the child, otherwise their imagination and guilt can conjure up a 'monster' far worse than the real handicap. The healing that can come from seeing a baby who is stillborn is beautifully expressed in this excerpt from 'Death of a Baby' by Judith Mott, published in the *Nursing Times* (12 January 1983):

The sister from our community nursing team walked in. She expressed the usual kind sympathy and concern for my health, but then asked if I had seen the baby. I told her that I was afraid of what he would look like. She firmly told me that she would go and look. When she returned, she said that he was fine, but his lips were blue through loss of oxygen. She confirmed that he would be cold and very pale. Then gently and kindly, but somehow conveying her own strength to me, she offered to go and get him. At that moment I just wanted to hold him and love him and give him the 'mummy hug' that was his right.

As I waited I felt no fear, just an intense longing and the excitement of knowing that at last I was going to have what had been promised for all those months. Soon she returned carrying a rectangular box. It was draped in a purple cloth like those used to cover an altar. She placed it on the clothes cabinet at the opposite wall of my tiny, single room, and I watched her remove the cloth and open the lid.

As she took out my baby son I think I experienced the most intense yearning to love that I have ever felt. My body was still painful and bloated and I felt the restriction as I leaned forward, but I know that I stretched out my arms. As she tenderly laid him down I was crying but feeling something that was very strong and very right. For those few, precious moments there was only him, me and the sister in the whole world. He was cold and hard, but I had expected this and it was no worse than the shiny, china doll I had kissed as a child.

From that moment our new son had his own separate identity and the feelings that belong to him will never impinge on the secure, established love that we have for our little boy who lives.

Neonatal death can be extremely hard for professional carers to deal with. Gavin Fairbairn makes a powerful plea for more emotional understanding and support in his article 'When a Baby Dies – A Father's View' in *Nursing Practice* (1986,1):

They took Hesther out of her special-care cot and gave her to me. I was in great emotional upheaval. This was my first child and I had agreed that she should be allowed to die. I had taken the word of the paediatric senior registrar that my child was unlikely to live and agreed that he should stop trying to make her live.

I was left holding Hesther while people, as it seemed to me, backed off into the corners of the room. I spoke to her and cried with her. As I welcomed her into the world I said I was sorry she would not be able to stay with us. I held out my hand towards the retreating figures and asked for help. They retreated further and further away. They seemed to vanish into every available corner of the special-care room and into the adjoining office – safe behind psychological or glass partitions, able to deceive themselves into thinking that what I wanted was to be left alone with my baby, able to ignore my outstretched hands and eyes. These caring and committed professionals abandoned me when I need them to stay with me and help me to be with my child. . . .

I wanted to take Hesther to [Susan]. I wanted to know that she was going to be all right: I wanted us to be a family for a while before Hesther died.

I went to Susan and showed Hesther to her: I told her she was very beautiful but she was not going to live, the doctors had told me so. Susan was very dozy, though she managed to come through the fog briefly to say hello to our daughter. It was a very sad time for us. It was a turbulent time for me – what to do? – stay with my wife or stay with my baby? In my mixed-up state it did not occur to me that I could stay with both.

After a few minutes I took Hesther back to the special-care room and left her to die in a cot. I went back to Susan: I had begun to believe that she too would die and I wanted to be with her if she was going to do so. She was my love, she was my long-standing friend, she and I shared the world together. I left my baby to die with people who would not hold my hand while I cried and I went to be with my wife.

My continuing concern, my guilt, my regret, is that I left my baby to die with strangers and went and sat with my wife. I remember now how I admired my father many years ago when he sat and held his dog while the vet 'put her to sleep' and I wonder what possessed me to let my baby die in a room full of strangers while I ran off and hid from her.

Cot deaths (Sudden Infant Death Syndrome)

Sometimes a seemingly normal baby dies unexpectedly and for no apparent reason. The death is a mystery and a terrible shock. Parents often feel that they were in some way to blame and go over and over the tragedy in their minds, asking themselves if there was anything they could have done to have prevented it. These guilt feelings are a perfectly natural reaction, but are usually quite unfounded. If relatives or a baby-sitter were caring for the baby when the death occurred, the parents can blame themselves for having left the baby. Occasionally a mother will also be blamed by her husband or relatives. It is important that all involved understand that in the present state of medical knowledge these deaths cannot be foreseen by parents or doctors.

Such sudden deaths invariably involve some sort of legal investigation and a post-mortem, which add to the parents' stress. However, since in nearly all cases the cause of death turns out to be unknown, this investigation can help parents to let go of their feelings of guilt.

Ray and Pauline lost their only son, Harry, in a cot death. They are not able to have any more children. They both found writing about what happened, talking about it to friends, and meeting other people who had experienced a similar death helped them in their grief. Having a 'Service of Thanksgiving for the Life of Harry' on what would have been his first birthday was helpful too. The following poetry is by Pauline and the prose by Ray. Men generally find it more difficult to express or write about feelings, but obviously have as much need as women to do so, so I hope this will encourage male readers who have unresolved feelings about a loss to write about it.

> The pain at birth to give you life – soon turned to joy.
> The happiness inside of me – was nothing I had felt before.
> Eight months of love I had – then you had to die.
> Why did you go to sleep that day?
> Why didn't you cry?

How do you put emotions into words about a cot death? My personal feelings changed weekly, if not daily, after the death of young Harry. I cried when I registered his death. I realized that all the registrar was doing was wiping my son's name off the computer, which meant henceforth he didn't exist. For an instant, I had doubts that he *had* existed. Thankfully this feeling passed quickly. Some days you can look at other people's babies and have control, other days you hurry past prams and pushchairs not daring to look. . . . I wonder if all the hidden doors in my mind concerning Harry have been unlocked or whether some will never open.

What I am sure of is you need to tell someone exactly how you feel and that person needs to be a level-headed listener who reflects your thoughts, not distorts them. . . . I feel my wife may be more deeply affected than I because she had to deal with the initial finding. She may be scarred deeper, especially as futile resuscitation was involved. Feelings of guilt and total uselessness prevail, sometimes leading to nightmares. Guilt is one of the hardest things to overcome, although there is nothing to be guilty about. 'What if' questions come flooding in and you know there is no answer to them.

After I've lost my baby, please . . .

Elsie, who suffered two miscarriages, one baby who lived for eighteen hours and one for five months, speaks for many parents with the following:

- Don't ignore me because you are uncomfortable with the subject of death. It makes me wonder if what happened means nothing to you.
- Acknowledge my pain, even if you think I shouldn't be feeling it because I've lost 'only a baby'. And please don't expect me to be 'over' this in a month (or maybe even a year or two): losing a baby is one of the most difficult of all life's experiences, and the depth of my grief will shock even me as it returns in waves, over and over again, long after everyone else has forgotten. And, please, be aware that holidays and the anniversaries of my child's birth and death will be particularly difficult.
- If you haven't yet called and a long time has gone by, tell me that you are sorry, that you just haven't known what to say, but don't say you've been too busy! This has been an extremely large event in my life, and it hurts to hear it has been so low on your priority list that you couldn't spare a five- or ten-minute call.
- If you invite me for lunch – and please do! – in the midst of my grief, expect to talk about my loss. It's all I'm thinking about anyway, and I need to talk it out; small-talk neither interests nor helps me just now.
- Don't change the subject if I should start crying. Tears, and talking about it, are the healthiest ways for me to release this intense emotion.
- Telling me that So-And-So's situation must have been harder to bear won't make mine easier. It only makes me feel you don't understand, or can't acknowledge, the extent of my pain.
- Don't expect that because my child 'is in the presence of the Lord' that is all that should matter (i.e., that I should not be hurting). I do believe, and I'm thankful for that; but my arms ache to hold my child *here*, and I miss him or her so much.
- Now is not the time to tell me all about your own birth experiences ... it reminds me, painfully, that you came home with a live baby and I didn't.
- Telling me I must be a very special person that God would send me such a heavy burden, and that 'God's will is best' implies that God did this purposely. I believe His will is best too, but I don't believe everything that happens (including my baby's death, or anyone being killed by a drunk driver, for instance) is God's will.

- Don't remind me that I'm so lucky to have the other kids . . . I am, and I know it. But my pain is excruciating for *this* baby, and the others don't take that away.

- No matter how bad I look, please don't say, 'you look terrible'. I feel like a total failure right now, and I don't need to hear that I look awful too.

- Don't say, 'I'm so glad you didn't get to hold him, or nurse her.' I am in agony because I didn't get to do those things. My arms ache to hold him, my breasts are full of milk meant for him, and the feelings of deprivation and missing my baby are so intense that I can't imagine you'd believe it is easier for me this way.

- Don't devalue my baby ('Oh well, better luck next time') – to me he was a very special, unique person who can never be replaced. (Besides, there may not be a next time . . .)

- Don't say, 'I know how you feel, I lost my mother . . .' It is not the same. We all expect our parents to die one day, after they have lived their lives, but I am grieving intensely for all the might-have-beens of my baby's life.

- When you ask my husband how I am doing, please don't forget to ask him how he is doing too. He also has lost his child, and if you ignore his hurt it says to him that his pain shouldn't exist, or doesn't matter.

- Don't say, 'You'd try again?' like I must be crazy. If you had my history, you might not want to face the menopause without doing everything you could to change it.

- If I snap at you for saying any of the above (or anything else), please forgive me and try to understand it came from my intense pain. (Your dog might bite you when you try to pick him up at the side of the road after he's been hit by a car; that wouldn't mean he hates you or is ungrateful, just that he's been hurt and your touch – well-intentioned though it be – has added more pain.)

- Hug me, tell me that you care, and that you're sorry this has happened.

- Be available to me, often if you can, and let me talk and cry without judging me. (Saying, 'Don't be angry' is like saying, 'Don't be thirsty' – my feelings are part of a normal grief response, and I will work through them more quickly and easily if you are not judgemental.)

- Just love me, and I will always remember you as a true friend.

Accidental deaths

Children are killed in accidents every day. For children between the ages of ten and fifteen, nearly half of all deaths are
due to accidents. Many of these are road accidents. Young
people who ride motorcycles are particularly at risk.

Accidental deaths tend to give rise to guilt as well as shock
in the grieving parents. Rebecca's four-year-old daughter
was knocked down and killed. Rebecca says she walked
round in a kind of dream for a long time:

> I didn't want to meet anybody I knew; I couldn't even go out
> shopping on my own. I felt I had failed as a mother, because
> your child just doesn't die before you. I felt guilty for letting
> her go out to play. I felt guilty too because in some ways it was
> a relief. She was a very demanding child, my first, and there
> were times when I felt I didn't know how to bring her up. Not
> that I didn't love her enormously, but there are all sorts of
> feelings that you have to sort out once they are gone.

As Audrey (a member of the Compassionate Friends, an
international organization offering friendship and understanding to bereaved parents) says, guilt is not logical. She
remembers feeling, after her son died in a car accident,

> 'My child died because I was too loving and he never built up
> the necessary survival kit to grow up and survive' and at the
> same time, 'I was not loving enough – I should have kept him
> so close to me that he would have been protected by me
> always.' I was feeling guilty for two opposite characteristics – I
> was torturing myself with guilt – but I couldn't stop. Now I
> accept that I am a mixture of over-loving and under-loving, as
> are most parents.
>
> On the other hand, my husband felt guilty because he had
> given our son a green car in spite of his in-built superstition
> that green was an unlucky colour. He still felt guilt even
> though he knew that people safely drive green cars all over
> the world. In fact, he still feels guilty, but now accepts the un-
> reasonableness of the feeling.
>
> . . . . Guilt is linked with anger. A child's death causes tre-
> mendous anger within us. Sometimes the anger can be
> directed at someone or something and we can say that was
> why it happened – admit that we feel angry at someone or

something. However, when the anger is turned inwards to oneself it can become guilt.

Rebecca felt unable to ask other children to play with her remaining child, as she felt unable to accept the responsibility of looking after them. Another difficulty she experienced was telling relatives:

> You can't imagine how dreadful it is having to tell your parents what has happened to their little grandchild whom they loved. It is ridiculous that so many of us can't talk to our own relatives. We don't want to upset them and they don't know what to say to comfort us. This is where the loneliness comes in: you try and keep your feelings to yourself.

Adrian and Linda's seventeen-year-old son and his friend were killed while riding a motor-scooter. Adrian cried all the way to the police station. He felt embarrassed, but at the same time sad, for the eighteen-year-old policeman who had to bring the news. Linda remembers going around in a daze after her son's death and not knowing what season it was. Adrian and Linda's big question, even as Christians, was 'why?' It was difficult to understand why their son and his friend should die 'when there are so many wicked people living in the world'. Linda says that at first she just wanted to die, and that for a long time her first thought on waking was that her son was dead. 'Once you can live with the fact that you will never know why your child died, you have started to come to terms with grief.'

Another father describes his feelings about losing his son, who was involved in a similar tragic accident that resulted in severe brain-damage and a coma:

> We entered the ward and sat beside him. There was even more apparatus than before yet he simply looked asleep. His skin was unmarked, warm and pink, and his chest moved with the ventilator. The nurses attending him talked to him, evidently well briefed in the fact that hearing may be present even in the absence of all response. They tried hard to raise our hopes after the doctors' foreboding.
>
> That evening his girlfriend arrived and she and my wife sat up with him all night while I went home and returned the next day with his elder brother. There was no change, only

the news that blood had been taken for tissue typing [Nic carried a donor card]. The implication did not escape us. We went out for a walk and toyed with a token lunch while he was reassessed. On our return we were told unequivocally that there was no hope of survival. . . . We sat beside the body that was our beloved son, brother, and boyfriend. There was an uncanny feeling about the scene. A few minutes earlier Nic was at least in one sense alive and there was hope. Now, although nothing had changed, he was dead and there was no hope. Yet so many signs of life continued: heartbeat, colour, respiration – albeit by ventilator – and warmth, although we noticed that his body was being allowed to cool.

The transplant surgeon arrived. He was very kind and said that there was an acute shortage of corneas as well as kidneys. We asked him to arrange for anything of value to be taken and said that we had no hang-ups about beating-heart donors. Keep him going for as long as would be useful. I signed the appropriate piece of paper and we went to say goodbye to our Nic. We made ourselves realize that all was not hopeless. Somewhere out there two people in renal failure would have the hope of their lives fulfilled and two who were blind would see[2]. . . . Then, for the first time since childhood, my carefully cultivated composure disintegrated and I wept loudly and openly and cared not who heard and saw.

We broke the news to those at home and then started telephoning. We found that we wanted to tell family and friends but it was hard to know what to say. . . . We discovered that we were attempting to console those who were trying to console us and that there was no consolation, only shared grief and affection. At the end of that first evening we sat quietly with a few of Nic's friends and read the lines of Laurence Binyon: 'They shall grow not old . . . we will remember them.' That was helpful in that the words said exactly part of what we felt. Finally that day came the night of weeping. I remember calling into the darkness the words of King David in the Old Testament, using Nic's name: 'Oh Absalom, my son, would God I had died for thee.'

The next few days were occupied by various activities and the expression of a whole range of emotions including unashamed weeping when thinking about Nick and describing the last hours at the hospital. I was surprised at finding how very much I wanted to perform irrational rituals. My eldest son drove me to the scene of the accident so I could place a flower there with a piece of rough wood with 'Nic' painted on it. Then I lay down in the ditch and bawled until my son helped me to the car. I wondered what the passer-by walking his dog thought. I went to see the smashed motorcycle and left a flower on it. Weeping, I was taken by the garage manager to his office and given coffee. I apologized and said that his job was mending broken vehicles rather than broken hearts, but that the two must often go together. At the funeral I followed another ritual and threw Nic's keys into the grave. I could not resent the machine that brought about his death as it had meant so much to him and was so much part of him that to hate it would be to hate him. I was thankful, however, that it was an insurance write-off as it would have been hard to have the machine back repaired but not Nic. . . .

Going through his effects was an interesting as well as a moving experience. I feared it would be distressing but there was a real delight as I found myself getting to know him in a new way after death even though I do not think that I had neglected him before. Joy and grief were present together as souvenirs of childhood rekindled memories of happy days. Letters from girlfriends certainly showed that he was appreciated. . . . We were thrilled to find the Leeds Medical School magazine in which he had had an essay on hepatocytes published. He had mentioned it but never shown it to us. We looked among our own belongings for tangible memories and were especially delighted to find we had kept the Christmas, birthday, and Mother's Day cards that he had given us during the year. We shall put them up at each anniversary for the rest of our lives.

. . . . What of those who wrote or visited to console? None could console. Especially welcome were those who had known Nic and whose conversation revived memories for cherishing. We did not mind recounting the events of his death.

. . . . Should we have banned the machine from our home? He was an enterprising lad who would have earned money somehow and kept a bike at a friend's home. Then we would have lost him another way if not both ways. We decided to accept him with his youthful ambitions. We made clear to him the risks of motorcycling and that he would receive no financial support from us except for training and equipment for safety. Indeed, he achieved the top grade in the local training scheme and had the best of helmets even though it was pushed in by a tree-stump like a thumb into an eggshell. We paid for car-driving lessons at the age of seventeen and made a standing offer of the use of a car even to take to Leeds. He would probably have refused the offer of a Rolls-Royce. Bikers are like that. I am simply thankful that there are no grounds for ill-feeling about his death. No one else was hurt. He never drank when riding. His machine was found to have been in perfect condition. He had not stormed off after a family row. We were in mutual harmony as son and parents and all our memories are happy. To the last we never lost him and he died instantaneously doing what he most enjoyed.

. . . . I do not find the answers to the questions 'why?' and 'why Nic?' in religion but in life. The first answer is in the counterquestion 'why not Nic?' Secondly, I discover that freedom of all kinds entails risks, and that means that the worst consequence, death, is going to happen to someone some time and by random chance, not with any form of fairness. Freedom of speech, political freedom, freedom to climb mountains, to drive cars, and ride motorcycles, costs lives. One of the safest places to be is in prison. We gave Nic freedom and he paid the price and our loss is our share in that cost.

Grieving for children

I remember a mother describing how much it hurt when she was asked, 'How many children have you?' She said she always included her dead son, but his brothers and sisters left him out.

It can be difficult for parents surrounded by anxious family and friends, and often with other children to care for, to create the emotional space they need to grieve. One of my counsellors during my psychosynthesis training was American. Her twelve-year-old son had accidentally drowned the previous year. She said she had come to England to give herself time to grieve. At home, her family and friends gave her no space. Here, as soon as feelings of grief and sadness began she used to treat herself like a child and take herself off to bed or sit and allow herself to go into the feelings. At the end of a year she felt her grief was complete, and she went to resume her previous life. She also remarried her son's father, whom she had divorced several years earlier.

One of the hardest things for parents is sorting out their dead child's belongings. Audrie described her feelings:

The toys and books I had frequently called 'all that junk' suddenly took on a new value, and the clothes had that wonderful personal smell. I used to think I was odd because I would put my head into Nick's wardrobe and sniff deeply, but I could still smell him there. It was with a great sense of relief that I realized that other mums did that too. The older your child is when he or she dies, the more possessions they have acquired, but whether we are looking at few or many, it is still hard to know the right thing to do with them. And of course, there isn't a right or wrong. What is right for one family may not be so for another. I used to be amazed by families who kept a child's room exactly as he had left it, but now, having lost a child myself, I can understand it. I personally didn't feel the need to do this, but I no longer find it strange that some people do.

One of the biggest mistakes I made was in wanting to give mementos to Nick's special friends a little too soon. For instance, I gave his beloved guitar almost immediately to his friend who had taught him to play (he actually used it at Nick's funeral), only to discover later that my daughter, who doesn't play the guitar, would have liked to have had it.

I found going into his room extremely difficult and didn't do it for some time, except to sniff in the wardrobe. It must have been some months later that I actually persuaded myself to go and sort out a few things, and even then I had a mental word with Nick and asked him to come in with me. I didn't like the thought of going through personal things, and seeing things he had written was very upsetting, but I knew it had to be done. I needn't have worried too much about the personal things as I learned later that his brother and sister had already been through the room and taken out and destroyed anything they knew he wouldn't have wanted me to see. We must allow our children their secrets.

It has taken me eight years to get the things I have kept down to one-and-a-bit drawers in a special chest, but I have managed it. I gave most of his clothes (the ones that were respectable) to a charity sale, and his personal possessions just seemed to drift off among friends. When it comes down to it, so little of it was important, because my values too have changed and I no longer worry about material things. It is nice to see the odd reminder of a special occasion in his life, but to me the real Nick is deep inside me and I know he would have wanted everything else to be used by others.

Parents' feelings of failure can be very strong. Fathers often find it most difficult to talk about what has happened. They often feel they have to cope while their wife gets all the sympathy:

> After the funeral of our twenty-two-year-old son, Mark, a friend pressed my arm gently as he was leaving and said, 'Look after Wendy'. He meant well, but in truth I was hardly capable of looking after myself at that point, let alone her. Yes, there were times when we were able to look after each other in those early weeks and months – but there were also times when we were lost and isolated in our own grief. But I as a father did not feel myself to be the strong one all the time, as cultural expectations would have it.

Bill Schatz, a bereaved father himself and co-founder of the Seattle Compassionate Friends, pointed out in one newsletter how aspects of men's traditional role as fathers can hinder their grieving process. Men naturally assume the role of protector, and may feel a sense of failure when a child dies:

> He shouldn't have let his daughter go to that party! He should have watched the baby closer! Furthermore, after the death of the child the family, individually and collectively, is in grief. Try as he may, the father cannot protect his family from the pain of grief. And finally, he is unable to shield them from the devastating effects of his own grief.
>
> Another role to consider is that of provider. This role commonly causes a father to return to work very soon after his child's death – long before the shock and numbness have worn off. . . . In a few weeks he may adjust to the work routine, but each night when he returns home, he finds the memories, the family in grief and the stark reality of the death of his child. He may find it increasingly difficult to come home and choose to escape through working overtime, stopping at the local bar for a drink or getting involved in some activity.

. . . This sometimes leads to extreme reactions, such as alcoholism or divorce.

Supporting your marriage

It is vital for parents to take care of their marriage after the loss of a child. The following suggestions first appeared in the US Compassionate Friends' *Valley Forge Newsletter* of Spring 1992:

- Don't expect your partner to be a tower of strength when he or she is also experiencing grief. Two people skiing down a mountain who each break a leg may love each other dearly, but it is hard for them to help each other down to safety.
- Be sensitive to your partner's personality style. In general, he or she will approach grief with the same personality habits as they approach life. They may be very private or very open and sharing – or some place in between.
- Find a sympathetic ear (not necessarily your mate's). You need someone who cares and will listen.
- Do talk about your child with your partner. If necessary, set up a time period daily when you both know that it is time to talk about your child.
- Seek the help of a counsellor if depression, grief, or problems in your marriage are getting out of hand.
- Do not overlook or ignore anger-causing situations. It's like adding fuel to a fire. Eventually there is an explosion. Deal with things as they occur. However, when an explosion does happen, realize that it's the grief talking so don't take everything said as a personal insult. Ignore a lot.
- Remember you loved your partner enough to marry. Try to keep the marriage alive – go out to dinner; take a walk; go on holidays. Think of things you both enjoyed before you had any children.
- Be gentle with yourself and your mate.
- Join a support group for bereaved parents. Attend as a couple if you can, but otherwise come by yourself. You will soon make friends and feel part of the group. It's a good place to learn about grief and to feel understood. Do not pressure your partner to attend with you if it is not his or her inclination. It is not worth having a disagreement

over and may make your partner antagonistic to your future involvement with the group.

- Do not blame yourself or your mate for what you were powerless to prevent. If you do blame your partner or personally feel responsible for your child's death, you may need to talk it over with someone. However, do try to forgive and think of the love the partner showed to the child when he or she was alive.
- Realize that you are not alone. There are many other bereaved parents – there are thousands, even millions, throughout the world.
- Try to believe again in the goodness of God and of life When you are ready, search again for joy and laughter.
- Recognize your extreme sensitivity and vulnerability and be alert to the tendency to take things personally.
- Read about grief, especially books about bereaved parents, written by bereaved parents.
- Take your time with decisions about your child's things. Don't move home until you have thought about it for many months If you rush into things, you may regret it.
- Be aware of unrealistic expectations for yourself and your mate.
- Remember there is no timetable to grief. Everyone experiences grief differently, even parents of the same child.
- Try to remember that your partner is doing the best he or she can.
- Marital friction is normal in any marriage. Don't blow it out of proportion. Try with all your efforts to keep your marriage together. Believe in yourselves and that you will make it.
- Try not to let little everyday irritants become major issues. Talk about them and try to be patient.
- Be sensitive to the needs and wishes of your partner as well as yourself. Sometimes it is important to compromise. After the death of a child, a husband often wants to make love more often in his need for comfort. A wife can be turned right off. Talk about this together and you will find, when you both understand it, the problem can be more easily resolved.
- It is terribly important to keep the lines of communication open.
- Work on your own grief instead of wishing that your partner would handle his or her grief differently. You will

find you have enough just handling your own grief. You may not be the best person to be your partner's therapist. Remember, when you help yourself cope with grief, it indirectly helps your partner.

- Expect to be on a seesaw. One day one of you is feeling better and the other is plunged into depression; then the seesaw goes the other way and the position is reversed. This may be a blessing in disguise as it might keep your family intact and still functioning with one parent being strong enough to take over. Although it is hard for you on a better day to cope with a depressed partner, realize this happens to all bereaved couples.
- As Harriet Schiff (author of *The Bereaved Parent*) writes: 'Value your marriage. You have lost enough!'
- Hold on to hope. With time, work and support, you will survive. It will never be the same, but you can learn again to appreciate your life and the people in it.

Single parents

In *The Bereaved Parent*, Harriet Schiff quotes Evelyn Gillis, whose daughter died in a car accident:

After we [single parents] recover from the emotional trauma of death or divorce, we create a new family unit of parent and child. As the child ages, and if we do not remarry, our relationship evolves beyond that of parent and child. Our lives become closely entwined. The child becomes a companion and helpmate. All our parental love and caring is given to this one child.

Upon the death of the child, we face the absence of support from another adult who would share the same feelings of loss and grief. After being told of the child's death, we alone carry the responsibility of the funeral arrangements. Even when help is offered by friends and family we must face these difficult final decisions alone.

After the funeral we are left to face the reality of the child's death in a house that offers nothing but silence. There is no desire to clean house, shop for and cook food, entertain. Doing these things for one person is not enough.

Only children

Edie, whose only child, Euan, died in 1984 when he was hit by a car, says grief after an only child, or all the children in a family, dies has additional complications:

- There is no one to parent – there is acute frustration in not being able to do what you know you can do, parent, and are denied because your child has died.
- You find you have a lot of time and energy and no direction for them. Fussing over your partner, the dog, a foster child; baby-sitting, or having your nieces and nephews over, does not compensate for your loss of directed energies.
- Your physical space – the house, car, even the shopping trolley – is not filled with anyone. It is quiet and sometimes the sound of that silence is deafening.
- If you cannot have another child, you have lost your future. You may never have grandchildren, and the question arises, 'Who will take care of me in my old age?', or, 'What do I have to look forward to?'

A grandparent's perspective

(This section was contributed by Margaret Gerner of the Compassionate Friends, St Louis, USA, who lost her granddaughter.)

Grandparents of a child who has died are sometimes referred to as the forgotten mourners. In most cases, we are. I think that we even tell ourselves we shouldn't hurt as much as we do, and tend to concern ourselves with our bereaved child's pain to the neglect of our own. We need to recognize that we, too, have lost a part of ourselves and we have a real reason to grieve. If we say to ourselves, 'He or she was not my child and I shouldn't hurt as badly', we are not being fair to ourselves.

As grandparents we have a double burden. We hurt because our precious grandchild is dead and we hurt because our own child is desolate. We feel helplessness and frustration in addition to our pain. But if we are to be helpful at all to our bereaved child we need to be helpful to ourselves also. As grandparents we have a special relationship with our grandchild. The relationship is usually one of unconditional love without the responsibility that parents have. We simply loved our grandchild and indulged him or her as we never could our own child. Most of us were loved in return by our grandchild in a very special way. Many of us were a link to the 'olden days' for them, and how they loved to hear tales about their mother or father when he or she was younger. There were times we baby-sat for our grandchild or fixed special foods that nobody could fix like Grandma. That special relationship is gone now and it will never be again. We miss that relationship and it hurts.

I miss my three-year-old Emily in so many ways. I miss hearing her talk. When she first began to talk I was 'Bamma', then I was 'Jamma', and by the time she died I was finally 'Gramma'. One time I repeated her dog's name just as she said it, 'Cappy' instead of 'Taffy'. I'd say 'Cappy', and she'd say, 'Noooo, Cappy'. After I repeated it a number of times she became exasperated with me and very emphatically said: 'Gramma, look at my tongue!' All I could do was squeeze her. She couldn't say her T's or P's. They came out as 'sh'. She would say, 'You're in shrouble.' I was reduced to jelly one day when I had done something she especially liked and she said: 'I'm shroud of you, Gramma.'

I can still hear her saying that to me, but today, almost five months after she died, I wonder if she is still 'shroud' of me. Am I still her Gramma to be proud of or am I falling down on the job? Am I allowing my grief to be expressed? Am I allowing myself to cry, to feel the stabbing pain in my chest when I realize, again, that she is dead? Am I allowing my anger at God to come out? Am I telling people, 'I'm feeling fine', when really my insides are in knots? Am I concerned only with helping my daughter, Emily's mother, when I should be helping myself as well? Am I accepting my humanness when I think I know all the answers to grief, but still hurt so badly? Am I attending to my own pain and my hurts and my grief in addition to trying to be a help to my bereaved family?

Anyone who has lost someone close to them experiences grief symptoms such as shock, numbness, fatigue, inability to concentrate, or depression. If we had a close relationship with our grandchild and saw him or her frequently, we are likely to grieve more deeply than for a grandchild we saw only a few times a year.

Some of us have other children who have children. We may resent their having 'complete' families of two or three children when our bereaved child may have had only one – the one who died. This is not an uncommon reaction for grandparents. I was surprised and appalled when I realized I was angry with my oldest son, who has three children, when my daughter lost her only child. But feelings aren't fact. I was not wishing one of my son's children should die, I was simply looking at how unjust life is, and my oldest son's family was where I focused. I felt guilty about this until I looked at my resentment for what it really was.

I think guilt is one of the strongest emotions we feel. In addition to feeling guilty that we have survived our grandchild rather than our grandchild surviving us, as we think it should be, we feel guilt at the things we didn't do. We feel guilty if we didn't baby-sit every time we were asked, or didn't spend as much time with our grandchild as we should have, or were too busy to fix that special meal. When these nagging guilts arise in me, I ask myself: 'Did I know Emily was going to die? Did I know I wouldn't have forever with her?' None of us will answer 'yes' to these questions. Even if we knew our grandchild was terminally ill, we always believed there would be more time. Many of us feel this kind of guilt even though it is irrational. We need to talk this out with an accepting person. We may need to simply forgive ourselves.

Grandfathers have an especially hard time handling their grief. Men in our culture are not allowed to be emotional. From childhood they are told to be strong and to take care of others – never themselves. Grandfathers may need to find their own ways to express their grief, to cry, to talk about their grandchild. One grandfather I know goes regularly to the cemetery alone. There he can cry without anyone seeing him. Sharing their emotions with another person is necessary for grandfathers if they are to successfully resolve their grief. Hopefully, grandmothers and grandfathers can share their pain with each other.

Some grandparents have lost a child of their own in some earlier years. The death of the grandchild will almost always revive the grief they felt over the death of that child. We may have gone years thinking we were 'over' our child's death, only to find that almost everything about his/her death and funeral will come back as though it happened only a short time ago. This revival of our child's death will likely be of such intensity that it will surprise us. There is a reason for this that I think is important to look at. If your own child died ten, fifteen or more years ago, it is unlikely that you resolved your grief. In earlier years (and still to some extent today) the griever was encouraged to put thoughts of the dead child out of their minds as soon as possible. We were told to be strong, 'keep a stiff upper lip', or 'keep busy so you won't think about him/her'. In other words, we were encouraged to suppress our grief. If we did that and did not work through it, it is almost certain to surface with our grandchild's death. It is important to be aware of this possibility so that if it does happen, you know that you aren't being silly or weak or deliberately bringing up painful memories. Be kind to yourself. Allow your grief to surface. Let yourself feel the pain of *your* child's death. Talk about it. Share it with your grieving child. It could well be helpful to both of you. It will certainly help you to empathize with your bereaved child.

Do

- respect your bereaved child's way of handling their pain.
- allow them to express their emotions and to talk and talk and talk about their child or the circumstances of his/her death.
- allow them to cry, even wail if they need to.
- allow them to express their angry thoughts or feelings of guilt.

Don't

- tell your bereaved child how he or she 'should' feel.
- tell them to 'be brave' or 'control yourself' or not to cry in front of the other children.
- tell them to 'think of all the good memories'.
- tell them to do or not do anything.
- try to rationalize their angry thoughts or feelings of guilt. It may be irrational guilt or anger, but to them it is real., and with time these emotions will lessen. Non-judgemental listening is what will help them the most.

We need to know there is no timetable for grief. We should be careful of our expectations of how our child 'should' be doing at this time. In the early months of grief our bereaved child may appear to be doing well. Then at four to six months they seem to fall apart. We need to know this is normal. In the early months our child does 'well' because s/he has not yet accepted the full reality that her/his child is dead. It isn't until they face that reality that real grief begins. This is the most painful and the longest part of the grieving process. This is the time we are expecting them to get better and when they get worse we can't understand it and fear for their sanity. At this time others turn away from them because they can't understand. This is the time they need us the most. How desolate they can feel if the two people they could always rely on now turn away from them.

How grandparents can help

Fatigue or even physical weakness is common among bereaved parents. There are numerous practical ways a grandparent can help out: preparing meals, doing laundry or grocery shopping; taking the surviving children for a day or an afternoon to give the bereaved parent some time to his/ herself.

If is my belief that one of the most important things we can do for our child is to physically hold them. Parental grief is so debilitating that there are times the bereaved parent would like to crawl up on their 'mommie's' or 'daddy's' lap to be comforted as they did as a small child. We need to be aware of this need and actually allow them to do this in any way possible. This can be physically hard because many of our bereaved children are adults, larger than ourselves, but we can find ways to put our arms around them, cuddle them and pet them as if they were little children. This need to be held is stronger when your child cries or is having an especially hard time thinking or talking about their child. Many times they are not aware of this need themselves, so we must take the initiative.

It will be painful to listen to your child talk about their child over and over. It will be painful to see them cry and hurt so terribly, but consider how important your care and concern for them can be.

As grief can be a cause for growth in our bereaved child, it can be a cause for growth in us. But the most important thing to remember is that our grandchild's death can lead to a lasting and beautiful relationship with our own child.

I am trying to attend to my grief as well as trying to help my bereaved daughter. I want my Emily to be 'shroud' of her grandmother.

6

Grieving children

A child can live through anything so long as he or she is told the truth and is allowed to share with loved ones the natural feelings people have when they are suffering. (*Eda Le Shan*)[1]

It changed my life a lot. I was always with adults, I had to grow up so fast. I had no one to play with. I was really depressed for a bit.

(Sally, whose brother died when she was seven)

There is a revolution taking place in our understanding of children. Until recently, the received wisdom in our culture was to shield children from the truth of loss, discourage them from feeling sad, and to believe 'they'll soon get over it'. Family, friends, teachers and carers unwittingly colluded in pressurizing children to suppress their grief; in over-protecting them. Because children's perspective on the world is radically different from adults' it was thought they didn't feel deeply. In fact, their openness to life and their dependence on others mean a child's world-view is fundamentally threatened by the death of someone close to them. Long absence – in prison, or hospital, for example – will feel almost the same as death to a young child: they can feel just as abandoned. And after one parent leaves or dies, a child may also lose the other, to grief.

It is now realized that children as young as fifteen months go through stages of grief. There is also evidence from studies in pre- and peri-natal psychology, and from adult survivors who have undergone psychotherapy, that even younger babies are deeply affected by serious losses, such as the death of a twin (see 'Healing childhood loss as an adult' in Chapter 1).

Even when adults do recognize the seriousness for a child of losing a parent, they may overlook the trauma of other losses. Many siblings have told me what a lonely experience the death of a brother or sister can be. So often when they meet someone who knows the family they are asked, 'How are your mother and father bearing up?' It is seldom recognized that the siblings also have a need to grieve.

A major loss may well entail serious secondary losses which may be almost as devastating for the child. I remember hearing about a boy of eight at a special school. He was an only child and when his mother died of cancer, his father decided to continue his career in the regular army. James was sent to live with an aunt in the country. In this way he lost his mother, father, familiar surroundings, school, friends, teachers and carers.

Children's need to grieve

Depression is a real risk if children are not encouraged to express their grief when the loss happens. Dora Black, a consultant child psychiatrist, found that there is a higher incidence of depressive illness in adults who lose a parent before the age of ten than in those whose parents live longer. Four times as many girls as boys are referred for psychiatric treatment. Girls under eleven are most affected by the loss of the mother, and from fourteen onwards by the loss of a father.[2] Grieving significantly lowers these risks, as I have found with the clients I have worked with.

Bereaved children may also experience learning difficulties or get into trouble at school. In a school where I taught there was a boy whose mother had died of cancer when he was ten. His father remarried within six months. The boy was given no opportunity to mourn. He became progressively more naughty and immature during his secondary school life.

Resistance to grief

The adolescent in the family is generally the most at risk here. They may feel they are 'too old for tears'. The eldest in the family may take on the responsibility of setting a good example and putting on a brave face. Children who had a difficult relationship with the dead person are likely to feel guilty, anxious and confused about their loss.

Many of the children in a special school I visited had difficulty identifying with adults due to their poor earlier relationships with parents whom they no longer or rarely saw due to either death or divorce. I remember nervously doing a visualization with a class of eleven- to twelve-year-olds. I got them to imagine they were a rose bush. One boy, whose father had died a year before, visualized his rose bush in a cemetery being looked after by the cemetery-keeper. He was able to cry and talk about his ambivalent relationship with his father for the first time since his death. His father had left his mother and he had seen very little of him before he died. He shared his sadness at not knowing his father or being there when he died or at the funeral.

A child's experience

The following account is by an older child looking back on a death that took place a few years earlier.

> The first thing I remember is not knowing how to act or what to do. I felt terribly alone and awkward. I was shocked. One minute it was a nice, normal day and the next minute everything was changed. I didn't know how I was supposed to act at school. Part of me wanted to tell everyone what had happened and part of me didn't want to talk to anyone at all. I felt guilty for getting some comfort from the attention (I asked myself if this meant I was 'glad' my brother had died), but on the other hand, I felt that people would think I didn't care when I said nothing. It hurt either way. One way I dealt with my grief was by being sarcastic and laughing whenever something painful came up.
>
> Home became a pain-filled place. My parents had been hurt very badly. They weren't the same parents I knew before the death. The biggest mistake I made in my grief was trying to 'fix' my parents' pain. I wished for and acted in ways that I hoped would change them back to happy, whole people again. . . . In fact, I couldn't do it. No matter how 'good' I was, or how much I tried to make our home pleasant; they were still sad. The bad thing was, by trying to make them

better I stuffed a lot of my own sadness, fears and worries inside. . . .

For years I rarely cried for my brother. I always thought that was strange. It was years before I was able to let the tears flow and then I cried for him and for me. I cried for Arthur because he was dead and I missed him; I cried for myself because of all I had missed. I missed feelings of happiness in myself and my family. I missed feeling safe and secure. I missed the attention my parents were no longer able to give me. I missed the years of carefree childhood that were ripped away. . . .

I now realize that my feelings about my brother's death were not the same as my parents' feelings. I used to think that I didn't love my brother because I wasn't as sad as long as they were. They hated the holidays, but I wanted the fun of the holidays. They couldn't be happy, but I could. . . .

I remember that I used to think about things I did or didn't do with my brother before he died. I felt guilty because I didn't play with him the last time he wanted me to. Of course, I didn't know at the time that he was going to die. I remember times when I got mad and yelled at him for no reason. I felt guilt about that too. . . .

My brother's death definitely changed my life. It brought pain and unhappiness, but it also brought an awareness of other people's pain and the ability to understand and help others.

The limits to grief

A normal child with the proper support should come through bereavement with no lasting ill-effects. In fact, this ability to take up the threads of normal life can often be hurtful to the remaining parent unless they understand that children dip in and out of grief and are unable to grieve for too long.

Friends of mine with two boys of five and seven lived in a small village and were members of the local church. The mother contracted terminal cancer and for more than four years she spent frequent periods in hospital. The care of the community and extended family ensured that the children had, if anything, more than usual care and attention. When the mother finally died and the father gently told the children the news, he was amazed when the younger boy said, 'When are you getting married again?' He wanted his life to return to normal as quickly as possible.

Helping children grieve

- Encourage children to attend the funerals of more distant family and friends (don't forget, it's their choice). In the case of a close family death, children and adolescents should be told what is likely to happen. They should be accompanied by a less involved adult who can comfort them and describe the event.
- Get together as a family and talk about the dead person. You can all grieve together instead of colluding in silence for fear of upsetting each other. It's helpful to children if adults can share how they are feeling also. Encourage children to talk about their feelings: your expectation that they are deeply affected will give them space to grieve.
- Making a scrapbook about the dead person can help family grief. This can be done either together as a family, or individually. It could include photographs, mementos from places you have visited together with the dead person, the funeral or memorial service, poems, writing, things the mourner(s) liked best/didn't like about the person. It is important not to idealize the dead person, but remember them, warts and all. Sharing what they didn't like gives children an opportunity to let any guilt feelings surface.
- Give photographs and things that belonged to the dead person to children, so they have something to remember them by, and as springboards for talking about them – 'Do you remember the chess game you played on this board with Daddy?' One father I knew who had cancer bought special watches his two young sons had particularly wanted, to be given to them on his death. Afterwards they proudly showed them to friends: 'Look at the watches Daddy bought for us'.
- Play can be helpful in facilitating mourning in young children. Encourage them to act out situations and fantasies; draw the scene where the death occurred; start them off with a squiggle and let them complete the drawing; use a toy telephone to talk to the missing person in heaven. Older children can be encouraged to read books around the subject of loss; to write poems, or letters to the dead

person. Pillow fights are good for getting out anger – they generally soon turn to laughter.

- Take children out (or ask friends to) as a relief from mourning. I went out with someone who had been widowed for a year and had one son of eleven. The son had not been out to any activities or played with other children since the death. The father had been so wrapped up in his own grief, he had completely forgotten his son's needs.

Talking to children about death

A child cannot grieve if she does not know what has happened. Unfortunately, when a parent or other person important to a child dies, adults often lie to protect themselves or 'spare' the child – in fact, this only makes them more anxious. Although the adult instinct is to 'protect' children, the truth in manageable doses is the wisest course. Children need to be told about death or loss in simple, jargon-free language that is appropriate to their age. The conspiracy of silence can be bewildering and frightening. They can find themselves alone with a tearful, withdrawn parent whom they cannot contact or comfort, and who no longer seems to be able or willing to meet their needs. Children need to be told something about the manifestations of grief in the surviving parent, and that it will gradually get better. Even worse, a child can be sent away to stay with a relative or friend and on their return, find the dead person's name isn't mentioned and it is almost as if they never existed. This can increase feelings of loss and fears of rejection when they most need love and support. From an early age, children are able to give and receive comfort and sense what is going on.

Jane told me of her father's death when she was four. She had answered the front door and been met by a policeman, who asked her to get her mother. She did so, and was then put in a room by herself while her mother talked to the policeman. Later that day, Jane was sent to stay with an aunt. A month later, on her return, her father was not there. She was never told what happened until she grew up. She always felt it was something she had done that must have caused his disappearance. In fact, he had died of a heart attack in the street.

John Bowlby says, 'If children are not allowed to share occasions of grief, fear and unhappiness, they will be driven in on themselves to bear sorrows alone. The earlier it starts, the more damage is likely to occur at a later stage.'[3] Rosemary Wells in her research into bereaved children talks about six-year-old William:

> After his mother died, William had appeared dry-eyed for weeks at the school where I teach. But he was quiet and withdrawn – not at all his usual self. His own teachers avoided talking about his mother for fear of upsetting him and embarrassing themselves. One playtime he took my hand and I sensed that he longed to talk about his mother but just didn't know where to start. I asked him where he went on holiday last summer and he began to tell me. 'Did Mummy go swimming?' I asked, and he looked up at me in sudden excitement. 'Yes! She had a smashing costume . . . it was red and had only one strap around the neck . . . and we tried surfing . . . and she said . . . ' He was off – all the feelings he had been keeping to himself came tumbling out. Every day for weeks William talked to me about his beautiful young mother, and eventually he was able to settle down once more into his school routine.[4]

What to say

Young children, in particular, can easily misunderstand what adults are trying to tell them. Tell the truth, and keep it simple. If you suggest Daddy has gone on holiday or gone to sleep, the child may be frightened that they too may die if they go on holiday/to sleep. Telling a child that God has taken from him the one he loves could destroy his faith. In the case of death from illness, it's a good idea to reassure children that the doctor helped the person not to suffer, and that even though he was unable to prevent them from dying, he can cure most illnesses.

Some children fear they will die like their parent. One three-year-old said, after his father died, 'I don't want to be four because it's nearer to death.' Another child said, after her mother had died, 'I don't want to grow up and die like Mummy – I want to be a boy and grow up like Daddy.'

The film *Where Is Dead?* suggests a good way to explain death to young children. The mother asks her young daughter, whose brother has been killed, to think of something they had enjoyed doing in the past. She then asks her to describe what happened, and tells her that it was what is called a 'memory'. The mother then tells her daughter that her brother is also a memory, so whenever she misses him, she can think of him and have a memory.

Keep the lines of communication open. You are bound to make some mistakes, but the more you talk about it, the less likely children are to stay stuck in misunderstanding.

How age affects response

Children, like adults, are individuals. They all go through stages of physical, mental, emotional, social and spiritual development, but the details for each child are unique. Young children process information differently from adults and this process changes as they grow. Children need to understand death in their minds, realize the social implications (So-and-so can't come and play any more), and get in touch with how they feel about it. Children tend to think of death as reversible until they are ten or so. They are used to playing games like cowboys and Indians – 'Bang-bang! You're dead!' and then they get up again.

Alfred Torrie, husband of the founder of CRUSE, who had three children aged eleven, nine, and four-and-a-half at the time, described their reactions to the accidental death of their pet dog. When informed of the sad event, the eleven-year-old responded at first by saying nothing. Slowly the tears welled up in his eyes and he began to cry softly. When he regained his composure he said, 'It's such a horrible thing – it's all over.' The nine-year-old listened quietly to the news and said, 'He has gone a long way. We'll have to get another one.' The four-and-a-half-year-old looked puzzled and said repeatedly, 'What happened? Why are you crying? Let's go and get him.'[5]

Very young children

Babies will be affected by their parents' emotional state and will also react to very close losses – a twin is likely to miss the other, for instance. Reactions may include being unsettled for a few weeks, losing weight, and having difficulty sleeping.

Toddlers (1-3 years) cannot understand the permanence of death and may ask repeatedly about the dead person coming back. At this time, their mother is usually the child's mainstay, so if she is not available, consistent substitute parenting is essential. Toddlers generally react by showing their insecurity and fear of separation. They may revert to baby talk, regress in toilet training, have nightmares or insomnia, and refuse to be left alone. Some toddlers search repeatedly for the dead person or act out the tragedy with their toys. Others become sad and subdued, losing interest in their surroundings.

'Magical thinking' stage (approximately 3-7)

This starts in an egocentric stage of growth when the child perceives that she is the centre of the universe and so believes her own thoughts, wishes and actions cause what happens to herself and to other people. Children who are not encouraged to share these thoughts may bury their guilt-feelings deep and subconsciously be affected for the rest of their lives. It is therefore particularly important to encourage these children to work through their grief and keep sharing what they are thinking. A couple of typical examples of magical thinking I've been told about by colleagues are, first, a little boy who had moved to a new area went out exploring and met an elderly man. When he returned home he told his mother about it, and said the elderly man was old enough to die. Two days later the man died, and the boy thought he had caused it. Another boy, whose father died after he had been angry with him, was out shopping with his mother when a car mounted the pavement near them. The boy thought it was his father returning to punish him.

When told about the death, children at this stage of development will probably react quite casually because they are used to playing bang-bang-you're-dead. Most likely they will cry and ask about the death at a later time, perhaps bedtime, as though you had never explained it before. This can be confusing for parents. The child may be frightened and remorseful that their jealous thoughts about the dead person made it go away. Their parents' preoccupation with the dead person may be seen as confirmation of their guilt, or they may try to comfort their parents in the way they themselves have been previously comforted.

Children may experience a compelling urge to recover the lost loved one, and will make every effort to search for them. Their magical thinking is reinforced by fairy and folk tales. Some children will think that if they are always good and endure bad things and wait for a very long time the dead person will return and all will be 'happy ever after'.

The child may re-enact the cause of death or an aspect of it such as the funeral. This should not be discouraged, as play is the means by which children integrate and master life's experiences. Some children become fearful that they may die themselves, or that they may disappear, or their parents might go away, and so do not want to let parents out of their sight.

Ailsa Fabian's book, *The Daniel Diary*,[6] written about her three-year-old son's reaction to the sudden death of his five-year-old sister is an intensely moving way of understanding a three-year-old's reaction.

Concrete thinking stage (8-12)

Children at this stage think in terms of either/or; good guys or bad guys. They have little ability to deal with subtleties, ambiguities or euphemisms. So care must be taken not to use figures of speech such as 'we lost your sister'. The permanence of death starts to be recognized, and by the age of nine or ten the irreversibility of it begins to be grasped. Children realize they themselves will die one day. By the end of this stage, a child perceives the finality of death in an adult way.

The following story shows an eight-year-old's reaction to the death of her brother:

It was nearly thirteen years ago that my brother died and yet it was only a few months ago that I talked to someone about it, about my thoughts and feelings at the time . . . My brother became ill when I was seven years old. Eventually he was taken into hospital and thus it all began. I felt very isolated, everyone seemed to almost ignore me and attention was centred on Mark (my brother). In retrospect the reason for this is obvious, but then it was a very different matter. When I went back to school I would be collected every evening by a friend and go to their house until about seven-thirty p.m. when Mum and Dad would pick me up. I used to go to bed early then, so I barely got home when I was sent off to bed. This routine seemed endless.

[Liz was staying with a friend when she received the news that Mark had died.] Bernie's mum came upstairs and said she wanted to talk to us. 'Mark has gone to the Angels,' she said quietly. I pictured Mark in a hospital bed with an angel on the wall above him. 'Mark died early this morning,' she continued. We all began to cry. Bernie's mum suggested a prayer for Mark. Later Mark's best friend's mum came over and after her, the headmistress of his school. I had been given a Leather Craft Kit and I strapped it into a buggy and walked around the room in front of the headmistress hoping she would say something; pay me some attention.

Mum and Dad came later that day to take me home. My auntie was also there. They all kept talking about 'Friday'. I knew why but I just wanted them to tell me. 'What's Friday?' I asked. 'Oh, it's Mark's funeral' came a reply – and they all continued to talk. I was never given the opportunity to go to the funeral. I was sent away to Leicester to stay with my cousins for the week. My auntie came back for the funeral, but I went to the zoo with my uncle and cousins.

When Mark died I lost my brother, my friend and my playmate. I felt lonely and I always wanted friends to come over to play. . . . I only wish I had been able to talk to someone about it all then – but no one wanted to listen. Being so young it was hard to find a friend to whom I could explain the loneliness, the emptiness and the loss and who would understand.

Teenagers and grief

Although teenagers will be able to understand intellectually about loss and death, they will not necessarily be prepared emotionally for the reality of often unexpected, untimely endings. Most people experience a see-saw of emotions at this age, and so their reactions to loss are likely to be more extreme than an adult's would be. Others will come through with fewer difficulties than adults if they are given permission and opportunity to grieve and included in what is going on. Boys may feel it's not macho to be affected by grief and put on a brave front, whilst girls may find their friends' endless chatter about boys, clothes and make-up desperately trivial. Since their friends are also likely to have little or no experience of loss, they may not know how to comfort the griever. This is why I believe loss and death education in schools is so essential. A teenager whose brother, sister, or close friend dies may also experience survival guilt (see Chapter 14).

Individual personality (as in adults) is the biggest determining factor in a teenager's response to loss. I remember friends of one family, where the father had died suddenly, contacting me because they were extremely worried about his fourteen-year-old son's reaction. He showed no emotion at all; but I soon discovered this was his usual pattern of behaviour, so for him this was in fact quite a normal reaction. I suggested he was given a keepsake and that opportunities were made as often as possible for the whole family to talk about the father.

Depression

Adolescents who have not understood what has happened, or felt cared for in their grief, can suffer severe depression. Louis De Costa, a social worker in a young people's counselling service in London found many adolescents were being referred for being sad and depressed when their fathers had recently died. 'They were described to us . . . as sad, withdrawn, having poor appetite, upsetting the rest of the family with uncontrollable behaviour, moping a lot, talking about leaving school, and feeling as if everything was too much.'[7]

In meetings they voiced feelings of personal helplessness, a lack of self-respect, and continuing depression. Their healing began as each teenager explored (with their social worker) the personal meaning for them of life with and without father; and looked at many of the experiences shared with him and the feelings associated with these incidents.

A teenager's experience of death

When I first realized that my grandfather really was going to die, I felt an urgency to talk to him, just to make sure that there wasn't anything I wanted him to know but hadn't got round to telling him. When I went to see him no real words would come, because previously we had never spoken very deeply to one another and this relationship didn't change just because he was dying. We still behaved the same way to each other, so I wrote a poem instead. I wrote with the intention of sending it to him but I never did.

The night he died I hadn't been able to stop crying but I didn't know why at the time because I wasn't told until the following morning. To my surprise, I was completely unmoved when I was looking at his body. It meant nothing to me. This cold, still body was totally empty. I read out the poem thinking that I should at least pluck up the courage now that it was in effect 'too late', but it felt quite pointless. Wherever his soul was, the part of him that I'd loved certainly wasn't lying inside the wax-like figure in this coffin. I knew then that I didn't have to put my feelings into words for him now, because he had moved on and could understand. I felt no regrets about not talking to him while he was alive. It was enough for me to know and be clear about how I felt and the poem helped me do that.

During the days that followed his death I didn't fully realize how things were going to be different, because at first nothing changed. So it was hard to come to terms with the fact that he was gone. Of course I cried a lot, but I also laughed a lot too and I think this was important. I'm glad now that I didn't suppress any of my emotions, although at the time it disturbed me because I thought it was wrong to be happy at such a time. When I got back to school all my friends stopped smiling or laughing when I came into the room. I presume this was to show sympathy towards me, but at the time it really upset me. It was their way of saying they cared, but what I really needed was someone to talk to me about it, not to give me big sad eyes. I was afraid to ask for this and so they never knew and I cried alone.

Looking back, I remember my confusion. How could it happen to me? 'This happens to everyone else, not to me,' is the common cliché, but that's how I felt. At the thanksgiving I was hit by the realization that the hundreds of people who had congregated in that church were there because they loved my grandfather, and to support us, his family, through losing him. He was gone. After this I would wake up with tears pouring over my cheeks, crying out, 'Please no! Tell me I'm just dreaming. I won't believe you're gone. Come back to me. Take me with you. Don't leave me!'

I have phases of feeling that after death you will eventually be forgotten, as will everything you do. So what is the point to living at all? If there's an after-life then perhaps you live again and again, learning something more each time, until you become a perfect being. But then what? and so what? Well, life is over all too quickly so I try to make the most of every minute and learn as much as I can, just in case I need the knowledge. There probably is a reason behind the apparent futility, and if there isn't I'd better enjoy myself until the day I'm the one in the coffin.

Helping teenagers grieve

- Include them in what is going on. Give them an opportunity to take part in services. Let them choose a keepsake.
- Expect mood swings and be sympathetic to them if you can; reassure teenagers that such reactions are normal.
- Be there for them and create opportunities for them to share their feelings and express their grief (especially boys who look as if they're trying to keep a stiff upper lip). Accept that they may prefer to confide in close friends or another adult who isn't so involved in the loss.
- Show your feelings, so they know they are acceptable. Explain about the kinds of feelings they may experience, and especially the range of conflicting emotions common in grief.
- Where appropriate, find a childhood comforter – a soft toy or teddy bear – for them.
- Guilt can be a problem when a parent dies, since it's part of normal development to separate from parents during adolescence. Suggest they write a letter to their dead parent, or talk to them internally, to express their feelings.
- If a parent has died, reassure the teenager that they don't need to take over that role or be strong to help the remaining parent. It can be difficult for teenagers to leave home,

or form serious relationships, knowing they will be leaving their remaining parent on their own.

Grieving children at school

It is quite common for divorced or bereaved parents to keep children away from school for company, although they may insist that in fact the child does not want to leave them. Children may well also cut themselves off socially and become isolated, with no friends. In fact, it is best for the child to return to school as soon as possible. Stability in areas outside the home at times of change is very important. The staff and children at the school should be informed of the circumstances, so the child is sympathetically treated and given the opportunity to talk about the dead parent.

At school, a child's anxiety may show itself in restlessness. 'Children who used to sit and do their work now roamed about the room constantly, and in the process began to interrupt classroom activities.'[8] Even if a child seems to be doing badly socially and academically, the reassuring structure of school life will be invaluable while s/he is grieving.

The need to involve staff and fellow pupils is highlighted by the case of a fifteen-year-old girl, who was very upset during a lesson I gave on bereavement. It was the first time, in the two years since the death of her father, that she had been encouraged to talk about him. On her return to school after his funeral, not one of the staff or children had made any reference to her loss.

Changing relationships

The disadvantages of having only one parent are well recognized. They include lower income, social isolation, parental preoccupation, and emotional over-dependence: all possible causes of problems in the children. The experience of married life is gone. All this may affect the children's later choice of spouse, their future married happiness and child-rearing, so special care must be taken to provide substitute experience – perhaps a teacher at school or friends or the parents could help with this.

For children, a mother dying is now a rare experience. Four-fifths of parental deaths are the father. When a man dies his children lose a model of manliness and a man's love. A father is often seen as the ultimate protection. Winston Churchill, who lost his father in childhood, said it was an experience to make or break you. A mother's death involves the loss of emotional support, of someone to talk to at the end of a school day, of someone who keeps in touch with the wider family network. It is important that an alternative sympathetic listener is found either in the family circle or school.

It is all too easy for the surviving parent to become anxious, impatient, and angry as they cope with the real material problems of housing and feeding the family on their own. There is a real danger that the parent will unconsciously allow a child to fill the role left empty by the lost parent. Many an older son, in cases of divorce or death, has broken under the responsibility of being 'the man of the house'. Fears of giving up his expected life-style and being different from his friends could all add to a situation where he opts out from any commitment at home. A boy's emotional and sexual development can be threatened. One mother had her eleven-year-old son sleeping with her for company after the death of his father. After his mother's subsequent remarriage, he was found exposing himself at school. Similarly, the older girl can become the 'little mother' when her mother dies, and feel she has to give up ideas of going away to college or university. Children need to be told specifically that it is not expected of them that they look after mother or father. That is the job of other adults in the community. If it is not possible to get additional help to cover some of the additional work, a family conference should be held to discuss a fair redistribution of jobs.

The death of a brother or sister may have profound and lasting effects on family roles and relationships. Children's grieving may be complicated by their feelings about their emotionally unavailable, grieving parents. Both parents may be so preoccupied that the surviving child feels isolated. This can cause a massive loss of self-esteem, because everyone seems to care more about the dead sibling than about the remaining child. Children may try and fill in for their missing sibling. In some cases, a dead brother or sister may continue to live with the family emotionally as a powerful ghost.

1 Quoted by Judy Tatelbaum in *The Courage to Grieve*.
2 *Family Intervention with Bereaved Children* (Rutter, 1986)
3 *Attachment and Loss* (Hogarth Press, 1980).
4 'I Can't Write to Daddy', *Good Housekeeping*, June 1984.
5 *When Children Grieve* (booklet for CRUSE).
6 Published by Grafton Books, 1988.
7 'Brief Intervention with Bereaved Adolescents', *Social Work Today*, vol.8 no.6.
8 Wallenstein and Kelly's research on divorce, 1980.

Unacknowledged grievers

Grieve for the loss, the separation,
– Why me, why me? –
Grieve for the loneliness, the rejection,
– Why me, oh why me? – (Sally Crosher)

This chapter looks at particular groups of people who, in Western culture, are still widely, and mistakenly, seen as not feeling deeply or somehow not needing to grieve.

Men and death

Because of the traditional cultural role men have as the protector and provider and the way they are often taught from an early age that 'boys don't cry', it is often difficult for them or for people around them to give 'permission to grieve'. Many men choose to show a stiff upper lip, or feel forced into that role by society. A male nurse-tutor described his reaction to his father's death, and how he wasn't given the opportunity to express his feelings, in an article in the *Nursing Times*:[1]

> One day, about two months after Dad had died, I returned to our local hospice, where I had been involved as a volunteer nurse for eighteen months. One of the staff asked me how Mum was and I said angrily: 'I wish someone would bloody well ask me how I am, because I have feelings, too.' Thankfully, my colleague handled my outburst skilfully and I felt able to discharge a lot of bottled-up emotions.
>
> I think this situation also illustrates how professionals are often not expected to need to grieve.

Guy Thorvaldsen, a writer and counsellor who has researched into the inner balance of the masculine/feminine aspects of man's nature and how this affects a man's experience of death, has contributed the rest of this section:

Most of my research has been stimulated by my own need to find some sort of inner balance between what I've been given as a man by our culture and what I experience in my heart and deeper wisdom as a human being. It is difficult for men to express a positive masculinity when the traditional authoritative father-figure archetype in our culture has modelled for us negative and destructive roles. We establish our identity through our *dis*identification with women. Men are mostly mother-raised and women are the 'emoters'. We gain a clear idea of what we are only by separating from that feminine world of emotions, sentimentality, receptiveness and nurturing. To return to that world, i.e., to express our feelings of weakness or fear, invalidates us as men, at least in the eyes of the patriarchal culture.

Another powerful ingredient of mother's world was its intimate connection with birth and a resultant reverence for the miracle and beauty of life, which cannot help but mourn for life lost. The mother, as primary provider, seemed to hold within her the power over *our* life and death. Again, in order to identify ourselves as strong, independent men, we needed to minimize the power of that connection. Despite our macho attempts to deny it, however, that childhood experience is still deep within us and the repression of that respect for life spurs us to act in fear of death. Consequently, we try to 'conquer' things like cancer and we kill others to defend ourselves against dying!

So when people, relationships or ideas do eventually die, the manly thing to do is certainly not to wallow in it. To grieve is to appear feminine and in essence to return to our original mother-ruled world – hardly a desirable identification for a 'real' man. We instead become stoic in the face of death, ably taking care of the funeral arrangements and returning to work as soon as possible. We turn to the next challenge as a response to the emptiness. Our pride as emotionally strong men simply does not allow us to grieve for things past.

I have come to learn, however, that in order to embrace our own aliveness we indeed *do* need to experience fully the pain of death. Our work and relationships are hindered, not helped, by blocking out feeling. Our hearts close down little by little with each unexpressed sadness. Slowly we cut off those people and states of openness which keep us vibrant and whole. Our masculine pride in our 'strength' is but an illusion. We die, on average, almost ten years younger than women! Men's suicide rates are consistently higher. Who are we fooling? I believe our inability to cope with the death experience is a major factor in this painful situation.

We must not be too critical of ourselves. What our culture has taught us about dealing with death has left us little choice in how we instinctively react. Our response to the need to disidentify with the first person in our lives who held the power of life or death over us, seemed to be to follow in the footsteps of Dad and stay away from our own [life]. In no way do I accuse mothers of instilling this fear of death into boys. Rather, I feel it is the absence of fathers in child-rearing which perpetuates the myth that the emotional, nurturing aspect of the home is not desirable. When we later reach the adult male world, we find our identity wrapped up in our abilities to protect and provide rather than those of feeling or being receptive. To die or to be physically or emotionally unable to cope in this breadwinner role signifies failure. It is simply not all right for a man to be unable to work without 'good reason' in the eyes of most bosses. Fearing to jeopardize our position, we tend to ignore the telltale signs of stress and wear on our bodies – indications that we are beginning to struggle as a man. Ignoring these signs in the long run invites premature death, the very thing we are fighting to avoid. Not giving ourselves time to express our fear of death, the pain of loss, or the despair of grief, severely undermines our health and our sense of openness to life and joy.

On the positive side, and in the proper context, our ability to risk our physical bodies in exploration, to accept death with honour, and to try to prolong life, are noble and wonderful qualities. But without feeling – the more intimate side of death and loss – those attributes remain one-dimensional images of 'macho-ness' and emotional invincibility. Until we become involved in the birth and rearing of our children, we will not transform the initial fear of vulnerability and death in our sons. Until we give ourselves full permission to experience our lessons of loss, the swallowed tears will slowly drown our hearts. We need to begin acknowledging our 'weak' points and nurturing ourselves, rather than pushing our bodies past their limits in fear that they will fail us, the heroic death-defiers. They will simply break – and die – with the strain of denial of our own mortality.

Our birth as whole, sensitive human beings will only come through our acceptance of the many aspects of the death process. I hope I and my brothers have the courage to move into this relatively new frontier for men. Goethe says, 'So long as we haven't *fully* experienced this, to die and so to grow, we are only a troubled guest on this dark earth.' Death is a gift and an essential part of life, not an enemy to be feared or defeated. Let us open ourselves to its riches and become heroes in our own hearts.

Gay bereavement

Dudley Cave of the Gay Bereavement Project gave me permission to quote part of his speech to the International Conference on Grief and Bereavement, London 1988:

When Lord Alfred Douglas wrote about the love that dare not speak its name, it was an exaggeration, and it is even less true today when we have gay characters in soap operas like *Brookside* and *East Enders;* when an openly gay MP – against the trend for his party – has been re-elected with an increased majority; and a person like Sir John Gielgud can speak openly of the man he shares his life with.

However they, like me, are a part of the tiny visible minority of homosexuals who are able to come out and speak for themselves and for the others. Most lesbians and gay men have to be discreet, secretive. Have to be discreet if they are to keep their jobs. For every gay person you can see, there are dozens of us out of sight.

Some lesbians and gay men only 'play the field', but many settle into relationships which are as loving and long-lasting as any marriage. (My friend Bernard and I have been together for thirty-five years.) For those who love in secret, the tangled web of concealing lies will cause problems in life, and when one partner dies, far greater problems. Grief must be hidden, there won't be any of those letters of sympathy which mean so much, and there can be no talking about the loss to colleagues at work or with neighbours. We heard of a bereaved man whose cover was so good that the neighbours' only re-action to his friend's death was to ask if there was a room to let. Those who love in secret must mourn alone.

Funerals can be disasters, with the real chief mourner, if not excluded by the blood relatives, probably sitting at the back, shrouded in private grief while all the sympathy is being directed to the blood family at the front. Clergy conducting services may be unaware of the real relationship, and if they know, may have negative feelings about homosexual love and let this come through the service . . . even if they do not go as far as one priest who prayed for forgiveness of the deceased's 'deviant lifestyle'.

Even when the relationship is fairly open and families appear to regard the partner as another son or daughter, they may well want the relationship concealed at the funeral. Partners are sometimes asked not to attend in case people should talk, or to attend but only as acquaintances. Such a funeral is a poor starting-point for good grieving. Lazare tells us that complicated grief can be expected when the loss is socially unacceptable, socially negated or if there is no sup-port network. For surviving partners of a secret love the loss *is* socially unacceptable, *is* socially negated and for most, there is *no* support network.

We soon learned from talking with bereaved lesbians and gay men that many doctors, nurses, clergy and others dealing with death and dying seemed unaware that same-sex partners would be as bereaved as spouses or families. It had just not struck them.

We found that many lesbians and gay men were dying in-testate and all too often the surviving partner lost the shared home on the death of the lover. The estate going to blood re-lations or, if there were none, to the Duchy of Cornwall. Without a valid will, a same-sex spouse cannot inherit any-thing. We then mounted a 'Write a Will' campaign and tried to educate the gay community to the facts of death – that even if they abandoned junk food, stopped smoking and practised safer sex, they would still die in the end, and that they should make provision for that day when 'we' becomes 'I'. We publish a will form which anyone can have by sending us an s.a.e.

The Gay Bereavement Project has three main aims: to help, support and advise lesbians and gay men bereaved by the death of a life partner; to educate all concerned with death and dying to the very existence of same-sex loss; and to educate the gay community to the facts of death – that, like it or not, we and those we love are mortal.

Mentally handicapped grievers

People with a mental handicap are often not allowed to grieve when a loved one dies, even to the point of not being allowed to attend the funeral for fear 'it might upset them'. In some long-stay mental hospitals and hostels, the death of relatives is kept at a distance. The people concerned can be told days, weeks, even months later. At a recent training course a member of staff at a residential centre told me the story of John, one of their mentally handicapped residents in his twenties. John had been told his father had died, but no arrangements were made for him to attend the funeral. A few weeks later, John asked other residents and members of staff to attend a service for his father in the local church. The simple service that he conducted himself showed only too well that he understood what was going on.

Maureen Oswin has made a great contribution to our understanding of the needs of the bereaved person with a mental handicap. She says it would seem helpful to establish the following principles:

- There is no reason to think that people who are mentally handicapped will not go through stages of grief, as do other people.
- Mentally handicapped people have as much right as other people to be given consideration when their relatives and friends die.
- Each person who is mentally handicapped is an individual and will grieve as an individual: there is no reason to expect them to react in some particular way because they are mentally handicapped.
- Some people who are mentally handicapped have particular disabilities and they may need some special help when they become bereaved.

Secondary losses can be an additional problem for people with a mental handicap after the death of a member of the family. These can include the loss of a confidant and someone to depend on; a change in lifestyle; and difficulty in communicating distress. P. Emerson's observation of grief reactions in the mentally handicapped showed that more than half the people he studied who suddenly began to exhibit challenging behaviour had been recently bereaved.[2] These secondary losses and changes of behaviour are illustrated in Jane's story in the King's Fund Report, 'Bereavement and Mentally Handicapped People', a discussion paper by Maureen Oswin:

Jane had lived at home all her life, the only child of elderly parents. She had never been to school but started attending the local Adult Training Centre at the age of twenty-five. She was very happy there and made many friends. She could walk and dress herself with help, but had very limited understanding of the meaning of money, or how to use public transport or shops. She could make tea and toast, and liked to help her mother with cooking and housework. She had considerable speech problems and had developed a form of signing with her parents. This was not much like any known form of sign language but the staff at the ATC had learnt some of her signs and used these in conjunction with a picture-board which her parents sent from home with her each day. When Jane was twenty-eight years old her father died. He had been ill for some months before his death and he died at home. His death was not a surprise to Jane and her mother: they had been looking after him together, with the help of a daily nurse. When he died Jane saw him in his coffin and she went to the funeral and helped her mother to prepare the simple meal that the mourners had together afterwards. Her mother explained to Jane that 'Dad has gone to Jesus and will get better and we will see him again when we go to Jesus.' On returning to the ATC a week later, Jane was encouraged to talk about what happened and she listened to the staff telling the other students about what had happened to her. She responded tearfully but bravely to the attention, the cuddles and sympathy of her friends amongst the staff and students. In her art class at the ATC she painted a series of pictures about her father's death and funeral; she made a vase in pottery classes to put on his grave; and for a few weeks the drama class in the ATC acted going to funerals.

For about six to nine months Jane suffered periods of depression and minor illnesses and she sometimes wanted to stay away from the Centre to be with her mother. But gradually she began to adapt to the changes which had been made in her life by the death of her father. She was helped by the loving support of her friends at the ATC and by her mother's always honest explanations about what had happened. She was also helped by the knowledge that she was a support to her mother in their struggle to help each other live without the father.

Gradually Jane and her mother settled into a secure but rather restricted style of life. They went out much less often than before as her mother did not drive and the father's car was sold. Their social life tended to be centred around the activities connected with the local club for mentally handicapped people and the ATC. They would attend functions, open days, concerts, garden parties to do with the local mental handicap groups, usually being picked up by members who had cars.

One day soon after Jane's thirtieth birthday party, her mother died very unexpectedly of a heart attack soon after she had seen Jane on to the ATC bus in the morning. The news was broken to her by the manager of the ATC, then a social worker took over as Jane was in a 'crisis situation'. The first problem was where she should go that night. One or two members of the ATC staff offered to accommodate her but the social worker advised them that this might be unwise and cause later complications as Jane was definitely going to need long-term residential care somewhere and it would be best if she was placed permanently as soon as possible rather than start off by living with members of the ATC staff. The social worker went to her house and got a case of clothes for her but did not take Jane as she thought this would upset her. Later that day she took her from the ATC to the hospital. Jane had never been there before and knew nobody on the staff or what the place was for.

A distant relative organized the funeral but Jane did not go. This was decided by the relative, who had never met her and only knew abut her as 'poor old Edward's defective daughter'. Over the next few weeks in the hospital Jane changed from being a secure, peaceful, happy woman to one who was described in ward notes as 'anxious, sometimes aggressive and quarrelsome'. She 'refused to co-operate in the hospital's activity centre', she lost weight, pinched a nurse who tried to bath her, and one night locked herself in the staff toilet She was moved to two different wards before she finally seemed to settle down into a pattern of rather withdrawn and passive behaviour.

Dr Lester Sireling, one of the main contributors to our understanding of the effects of bereavement on the person with a mental handicap, quotes the Mencap advertising copy which says, 'They may not think as fast, but they feel as deeply', and advises us to remember this and act on it in times of crisis such as bereavement.

---

1 11 July 1990 (vol. 86, no. 28), p.51.
2 'Covert Grief Reactions in Mentally Retarded Clients' *Mental Retardation* 15, 1977, pp. 44-5.

Recognizing Loss

He who has a why to live for can survive any how.

(Nietzsche)

8

Divorce

Relationships are there to grow a part of us. When we've grown that part, we need to either deepen them or move on. (Anon)

Many people who go through a divorce do not give themselves the emotional space to grieve fully. It is common to deny the full reality of such a loss by refusing to see the positive aspects of the relationship you have lost; or to stay stuck in anger or guilt. If you suppress your sadness to stay in control, you add to your stress. If you don't keep moving through the stages of grief, you won't ever leave your old relationship emotionally, and are likely to sabotage future relationships by unconsciously bringing all your old emotional baggage into them. If you are still feeling hostile to your partner, you have not completed your grieving.

Divorce is a great challenge, practically as well as emotionally. Just when you are feeling at your most unhappy and confused, all kinds of practical things need doing that you may well have never done before – new housing, financial, and legal arrangements have to be made. The fact that it has become much more common (one in three marriages in the UK and one in two in the USA break up) does not make the process any easier for the people concerned.

When break-ups appear to be only one partner's choice, the other can feel betrayed. There can be strong feelings of guilt – 'If only I hadn't worked late so often'; 'If only I hadn't spent so much time with my hobbies/friends/sports/children'. It is only recently that divorce in the West has lost its social stigma. There can still be a strong (possibly unacknowledged) sense of shame and feelings of personal failure.

From blame to acceptance

Many people who see themselves as the 'innocent party' in a divorce nurse feelings of self-pity, bitterness and resentment. Their attention is focused in the past and they may try and persuade family and friends to take their 'side' and to turn against their former partner. The problem with this victim-role is that it is disempowering. Unless you are willing to see your situation differently, you will stay stuck in the past emotionally. To be really alive (and open to new relationships), you have to be willing to experience your vulnerability and feel all your feelings. In other words, to move all the way through your grief. Although blame, and anger, may be an essential stage in your grieving process, in the long-term, putting rigid labels on people or situations will only prevent you from experiencing them fully. It's more helpful to be willing to see that no situation or person is completely good or bad – and that as you change and grow, so your experience of your past will also change.

Divorce can be a serious blow to self-esteem. When any relationship fails, for whatever reason, the initial separation is generally felt as rejection. Many people conclude they have failed the challenge of intimate relationship. Divorce can thus be a blow to self-esteem in a way that death is not. One way to prove to the former partner that you are 'OK' is to notch up 'successes'. This can take the form of an obsessive need to acquire material goods, to take a lover, or to get ahead in some way. I know of a banker who, on being left and divorced by his wife for another man, bought himself a Jaguar and found a new job with a higher salary and more responsibility. The job involved working more hours, which he used as his reason for not having girlfriends. His self-image was so poor he had a toupée fitted to hide the start of baldness. Luckily, he did get beyond this stage and later remarried: he and his new partner are now able to laugh together about this episode in his life.

Mary, whose husband, Gordon, left her for another woman, says she had deep feelings of anger, resentment and jealousy towards him. She used to 'spit vitriol' at him when he came to collect the children. She saw a counsellor who advised her to change tack and invite him in for tea, rather than shout abuse at him on the doorstep. To her amazement,

Gordon immediately responded positively, and Mary's healing process had begun.

Forgiveness is a powerful tool in transforming your experience. I'm not suggesting you should forgive the other person to make *them* feel better (or to prove you're a nice person), but to free yourself from old situations, and from the burden of resentment and judgement you will have to carry if you don't. If anything, the most important person to forgive is yourself. You may be secretly really mad at yourself for having got into such a situation – maybe you feel you should have known better than to get involved with your ex-partner in the first place! Forgiveness is really about being willing to change your perceptions – of yourself, of what happened, of the other person. Holding on to old anger not only limits you emotionally, but may contribute to stress-related illness. Letting go of judgement will allow you to recognize the good things that happened in your relationship, and to feel your sadness at losing them. You may also realize you have positive feelings about the separation – relief, perhaps, and the excitement of new opportunities.

Once you have dealt with your initial pain at the break-up, it may be helpful to see that you still have a relationship with your ex-partner, even if its form has changed radically. If you have children, it is important for all of you that you and your ex-partner nurture a continuing relationship based on respect and communication that will support you both. If your partner is uncontactable, you can still experience an emotional communication with them, and deal with unfinished business as you become aware of it, by writing letters.

Mary summed up her experience to me:

Five years on I still feel the loss of family life, and expect I always will. I am surrounded by others in the same situation, proof that the nuclear family is breaking up. I still feel pain occasionally, but also experience a lightness, as though I am coming into the sunshine. Gordon has given me my life on a plate and I try to stop fantasizing that everything would have been all right if he had stayed. The truth is, his cutting edge would have run through us all. . . . I feel greater compassion for him, for myself, and others, and know that we are all doing our best in patterns of confusion.

What you can do

- Talk to a variety of friends about how you're feeling, so you get a range of responses. Don't encourage friends to support you in a victim role.
- Work on improving your self-esteem (see Chapter 2).
- Get in touch with your feelings (see 'Denial' in Chapter 4). Don't hide your tears from your children: they could give them permission to grieve too.
- Deal with your anger (see 'Anger' in Chapter 4).
- If you're stuck in hurt and anger, try putting yourself in your partner's place. This may help you to understand what *they* have lost, and to have compassion for them.
- Realize that it's safe to heal your relationship: it doesn't mean you have to get back together again. You can work daily with visualization to move into forgiveness. Use the relaxation technique suggested in the Appendix; then imagine you are standing at one corner of a field and your ex-partner is at the opposite corner. See if you can get a little closer to them each time you meditate. You may notice their appearance changing, or the way they move. Once you're within earshot, try telling them how you feel, and see how they respond. It's good not to have a time-table for this exercise; don't judge yourself if there are days when you seem to be going backwards. You are complete when you can see them with complete peace in your heart.

   Another powerful method is writing letters. You can begin with real hate letters, burning them as soon as you've finished. Your ultimate goal is to produce a letter which says how you feel in a non-blaming way ('When you did such-and-such, how I felt was . . . '); a letter that you would feel good about receiving if someone sent it to you. Your goal is peace in your heart.

When I need to forgive myself, I picture myself as I was at the time that needs healing: what I was wearing, what my surroundings were, how I was feeling, and I tell myself 'I forgive you'. I then imagine giving myself a big hug, and bringing myself into my heart and feeling surrounded by love.

Filling the vacuum

It is common to feel incomplete for a time after a separation, rather than a person in your own right. This feeling of being incomplete is the essence of loneliness. Your number-one priority becomes having a partner, a lover or getting married again – anything to fill the emotional 'hole' and avoid feeling your grief. Rushing into a new relationship before grieving for the previous one, or facing your loneliness, often results in a person recreating a similar kind of relationship. I am convinced this lack of exploration of the previous breakdown is one of the main reasons for such a high failure-rate in second marriages. Approximately two-thirds of divorced people remarry, but the figures for break-up of second marriages are even higher than for first.

If you have left one relationship for another, you may find it difficult to find the emotional space you need to grieve the first relationship. It's easy to stay in denial, but you may find your suppressed feelings coming up unexpectedly, projected on to your new relationship. It may be that you need to recognize your new relationship is really a device to enable you to leave your marriage; and that you need to face what was really wrong with your former relationship. Or it may be a matter of recognizing your own need to grieve and talking to your new partner about it so you can give yourself a chance to feel all your feelings.

It is not easy to stand alone again after sharing a life with someone. Our culture tends to think of people in pairs, and most of our social laws and customs are based on marriage and the family unit. Other people may see you differently now you are single again. Women on their own can be seen as a threat to other marriages, especially by other wives. Husbands may see divorced or widowed women as 'easy game'.

What you can do

- Wait at least six months before getting involved in a new relationship. Give yourself time to grieve, and to experience your independence.
- Nurture your friendships – the old romantic idea of finding all your emotional fulfilment in one person is

unrealistic. You may discover emotional support and new friends by joining a women's/men's group.
- Work on your self-esteem (see Chapter 2).
- Look for opportunities to develop new talents and interests. Aim to feel whole and fulfilled as an individual.

Children and divorce

One in five children experience the loss of a parent through divorce or separation. In many cases the effect on their psychological development may be more traumatic than if the parent had died. Marriage breakdown and events leading up to it are always hard on the children involved. They may not always show their distress or realize at first what the break-up will mean to them. Marriage is generally still regarded in our culture as the foundation of family life, and research shows that, except in the case of violence, most children want their parents to stay together. Children may be caught in the duel between parents. Their responses to the situation can range through disorientation, wildness, a show of strength, shutting off from those around them, and asking questions like, 'What are you doing? Why did you have me?'

It's best to be direct and simple and tell your children what is happening and why in a way they can understand. The worst course is to try to hush things up and to make a child feel he must not talk or even think about what he senses is going on. Unpleasant happenings need explanations, which should be brief, direct and honest. Professor Caplan, the Scientific Director of the Family Centre for the Study of Psychological Stress, says that, ideally, pre-school children should be told a week or two before the family's break-up; five to eight-year-olds a month or two before hand; and older children should be given longer notice. The parents' marriage will have been the whole of the children's life up to the separation. Therefore it is important to let them ask questions and to encourage them to talk over the past and recall highlights of their childhood – to reaffirm the good that came out of the relationship.

For children, divorce not only means the partial (or, in some cases, total) loss of a parent, but also frightening changes in the whole familiar structure of their lives. They will need to grieve and may need to be encouraged to express their feelings (see Chapter 6). Parents can best support children in this by being willing to go through their own grieving process and by ensuring the lines of communication remain open between all members of the family.

This is a huge change for children and it will take a long time for them to come to terms with what has happened and to adjust to the division of their family into two separate homes. It is a good idea to make clear to children that their parents' decision to divorce has been made because of adult problems and the children cannot alter that decision. Young children can feel they have magical powers and have caused the divorce. Often such mistaken conclusions are due to their not being included in, or kept informed about, what is going on. Laura was five when her world fell apart:

My mum went upstairs and packed her bag, she put her coat on . . . she opened the door and she said, 'I'm going away for a few days.' And then I said, 'Why are you going away for a few days?' and then she didn't answer and walked away. Then I started crying and I thought I'd never see her again.

Five years on, Laura can look back calmly at that terrible moment when her whole life crumbled. At the time, however, convinced that she was somehow to blame for the break-up of her parents' marriage, she retreated into a cocoon of guilt and confusion. It is vital to make it clear to children that their parents intend no longer to be husband and wife because they have stopped loving each other and cannot live peacefully with each other; the divorce has *not* been caused by anything the children have done.

Children need to realize that divorce is common, and they should not feel ashamed it has happened. Tell them it's OK to talk about it to their close friends and teachers – emotional support from outside the family may help them a great deal. They are likely to feel they have lost control of their lives. You can help them feel more powerful by involving them in practical arrangements: suggesting different ways they can see their other parent, so they have a choice, for example; or making joint decisions on family outings and treats.

Pressurizing children to take sides in an ongoing feud between their parents is likely to damage relationships all round. If you are still feeling angry with your ex-partner, you may need to explain to your children that when you say bad things about the other parent, it's because you're angry. Don't use your children as go-betweens: it puts an unfair burden on them. Beware of unconsciously making one child a scapegoat for their absent parent. I suffered in this way myself – my parents parted when I was six months old and my mother was so upset with my father she didn't keep as much as one photograph. I never saw him again, but my mother frequently told me I was just like him. Since all I heard about him was bad, I therefore assumed I must be bad too. It took years work on myself as an adult to undo the damage. I still find it difficult to acknowledge my strengths.

Children may be reluctant to visit or talk to the parent who has left them, especially if s/he has a new partner. You can support them, if you are the one living with them, by explaining how it is possible to love someone and not like what they do. If you are in the position where your children are reluctant to see you, encourage them to tell you how they feel, no matter how negative it is. It may take time to rebuild their trust in your love. It's good for both parents to make it clear they want the children to maintain close links with each parent; and that both of them intend to continue to love and care for their children throughout childhood, no matter what may happen in the future.

Adolescents, in particular, who lose a parent of the same sex will find the loss of a role model challenging. The parent who has left may not be willing to remain closely involved with his/her children. It is important to maintain some form of contact, if at all possible. This can help children deal with their fantasies, which are often much worse than the reality of what is happening. It can lessen their feelings of rejection, and prevent them believing the separation happened because they were bad. It will also help them deal with their fear that they may never see the other parent again.

It's important to keep feelings of love alive at home. It's easy for a grieving parent and children to withdraw from intimacy – children may shrug off hugs and become 'super-cool'. You may all feel a little self-conscious at first, but parents can take the lead in asking for hugs: the armour should soon dissolve.

9

Living with handicap

He filled every corner of my life,
  he gave everything worth giving,
He taught me to love, he touched my soul;
  loving him made life worth living.
There isn't a normal child in this world
  who could give the love he gave:
His love was unconditional
  and I will take it to my grave.

(Dany Sherlock)

Whether you have a family member who is born or becomes handicapped, or you yourself become disabled, it's vital to feel your grief for what could have been. Until you experience all your anger, sadness, fear and guilt over your lost dreams, you will be closed to the possible gifts offered by the new reality. It is a great challenge to live *with* your loss, especially if the diagnosis means that further disablement, even death, is likely. Frequently, it is not only the handicapped person who has lost his previous life-choices, but also his immediate family. Many of the people who have contributed stories to this section do describe, however, the wonderful love and aliveness that can be experienced in what may seem unlikely situations.

Handicap involves so many practical problems both for the disabled person and their family that it can be difficult to take the space to let go and grieve. Rachel came to one of my workshops; her husband had had a stroke several years earlier. They have an eight-year-old son. Rachel said, 'I realized I needed to grieve, but found it difficult when having to hold on to all the practical tasks.' During the workshop she was able to grieve for the loss of the man she married. He can no longer talk, nor take part in their earlier intellectual life, or the work they shared. She has also lost the companionship of his friends, who no longer visit.

The thought of handicap brings up fear in most people, and Rachel's experience of old friends dropping away is unfortunately common. It is vital to stay focused on the individual, to see who they *are* rather than who they are not. It is easy to stay distanced by labelling other people, but the gifts of love are about connection, not separation. Maybe if we each knew that it is who we are that is valuable, not what we do, we would find it easier to stay open around handicap. It can be very helpful to work on your hurt child around this area (see Chapter 2).

There does seem to be a positive gain for some parents of disabled children. They see their 'special' child as having brought out from within themselves an understanding, joy and compassionate love that they would not otherwise have experienced. 'It took a tiny, mentally retarded boy to teach us this most precious lesson of unconditional love,' writes Leona Boshoff.[1] Many of these 'special' children are described by Dale Evan Rogers as having 'purity of thought and an amazing capacity for love'[2]. The experience of having a handicapped child can be very different from the common assumption that they are a burden and not lovable like other children.

Handicapped babies

He weighed 4 lbs 6 ozs at birth and 14 lbs 6 ozs at death. He spent thirty-four weeks in the womb and should have stayed there forty weeks. He lived for forty weeks. He should have had forty-six chromosomes in each cell but he had forty-seven. He was born on 14 February, St Valentine's Day, and died on 20 November. His heart failed him. He was called Will. He was my son.

The bald facts of the brief life of a mentally handicapped child with a severe congenital heart defect might sound to some like a tragic aberration in the normal cycle of human reproduction. As such, they regard it as best ended and hopefully forgotten. To me, the nine months of his life was an affirmation of life. As such it could never be 'best ended' and should not be forgotten. (Sarah Boston, *Will, My Son*)[3]

Parents of a handicapped baby need to grieve for the loss of a normal child before they can accept the handicapped one. They will probably have to contend with irrational feelings of guilt (see 'Stillbirths' in Chapter 5). The presence of a handicapped child in a family can aggravate any previous marital strain, and sometimes result in the marriage breaking up. In some cases, friends, family, and even professional carers can react defensively to the thought of a child not being 'normal'. One of the things that can hurt bereaved parents most is the expectation that they will be relieved if their child dies. This sort of insensitivity, and attempt to remain detached, is vividly illustrated in this article by a doctor:

A visit from the parents of a baby with a rare genetic defect that means it is unlikely to survive a year. That morning I received a letter from the hospital paediatrician, saying that he had told the parents their baby was like a mouldy loaf of bread. You could cut off the mould on the outside, but unfortunately the mould went all the way through and the loaf would eventually be thrown away. No wonder the parents looked at me with such hostility and desperation. How could I build a relationship with them?[4]

Cindwen told me of her and her husband, Charles's, experience with their second son, David:

I suppose that to truly understand about David you have to go back to when I was pregnant. It was an horrendous pregnancy because I kept haemorrhaging – nine times in all – but with each bleed and subsequent scan I grew very close to David. We already knew he was a boy because I'd seen on one of the scans and so we chose his names, David Huw.

During the ten days that I stayed in hospital [after the birth], he became jaundiced and then developed respiratory distress syndrome following an awful chest infection which the whole family shared. He nearly died then but pulled through only for us to discover that he had a hole in his heart.

It broke my heart to have to leave him behind in the special care unit, and each time we visited him it seemed there was more bad news. He wasn't feeding properly and I had to abandon my hopes of feeding him myself as I had done with our elder son, Robert, for eighteen months. It was a huge disappointment, but I realized that his welfare was more important than my ideas of motherhood. He was such a little fighter, he deserved the best. He was also the image of his big brother.

At last, after three long weeks, I was due to go in for bonding – unnecessary, I thought, for already I loved him so much, but to be able to hold him and cuddle him as much as I wanted was heaven. We were told that the consultant paediatrician wanted to see us both before we could finally take David home, but although a little concerned, we weren't too worried. I was happily cuddling David, and Charles was drinking his coffee, when Dr Semmens came into the room looking very serious. 'I'm afraid I have some very bad news for you,' she said, and I immediately asked if it was his heart. 'No, something more serious than that. There is no easy way to tell you but I'm afraid that David has Down's syndrome.' As I burst into tears and hugged David she very patiently and kindly went on to explain what it could entail but that there was no reason that David should not lead a normal life. She was so wonderfully kind and sensitive, but I still really appreciated the hug which Jeanette, the sister, gave me. To be honest, without the unfailing support of those two wonderful women and several others, I don't know how we would have coped.

Another unfailing supportive friend was Lorna, my health visitor, who burst into tears when I told her and yet gave me some very good advice: the only thing that had changed about David was what I knew about him – not our love for each other. And also, those who care matter; those who don't care don't matter.

To come to terms with handicap you need to grieve for the child you feel you ought to have had until that wonderful day when you see beyond the label and realize that your child *is* perfect, and very special. One important step was being able to go to a marvellous pre-school centre for handicapped children – the Nissan Centre – where the love and devotion of all the staff is a true inspiration. I loved going there (and so did Robert), and made some special friends for we shared a common bond – our children were outside the 'norm' yet each had been blessed with a special gift: a far greater capacity to love than ordinary children have.

My love and pride in David grew with each achievement – his development was spot-on average – and each illness that he managed to overcome, defying death twice. Robert adored his little brother, now nicknamed Dody, and used to help with the special portage exercises we used to do to aid his normal development. We had so much love and support from everyone, apart from our families and some now ex-friends. It was a hurtful but also a richly rewarding time – a period of intense emotional growth, of learning to accept the unacceptable, of facing up to many unpleasant truths and of learning to fight the prejudice and intolerance which exists both in society and, sadly, within the medical profession towards mental handicap. There are some notable exceptions to that last statement but alas they are in a very small minority.

[David became ill at Christmas and the doctor found his liver and spleen were enlarged.] I said the dreadful words, 'It's leukaemia, isn't it?' and I knew then that David was going to die.

He had one month of treatment, which was truly horrendous. Agonizingly painful for Dody and for me too because I was determined to stay with him throughout his treatment, to do whatever I could to help him because I loved him so deeply. I could give him nothing but my love, the last gift a mother can give. I must say that both the hospital staff and the Nissan Centre were wonderfully supportive and so were our true friends. I couldn't accept, and still can't, the fact that somehow having leukaemia should suddenly make Dody more socially acceptable, his Down's conveniently forgotten. To deny his Down's syndrome is to deny precisely what made Dody so very special and precious, much as I wanted him to be treated as a normal little boy. It may seem a contradiction in terms, but it's the way it was and is.

Anyway, during that month it became increasingly obvious that the treatment wasn't working and I had already decided that Dody should be allowed to die with dignity and at home – he hated the hospital – surrounded by all his favourite things but above all, secure in our shared love. Dr Semmens was again wonderful and she cried as she told us the treatment hadn't worked and asked what we wanted to do. There was no choice, but to be allowed to feel in some small measure of control was crucial. I can never thank her deeply enough for allowing us our dignity.

That final month had a kind of beauty of its own for we were cocooned in love and developed a strength neither my husband nor I knew we possessed. I was so glad to have Robert to cling to as well, for he needed so much love and reassurance about what was going to happen. Many people said we shouldn't have told Robert, he couldn't understand – he was too young at two-and-a-half. Well, they were wrong, because he loved Dody and deserved nothing less than the truth. Because I love him I was able to gently explain and find the right words to tell him that Dody was going to die. Although towards the end Dody was unconscious for most of the time, he awoke to smile goodbye to his special friends, Lee and Lorna – his portage teacher and health visitor – and he gave Robert a little hug and a very special smile. I shall always treasure those moments just as I shall be eternally grateful to Jeanette, the sister, who was kind enough to stay with me as Dody was finally dying, taking it in turns to cuddle him. Somehow it was only right that someone who had been there at his birth should be able to help him on his final journey. He died in my arms at ten past midnight on 26 February 1988 – just 15 months old.

Nothing can ever prepare you for the mess of emotions which follow the death of your child. The physical pain, the dreadful ache in your arms, the total emptiness. The utter despair and loneliness, the overwhelming anger, the desire to hurt as much as you are hurting inside. But grief is a totally selfish experience and an unbelievably painful process – a true journey of self-discovery through madness eventually to find strength and peace, after you allow yourself to heal. It's like a festering wound which does eventually heal in its own time, leaving you scarred, yes, but it's a scar to be proud of, leaving you forever changed.

For me, Dody's life was a celebration of courage, fighting against the odds, but above all it was about love both given and received. An ordinary child has to learn how to love, but Dody gave so much love from his traumatic arrival in this world to his traumatic departure and I count myself as blessed for having known him. I guess that's the difference between a 'handicapped' child and a 'normal' one and why perhaps the sense of loss is so huge. I love all three of my children deeply but for me Dody will always be fifteen months old whilst Robert and Jessica (she was born almost a year after David died) grow older.

Although at times it was like a living Hell, I can now see the experience as a very positive one, something which has enriched my life. I truly believe that we are never given more than we can cope with but it is up to each of us to decide whether we profit from such experiences or whether we lose by it and let it ruin our lives. For me, life is for Living.

The loss of a handicapped child

One of the things that can hurt bereaved parents most, and complicate their grief, is the common expectation that they will be relieved if their handicapped child dies. Pauline found herself constantly repeating 'This is not a blessing' to medical staff when her twenty-seven-year-old son Gary, who had Down's syndrome, was on a ventialtor in an intensive care unit after a road accident. (He survived for four days, dying on 10 November 1989.)

> Why did I feel it necessary to keep stressing this? Did I feel that they might not fight for a disabled boy's life as hard as they might for a 'normal' one? Of course not. Logically I knew this, and yet I kept repeating, 'Don't you understand, he led a full life, this is not a blessing'. Little did I know then how many times thoughtless remarks would have me screaming these words again in my mind, even though I seldom voiced them (perhaps I should have). Things like: 'At least you know his end', 'At least you do not have the worry any more', 'It's a blessing in the circumstances'. It isn't 'easier' to have lost a handicapped child. Who would dream of saying such hurtful things to other bereaved parents?

Margaret Hayworth, editor of the UK *Compassionate Friends' Newsletter*, says there are some common experiences in grieving for a handicapped child:

- The void after their death is greater because the household routine has been geared around the child's needs. One mother said after her son died in hospital: 'I feel like a big part of my family (the nursing staff) and life are missing.'
- Parents are likely to experience more blame and guilt, especially with a hereditary or congenital disability. Also,

some parents may feel guilty because they experience feelings of relief at now not having an increasingly tiring,
time-consuming, difficult situation to deal with, even
though they loved their child deeply.

- The 'why us?' thoughts carry with them a double
  questioning. Not only 'Why did our child die?' but also,
  'Why was our child disabled?'
- Parents of a disabled child will have experienced some
  grief already, when they first realized their child's condition.

Older children with handicaps

Julia and Barry's son, Ashish, has muscular dystrophy. This
hereditary disease affects boys and is usually undetected at
birth. Gradually, their muscles deteriorate and by the time
they are eleven (like Ashish), most boys are unable to walk.
Eventually, the respiratory muscles are affected, making it
difficult to recover from chest infections, and often resulting
in early death. Julia describes how Ashish's handicap has
affected them all:

I knew before he was born that there was something wrong.
There was no way of proving it, so I didn't tell the doctors, as I
thought they would think I was being silly. There were no
obvious signs until he started walking at eighteen months.
Barry and I took him to six doctors before he was finally diagnosed at three years old. Each time we visited a doctor who
said all was well, we said, 'Thank God,' but would look at
Ashish afterwards and realize there was definitely something
wrong.

When he was finally diagnosed at three, it was a long-
drawn-out affair. Barry wasn't able to come to the first
appointment. I was told it was muscular dystrophy and that I
was not to consider having any more children until a proper
diagnosis had taken place. I went home and phoned a friend
with a medical dictionary to find out what muscular dystrophy was, as the doctor didn't tell me.

Six weeks later there was a biopsy and four weeks after that
we were told Ashish definitely had muscular dystrophy. In
the time in between I cried for a whole day. Barry said, 'I wish
you wouldn't, you don't know for certain.' This reminded me

that, as a child, I'd never been given space to have feelings and express them. I'd been sent to boarding school at six when my mother had a nervous breakdown. I learnt then that tears were an inconvenience for others and I never felt I was given permission to grieve. For three or four months after Ashish's diagnosis, wherever I was I would steer the conversation around to muscular dystrophy, so I could tell my story. I found I needed to *hear* myself, over and over again, talking about what this diagnosis meant. But I couldn't cry.

Barry found it difficult to talk about it. He put a lot of energy into the practical side, like building a wheelchair for Ashish. Whereas I prayed to God for strength to deal with it. I needed to grieve for the loss of the dream I had had for Ashish growing up. I realized he would never reach manhood, tower over me, put his arms around me. It was also very difficult to accept the fact that I must never have any more children. I had always wanted four or five boys. I would look at sixteen-year-olds growing into manhood, vulnerable and innocent, and realize Ashish would never be like that.

Julia said the things that had hindered were the difficulty her husband had in the early days in talking about what had happened; and her own denial of what was happening. She emotionally disconnected from Ashish. Julia realized she was protecting herself – she feared if she was too attached she would miss him more.

What helped Julia most was her change of attitude. When Ashish was eight years old, she decided she didn't want to look back through life and realize she had wasted the time they had together. She spent three days going through photos of Ashish since he was born and putting them in albums. Julia said it was her way of saying goodbye to the healthy child she had dreamed of and accepting Ashish as he was. She allowed herself to weep over what she had missed. She now feels positive about Ashish and what he has achieved. This in turn has allowed Ashish to change and be himself and not to feel he has to try and please his parents all the time (as Julia had with her parents). He is able to express his feelings more freely – his anxiety, sadness and anger. He draws endless pictures of Superman and Batman, his heroes, and is attracted to naughty boys who do things he can't.

Julia and Barry now feel relieved they have come round in time to accept Ashish as he is, rather than their dream. They now realize that in reality they haven't much time with Ashish and though they accept they will never be grandparents, they don't want to miss out on the joy of being his parents.

Becoming disabled

For an older child or adult who becomes handicapped, it's important to grieve for the loss of the person they thought they were, or were going to be. There is likely to be a serious dip in self-esteem and a time of depression as well as strong feelings of anger before it's possible to build a new self-image. It can be difficult to visualize a positive future, and the loss of earning power and status (whether real or perceived) can mean insecurity and anxiety. In *Loss and Grief in Medicine*,[5] Peter Speck talks about the experience of becoming blind: 'The initial reaction to loss of vision may render the person immobile, expressionless and depressed. The person may be preoccupied with the total dependency that they feel and the loss of individual freedom.'

Catherine Pointer became disabled in an accident in 1983. A car suddenly cut across her path as she was on the way back from church with her husband, son Jonathan and daughter Rachel. The car swept them all along with it. Catherine's husband went into intensive care and made a gradual, almost complete recovery. Although Catherine knew immediately she was partly paralysed she didn't cry as she felt that with her husband so ill, 'one of us had to cope'. Within a short space of time, their daughter Rachel died – on Jonathan's fourth birthday. Jonathan's physical injuries were minimal, but the psychological effects of the accident, and his mother's disability, have had long-term consequences.

In the early weeks in her local hospital, Catherine didn't find the atmosphere conducive to grieving. She cried early in the morning, when the staff were writing their reports and there was no one about. She also talked and grieved with the visitors she knew would understand (most people wanted her to be cheerful). Those who helped were friends from her church and the National Childbirth Trust. The most helpful of all were her former vicar and his wife from London, who told her they felt it a privilege to be with her. 'One of my biggest difficulties was having to ask other people to get things for me or hand them to me. I'd never had to do it before, so often I didn't remember to ask for things until it was too late.'

Once Catherine's condition stabilized she was transferred to the National Spinal Injuries Centre at Stoke Mandeville Hospital, where she stayed for nine-and-a-half months. To begin with she was on a high dependency ward with four others. For the first two weeks she didn't cry. The focus was on rehabilitation, and there was no acknowledgement of her need to grieve for the loss of her daughter and the use of her legs.

I felt the need to talk and share at a deeper level. I had no affinity with the other patients and felt isolated. I cried when a group of Brownies came to visit. I was reminded that my daughter would have been in uniform by now. It was Christmas, and they sang Rachel's favourite carol, 'Away in a Manger'. The Brownie leader stayed and talked to me.

Some visitors from the local church also helped Catherine grieve. When her condition improved, she found helping in the medical library, and talking to the librarian, was supportive. A wheelchair-bound physiotherapist said, 'You may never grieve for the loss of the use of your legs, because of the major loss of your daughter.' In fact, it was two years before Catherine really grieved for her legs.

Catherine has lost much of her mobility and freedom: she is confined to a wheelchair. Her daughter's grave is inaccessible to her. It now takes Catherine two hours to get ready in the morning. She has to have a specially adapted car and needs help to do jobs around the house. She still feels anger and frustration at times, at her lack of mobility and the fact she is no longer able to bring in a professional salary. Nine years on, the claim for damages from the accident still hasn't been settled.

When describing how her experience had changed her, Catherine quoted Blake's lines, which are on the commemorative plaque under her daughter Rachel's memorial tree:

> To see a World in a grain of sand,
> And a Heaven in a wild flower,
> Hold Infinity in the palm of your hand,
> And Eternity in an hour.

She says:

> I feel much better equipped. I am much more compassionate now and aware of the pain in the world. Previously, I had no real understanding of what it was like when people died. Now I'm less active, I'm more contemplative. What matters is what you do with every situation and how you let God work through you. I now work as the honorary librarian for Compassionate Friends, sending out books, tapes and videos, and also listen to and support other bereaved parents.

Spiritual healing

Especially when conventional medicine can't help, holistic or spiritual healing can open up new possibilities for people, particularly emotionally. Such support can be valuable to carers as well as those who are handicapped. It's important to make sure, as a carer, that you yourself are nurtured also.

Barbara and Stan Proffit distribute my teaching packs. Barbara describes their experiences of alternative healing:

> The big change in our lives started with the birth of our third child, Karen. All seemed to be fairly good until we discovered that she was mentally handicapped and according to the doctors would probably be 'a cabbage' for the rest of her life. We did not go along with this view, so turned to spiritual healing. This was a great help to all of us, especially to me as a mum because of the feelings of guilt I had at the time.
>
> Gradual improvement in Karen's condition led to Stan and I forming our own prayer group for healing. Karen is now twenty-five, can swim, ride, tell the time and read and write, although behind for her years. She is very loving and concerned for all, and even gives healing touch to family and friends.
>
> Change number two occurred whilst I was doing part-time nursing on the district. I was diagnosed as having Parkinson's disease and had to give up my beloved nursing. I lost more and more movement, ending up in a wheelchair. Then Stan was made redundant, which was a blessing really as he was able to look after me. I had more therapy and healing, and slowly began to improve. I had been practising yoga since

before my illness, and breathing control and relaxation have helped me a great deal.

I still find it hard at times to accept having a mentally handicapped daughter and not being able to move freely, but I am sure Stan and I have grown spiritually and come closer together due to these changes in our lives. I should add that the wheelchair is now dispensed with. I am able to walk some distance each day and have achieved as much as three miles on more than one occasion. This surely must be a Healing Influence working through me. I am eternally grateful for this and to those who have helped me in this way.

Karen, Stan and I all pray that whoever reads this may perhaps find as we have done over the years, fresh hope and encouragement to K.O.K.O. (keep on keeping on).

1 'Death of a Disabled Child' by Margaret Hayworth, in the UK *Compassionate Friends Newsletter*.
2 *Angel Unaware* (Spire Books, USA, 1963).
3 Published by Pluto Press, 1981.
4 'Tell Me, Doctor', in the Living column of the *Independent*, 10 October 1991.
5 Published by Balliere & Tindell, 1978.

10

Life-threatening illnesses

We cannot stop the bird of sorrow landing on our shoulder, but we can prevent it nesting in our hair. (Chinese proverb)

The value of grieving and allowing yourself to experience all of your feelings around a life-threatening illness is that it allows you to accept how you really feel in each moment, and enables you to choose how to live with the situation. It's tempting to feel that if you deny the reality of the illness it will magically cease to exist. Unfortunately, suppressing your feelings is more likely to disempower you – either you cannot act for fear of making your illness real; or you stay stuck in guilt or anger and see yourself as a victim; or your suppression of your feelings results in depression.

Discovering you have a life-threatening illness is an immense challenge. Your whole life is liable to be turned upside-down, putting enormous strain on close family and friends also. Such a diagnosis can result in serious secondary losses. In one family I visited as an education welfare officer, the mother had had multiple sclerosis for ten years and was in a wheelchair. Her husband, who had been devoted and looked after her every need, had left her suddenly some two years earlier for another woman. She was therefore left with a treble loss: MS and the handicaps it had brought; the loss of a husband; and the loss of a father for her son, who was still at school. In the two years I visited her she attempted suicide and I prevented her on several occasions. A few years after I left my job I heard that she had made a successful attempt. I often wonder if I did the right thing in stopping her earlier. Sometimes the challenge of life is just too great.

Suppressed grief and illness

Denied feelings about past losses can be an important factor in health. Anorexia nervosa, for instance, is often thought to result from a rejection of adulthood, caused by unresolved emotional problems involving other family members. The daughter of a friend of mine became anorexic in her mid-teens when her parents' marriage was breaking up. The condition only lasted about a year and she resumed normal eating once her parents had sorted their lives out and she felt able to communicate with them both easily again.

It is also interesting to see the link between death and anorexia. Dr Robert McAll, a Hampshire doctor, found that in fifteen cases which he handled a member of the family had died without being properly mourned. As soon as the sufferer was persuaded to take part in a church service of mourning, improvements began, often dramatically. In a letter to the *Lancet*[1] he suggested that 'hidden guilt, either in the patient or a close member of the family, may be a causative factor'. He described one of his patients, a girl who, aged eleven, had spent months in hospital after a car accident. Only when she was discharged was she told that her father had been killed in the same accident. No member of the family had attended his funeral. The girl immediately began to refuse food. By the age of eighteen she weighed five stone and hospital treatment had achieved nothing. Dr McAll arranged for a priest to hold a church service for her father, which the girl attended with her mother. The following day the girl started to eat normally. 'This girl was saying she loved her daddy and was going to join him. Not eating was a polite form of suicide. Her father's spirit was haunting her.'

The family's need to grieve

A health visitor colleague of mine, Kay, told me how she found herself going through the stages of grief as she dealt with her elder daughter's anorexia. To begin with, there were a few years of confusion and denial before Ann was diagnosed at the age of seventeen. Kay and her husband had not been able to agree on what should be done; and Kay later realized she had constantly pacified and over-protected Ann when she stirred things up in the family.

Later, Kay grieved for Ann's loss of femininity; the fact that she has had no boyfriends, no periods, and thus no opportunity to have children; the fact that she wants to be a little girl all the time; and most of all that she doesn't enjoy life.

Kay said she also experienced anger at her husband for not letting her do something about her daughter's eating disorder earlier; at her mother for being critical rather than supportive; at herself as she felt she had failed as a mother; at the medical student who delivered Ann too rapidly (she has had various problems since birth); and at her husband's family for not giving support. Kay also resented Ann's anorexia and how it has dominated all their lives.

Guilt has also been a challenge for Kay. She felt that, as a trained nurse, she should have been able to do more for Ann when she was a baby and small child. Secondly, Kay was always dieting and feared Ann may have emulated this. Thirdly, she tends to be a perfectionist, and Ann is too.

Kay and her family have opened up to outside support. She has found the 'Wise person' meditation (see the Appendix) helpful. She visualized leaving her daughter with the wise person and then meeting Ann again at the bottom of the mountain. Kay says that really helped her in her process of letting Ann go and arriving at the stage of acceptance.

One of my clients described the pain and frustrations of being emotionally involved with a life-threatening illness but not in a position to do anything directly. She came to see me with severe depression after her nephew, who had been like a son to her, had died of anorexia nervosa while at university. Ken had been a first-class athlete and a brilliant student:

I am trying to put down some of my thoughts about Ken's anorexia. The worst parts of this illness were the secrecy; the denial that it was anorexia; the feeling of helplessness, of being unable even to share the worry and pain or to offer comfort and to gain some back. Alongside this was the terrible fear of the likely outcome, especially since I knew of a boy of a similar age who had already died. It was awful having to watch a beautiful, full-of-fun, athletic man turn into an anxious, withdrawn near-skeleton. When all the other physical tests were being carried out, there was relief when he didn't have leukaemia, heart trouble, etc., but each negative result led inevitably to only one explanation. For me, being excluded from a lot of what was happening made me feel worse, as if I was perpetually carrying an enormous stone in my stomach. When he became so weak he was hospitalized, I spent a lot of time with him; but I couldn't risk showing the depth of my anxiety in case he decided he didn't want me there. I knew that seeing his grandma's anxiety had made him stay away from her and her continual questions about his eating drove him mad. So I had to 'zap' myself up to go in and walk a tightrope between showing I loved him and keeping things light and fun; taking things, yoghurts, crosswords, etc., each carefully chosen to try and help.

The lull of the next eighteen months of him surviving, although painfully thin, holding down a job and then returning to university, didn't take away the anxiety feelings but gave a glimmer of hope that maybe he could survive, even if not as we would have liked him to be. At least he seemed to be a bit happier and glimpses of his old humour shone through at times.

When he died so suddenly, each member of the family seemed to react quite differently. For my mother it seemed almost a release from her continual anxiety: she said, 'At least his suffering is over' – almost like where death follows a slow cancer which you know there can be no recovery from. For my husband and another sister it was just confirmation of what they felt was inevitable: the end of an ongoing problem that had been causing them hassle and that they had decided to wash their hands of some time before. I blamed myself for pussy-footing around. I felt that if I had really accepted that he could die without very specialist help, I would have fought my sister, brother-in-law and even the sick Ken until I'd got him into the unit in London which appeared to have been the only hope. I had been petrified of causing trouble which would not have resulted in him being helped and might have led to my being excluded completely and Ken feeling even more unhappy. This is what happened when another of my sisters criticized his parents' way of handling things – his re-action was, 'My parents are perfect: it's me that is no good'. When he died, I felt I had let him down: it would have been better to take the risk and just possibly have persuaded him to go, rather than leave him to suffer eighteen months' more pain and to die in the end anyway.

My feeling of devastation was made worse when I dis-covered how little food there had been in his room, which made me acutely aware of his physical suffering. I didn't have the time and space to grieve, so I just turned everything inward: taking control; carrying out all my responsibilities to family, work, college, automatically, whilst dying inside. I don't know that I would have reacted differently if he had died in some other circumstances. I just feel that the strain of the six years of his illness; the impotency of being unable to help yet not feeling it was like leukaemia or cancer and beyond medical treatment; watching his physical and mental distress, and people's reactions to him dying of what is seen as a female fashion problem; and listening to remarks like, 'Well, he did it to himself – all he had to do was eat!'; all made what would have been tragedy in any circumstances a hundred times worse to bear and to come to terms with.

Taking charge of your illness

Jean was forty-two when she was told she had breast cancer. Her story shows the value of taking responsibility for yourself. It's easy to go along automatically within the medical system and not really confront what's happening inside you. In terms of the stages of grief: to stay stuck in a certain amount of denial rather than opening up to your feelings of anger, sadness, guilt, and fear. This is not to say that your doctor may not advise what is in fact the best treatment for you – but if you consciously *choose* his treatment your positive attitude will make a positive outcome more likely.

To be told that you've got cancer is a tremendous shock. I felt numb and very frightened. It was three months from my seeing the consultant and showing him the lump on my breast until anything was done. I was lulled into a state of false security when the consultant said, 'I don't think there is anything to worry about. Wait two months.'

I played bridge the day before the biopsy and was asked if I was nervous. I was quite brassy and said 'No!'. I waited a month for the result and finally rang the consultant's secretary. She read the letter to me over the phone. It said, 'No sign of any malignancy, but some hormonal changes. Come and see me in three weeks' time.'

I walked into the consulting room and was told, 'You'll

have to have a mastectomy. I'll also do a biopsy on the other breast and you might have to have a double mastectomy.'

I don't remember the drive home. I was in a state of shock at the thought of the disfiguring effect of losing one or both of my breasts. I felt I would never be attractive as a woman again. It felt like the end of my femininity and of anyone ever finding me sexually attractive. I rang a hospital doctor I knew who was head of a clinical department and he arranged for me to have a mammogram. This showed nothing wrong with my other breast.

From that moment on, I stopped waking up in a sweat thinking 'this is all a ghastly mistake', and hoping it would go away. I felt very angry that the consultant had written to say I had no malignancy, then when we met said I had cancer. I decided to change to a new consultant in London. This was the start of my being able to take control of my life again. I was busy organizing our business so it would be covered whilst I was away. I also had to find someone to look after the children. I was determined I didn't want to hide the fact I had cancer. I told my children about it. I said, 'You may have heard lots of stories about cancer, but I'm going to get over this and be OK.' They seemed to believe this and appeared fairly unconcerned. My husband shut off and pretended it wasn't happening. I felt angry that he couldn't cope with it, then realized he was so frightened he just couldn't deal with it. I had to get away from the fact he was non-caring and rely on friends and children who could support me. It was a wonderful bonus that I looked healthy and didn't feel ill. I had no pain or discomfort and went in for the major operation in extremely good health with tremendous support from my friends and children. I rationalized that I had had forty-two years of having an attractive body, which some never have. I could have had cancer when I was twenty-five and no time to enjoy my attractiveness. By the time I drove up for the operation, I had done all my crying (I only cried when I was first told; after that I got on with it.)

I joked about the operation before I had it. Afterwards I realized it was not visible to others, except those very intimate to me; and that my physical life would not be affected in any way. I told myself, 'I'm having this operation and this will be the end of it.' I only felt upset about the loss of my breast before the operation. Afterwards I found no one treated me any differently.

What helped me most was the love and support of friends and family. My sister flew over from America when I was first diagnosed. A friend had me to stay to convalesce after the operation. Another friend's husband, whom I hardly knew, scoured book shops looking for a particular book for me written by someone who had overcome cancer.

Before the operation I had felt almost on a high; with my adrenaline charged up. But about six months later I became very nervous. I felt every twinge was going to be a recurrence. I found later that this depression is common after operations. It reminded me of when people die and everyone copes well until after the funeral, whilst lots of things are happening. Then it all catches up with you. For me, this stage lasted eighteen months.

A neighbour of mine had a mastectomy at the same time as me. When I saw her a year later she had been given six months to live. This may well have contributed to my later despondency. For the first time I thought, 'Cancer is something that kills you.' When I had the operation I believed if the cancer was removed early enough there was no problem; it was only afterwards I discovered that survival was not as good as I had thought.

I imagine anyone who has been through this experience sorts out their priorities. I've always been a bit of a perfectionist. I don't worry nearly as much as I used to. I now think, 'This isn't really important: why am I worrying about it?' I don't feel sorry for myself anymore. I don't feel 'if only'. If I feel slightly depressed, I think of what could have happened.

As time goes on I realize how amazingly lucky I was. I imagine cancer could change lives tremendously. It's made me much more relaxed about life. Three of my friends have cancer at the moment. One of them, invasive breast cancer. I've had friends who gave in when they were diagnosed. Others were resilient. At the time I had cancer, I didn't realize how much mental attitude has to do with recovery. I felt it was normal to be positive. Whether my mind shut out the negative aspects, I don't know. All my tears were about the loss of my breast, not fear of losing my life. I do remember the sister in the hospital where I had the operation saying, 'I'm sure you're going to be absolutely fine: you have the right attitude.'

Facing the challenge

MEMORANDUM
Gossip, Thursday 21 August 1989
(I actually heard this from two middle-aged women who were leaning across the garden fence, talking about me)

That's him you know
Who
That chap with you-know-what
It never is
It is you know
I saw him on TV as bold as you and me
Bloody cheek
He should be locked up and throw the key away
They never did that in my day
What? Threw the key away
No, what he did
What's that then?
Well it's personal isn't it
Oh, you mean,
Don't say it,
Say what
What you were going to say
What was I going to say
Oh, never mind you will only *gossip* anyway

(Jon Varker)

HIV/AIDS is not only proving an incredible challenge to the thousands of sufferers and their families all over the world, but is also pushing governments, health services, local authorities and individual carers to explore their attitudes. Jim Kuykendall, Ealing and Hammersmith's HIV/AIDS Co-ordinator says, 'Care-givers have had to review entirely how they work and how they can transfer this good practice to other situations and clients.'

Jon Varker's story has made a major contribution to demystifying HIV and AIDS and to dealing with the fear element, two of the major things I have tried to achieve with my bereavement work. Jon was diagnosed HIV-positive in October 1984 and as having Karposi's sarcoma, one of the conditions of AIDS, early in 1986. He has now been told that he is the second longest-living person with AIDS and Kar-po's sarcoma in the UK. He has had radiotherapy more than seventy times. His left lung collapsed six times from 1978 to 1983 when he had two large tumours and several small ones removed from his lungs and the lungs were lined so they wouldn't collapse again. He has been told he fits all the terms for long-term survivors. In 1986 the doctors gave Jon eighteen months to live. Jon decided not to believe them, and the outcome is 'I'm still here today'.

Jon and his partner, Graham Peter, went to live with Graham's parents, who had been supportive from the beginning. Their unconditional care and love always astounds Jon. Jon says having a stable relationship for the last fifteen years was one of the things that helped him most. In the past everything revolved around Jon and his death and making sure Graham was financially stable. Then, sadly, the tide changed and Graham died. Jon has since planned and organized his own funeral.

After living with AIDS for over a decade it's hard to look back and see what it was like at the beginning I do remember that when people said negative things to me, I would always try and turn them back to something positive. I have a need-to-know mechanism which helps me cope. Because I need to know what's going on in my body, all the decisions that are made about my treatment are taken jointly by me with the doctors. I also decided that in addition to allopathic (conventional) medicine, I would introduce complementary therapies to suit my own needs. At the same time, without realizing it, I started to work on my own inner being, to contact my energy within.

My breakthrough first started with the AIDS Mastery workshop, which empowers people to live in the present moment. This workshop set me on my way and made me realize there was something more within me I needed to find out about. It put me back in control of my life. Once I recognized this gift, I was able to work on it. I next attended the Warrior Within workshop, which through physical challenges again helped me develop my inner strength. As I left the site of the course, I was given the strength to call out to people by the side of the lake, 'I've got AIDS and I'm proud of it!'

Throughout the past decade I've had my ups and downs, seeing people going through incredible different stages of their AIDS-related illness and going to many funerals. But there is also the lighter side of me, the child within that is like a toy in the cupboard: when that's brought out I can go with it one hundred per cent.

I think that now, ten years on, I really know who I am and where I'm going. I have no time for what I call crap/waffle in the world from other people. If someone wants to ask me a question I'd rather they asked the question outright than beat around the bush. Whether they get the answer they want is their problem.

People say to me, 'You give so much. You have an insight into people's distress. You have a calmness about you that makes me want to talk.' They don't recognize the part of me that hurts or has needs. That's all part of the Jon with AIDS. Before I had AIDS I didn't know who I was or my direction in life. Now, having AIDS, there is meaning and unconditional care and love, even for people who are still frightened.

If I hadn't done this work on myself, helped others and found inner peace and energy or life-force, I most definitely wouldn't be alive today. It is very important for people to understand that although they are the centre of their own universe they are not the centre of the universe at large.

If they produced a pill to cure AIDS tomorrow, I'd be at the back of the queue for it. I'd have a fear of going back to what life was before AIDS and losing my sense of self now my life is so enriched and fulfilled.

Jon put this message over very powerfully in a speech he did for World AIDS Day:

Living powerfully with AIDS is a real possibility. One thing I have learned from working with people with AIDS is just how powerful the human will, the human spirit and the human heart are. People with AIDS are not victims. People with AIDS are people with choices, people with passion, people with creativity. It takes power and creativity to exercise choices that nurture and enrich lives in the face of a health crisis. People *have* AIDS; they do not become their condition.

When AIDS first emerged, the likelihood of creating miracles seemed pretty remote. I believe in miracles: I see them all around me. I don't know how to make them happen, but I see the possibility of creating an environment for them to appear. The first step is perhaps to redefine the word 'miracle'. It may not always look like the parting of the Red Sea, or walking on water. A miracle may be a remission; sometimes a miracle is living through opportunistic infection after infection. Sometimes it's dealing with our families. Sometimes it's discovering that healing may be leaving the body; and sometimes a miracle looks like falling in love with yourself. There are medical miracles: there are some people with AIDS who have been alive and well for a long time. There are also those who say that, oddly enough, AIDS is the best thing that ever happened to them. Until they were diagnosed, they were living a life that was not nurturing them. They were unaware of the love that was all around them; they had not allowed true intimacy in their lives. It seems that when a person is confronted with the likelihood of losing life and chooses not to be victimised, then they can discover the beauty and wonder of life around them, and their own beings. Now, that's a miracle. Now we need to look at the choices: the quality of our lives is not determined by circumstances. It is determined by us. We determine how events affect us. So our first choice about AIDS is how we deal with it.

What you can do

- Keep using the suggestions in Chapter 4 to help you get in touch with and express all your feelings around your illness, or the illness of someone close to you. The 'Wise person' visualization (see Appendix) can be particularly helpful.
- Keep the lines of communication open. Don't shut off, imagining you're 'protecting' the ill person (if you're the carer); or deny your reality to friends or family.
- Forgive yourself if you think you've made mistakes in dealing with your illness. Give yourself permission not to be perfect, and imagine giving yourself a hug. It may help to do some inner child work (see Chapter 2).
- Do your own research on the particular illness you are involved with, so that you can understand what professionals say to you, and equip yourself to be involved in deciding what care is best for you.

- Join a support group for your particular condition. Meeting other people with a similar condition can make you feel less alienated.
- When you are fearful or anxious, say 'I choose love' (which is the opposite of fear).
- Look at holistic, complementary care alongside conventional medicine. Such alternative therapies can be particularly valuable in strengthening your life-urge and supporting your emotional wellbeing This kind of help is invaluable also for family members under stress.
- Be willing to perceive unlooked-for positive effects of the situation.
- Whether you're a carer, or the person with the condition, explore your relationship to the illness. Unresolved hostility can be unhealthy. You can try writing to the illness and write its replies back to you; or hold conversations with it inside your head.
- Live in the present as much as possible. Meditation can help with this. Try literally living life half an hour at a time when things are difficult, thanking God or whatever you believe in for having got through each thing you do.

---

1 Quoted in 'How Anorexia Was Cured by Mourning' by Oliver Gillie, *The Sunday Times*, 24 August 1986.

The Experience of Death

To die must be a really big adventure.
(J.M. Barrie, *Peter Pan*)

11

Dying

Death is one of the greatest taboos. It doesn't square with our worship of youth. But the truth, after all, is that we are all terminally ill. Once we recognize that, we can enjoy the life we have left.

(Elisabeth Kübler-Ross)

When a person is dying their family can find themselves in a crisis situation. Their joys and regrets from the past, the demands the present situation is making on them, and their fears of the future are all brought into stark focus. The whole family may experience guilt, depression and discord. The emotional stages of death are very similar to the stages of grief: this is also an opportunity for healing. In this time of crisis there is the possibility of resolving old problems and finding reconciliations that greatly strengthen the family group.

If this time is to be used fully, there needs to be some degree of shared awareness. Truth needs to be available (though not forced on people), so that the family can travel together. In general, sharing is more creative than deception. The often surprising potential for personal and family growth at this stage is one of the strongest objections most hospice workers have to shielding a patient from the truth, or to legalizing early euthanasia. The most important things for people who are dying are that they are surrounded by love and compassion, are allowed to die with dignity, and to be at peace. I also believe a dying person needs to feel in control of the remainder of their life.

The dying have their own special gifts to give those who will still be there after their death. I asked volunteers at a hospice why they were doing it: 'This is the happiest place I know,' they chorused. My colleague, Uthe, says: 'I've learnt how to live by working with the dying.' Apart from the courage, endurance, simplicity, and often humour she has seen in her patients, she says she has learned to live in the present and clear any misunderstandings with people close to her as they happen.

I remember the gasp that went up when Anthony Bloom, head of the Russian Orthodox Church in England, said:

> I wait for death like a bridegroom waits for his bride. I can't understand why so many people are frightened of dying when they seem to get so little enjoyment out of life. . . . Death is the touchstone of our attitude to life. People who are afraid of death are afraid of life. It is impossible not to be afraid of life with all its complexity and dangers if one is afraid of death. This means that to solve the problem of death is not a luxury. If we are afraid of death we will never be prepared to take ultimate risks; we will spend our life in a cowardly, careful and timid manner. It is only as we can face death, make sense of it, determine its place and our place in regard to it, that we will be able to live in a fearless way and to the fullness of our ability. Too often we wait until the end of our life to face death, whereas we would have lived quite differently if only we had faced death at the outset.

I think it's valuable for everyone to ask themselves: what would I do if I only had six months to live? Why aren't I doing those things now? In *Who Dies?* Stephen Levine suggests healthy people should use illness

> as an opportunity to investigate our relationship to life, or to explore our fear of death. How often, for example, is one encouraged to contemplate the aches and pains of flu as a preparation for death, as a means of melting the resistance to life? Struggling for satisfaction from moment to moment, we think of ourselves as either fortunate or unfortunate, little realizing the teachings of impermanence.

The taboo of death

> We are in the middle of an astonishing worldwide conspiracy.
> What could be called a macabre game of 'hide the body'. . . .
> How many dead bodies did you see today; this year; in your
> lifetime? (Barry Long)[1]

A survey in the 1970s showed that ninety-eight per cent of
people had not discussed the topic of death with friends.
There are many people who don't think about someone
dying until it happens to them. They then are totally unpre-
pared, on every level, for what happens.

Medical education is geared to curing people, and somebody dying represents a failure to many doctors. Doctors and
nurses in the UK generally only receive about half a day in
their entire training dealing with the emotional aspects of
death and dying. As Dr Michael Simpson said at one international conference: 'The modern deathbed experience
would have been regarded as science fiction some ten years
ago.'

Dying is an emotional challenge not only to the person
concerned and their immediate family, but to the professional carers involved and other friends and relatives. We are
all afraid of the unknown, and death has become increasingly hidden from us. If you are involved with an anticipated
death, you may find yourself battling against pressure to
sweep the whole experience out of sight; in danger of losing
the opportunities for growth and love, as well as the emotional risks, that involvement offers.

The emotional stages of death

> Dying is usually a process that is as active as it is passive. It is
> as much a doing as an undergoing. It involves active choices
> and attitudes as well as letting go. It's a final dance with
> elaborate steps, and we usually have to improvise. Of course,
> some people die in a flash without ever knowing what hit
> them, but others like my dad prepare for death, aware of it as
> a process. (Gabrielle Roth, *Maps to Ecstasy*)

Elisabeth Kübler-Ross, one of the greatest modern teachers about the process of death, says in her book *On Death and Dying* that dying people go through the following stages:

- Denial and isolation
- Anger
- Bargaining
- Depression
- Acceptance

Hope is a fundamental emotion that is likely to be experienced on and off during all these stages, until immediately before death: it sustains patients through their weeks and months of suffering. It is hope that allows us to 'live until we die'. Of course, for some people there *are* long-lasting remissions, or miracle cures. Doctors and carers who share the hope that something unforeseen may happen (while also dealing with the reality of the patient's condition now) are the most helpful to patients. It is important not to insist on hope at times when the patient may be feeling other emotions, and especially when they come to a final acceptance of death.

Denial and isolation

Elisabeth Kübler-Ross said that of 200 people she interviewed, nearly all reacted to the diagnosis of terminal illness with 'No, not me. It cannot be true.' Some people (and some families), stay in deep denial until the end, but for most, this is a temporary defence, which will soon be replaced with partial acceptance. There is unlikely to be a clear-cut end to this stage: nearly everyone will use some denial from time to time. Elisabeth Kübler-Ross quotes the saying, ' We cannot look at the sun all the time, we cannot face death all the time. These patients can consider the possibility of their own death for a while but then have to put this consideration away in order to pursue life.'[2]

Dr Dora Black, speaking at the Second International Conference on Children and Death, said that many consultants fail to recognize the terminal stage of illness in children and continue to treat them rather than taking the decision to stop their attempts to cure. In this way children can die without acknowledgement at the end. Children appreciate the opportunity to say goodbye to friends and family. They also like the opportunity to give their possessions to friends and siblings without them feeling guilty.

Anger

'Why me?' It's common to look for someone to blame – yourself, God, the doctor, family – whoever possible. When she found she had cancer my mother searched for a reason and blamed garden sprays and smoking. There can be deep frustration, too, at having all your plans and dreams taken away. You may feel furious at everyone around you who is still active and independent. It's important (even if difficult) for carers not to take such anger personally, but to recognize the hurt and fear beneath. Taking time to listen, and showing your respect for the value of the patient as a worthwhile human being will help a great deal.

Bargaining

'If only . . .' If you stop smoking/eat special foods, etc., the doctor will save you; or if you forgive your enemies, God will reprieve you. Often there is irrational internal dialogue based on personal superstitions. The bargaining is often for more time – just until spring/some special occasion. Sometimes such bargains are the result of underlying guilt: a feeling of not having been good enough or not deserving to live unless an impossible effort is made to be perfect.

Depression

Feeling despair, emptiness; that there's no point to anything. This can be seen as a kind of preparatory grief for impending losses. When someone dies they lose not only their physical body, but familiar surroundings, family, friends, interests, work. They may have regrets for all the things they haven't done. Comfort can be had from going through their lives and focusing on what they have achieved; and from dealing with any unfinished business – both emotional and practical.

Acceptance

This can be the time when the family will need most help, as the patient will generally withdraw more and more and not want to be disturbed by the troubles of the outside world. When they have overcome their envy of the living and mourned the impending loss of so many important people and situations, they can be empty of emotion. They will be tired and weak and sleep a lot. This stage may unfortunately coincide with a partner or close relative wanting them to stay alive, or being hurt by their withdrawal (seeing it as rejection). Some people keep on fighting because the people close to them cannot accept their death. Patients frequently ask to see fewer and fewer people; they are gradually separating themselves from friends and family. They may prefer people to sit with them quietly rather than talking.

As with the stages of grief, (see Chapter 4), this model is simply a structure for looking at your emotional experience, which can be used if it's helpful. Not everybody experiences all the stages, or in this order. It is most common for people to experience more than one stage at a time, and/or to move backwards and forwards through them. If you are caring for a dying person, you may find this model is closer to your own emotional experience than theirs. Feel your feelings and remain open to the experience as far as you are able.

Facing the news

Forty years ago it was regarded as ethical not to tell a patient or their family that they had a terminal illness. Now, thankfully, that has changed. We owe a great debt to Elisabeth Kübler-Ross, whose work and research has greatly increased our understanding of the experience of dying. In her early days when she suggested an interdisciplinary seminar on death and dying it was refused with utter disbelief by everybody she approached. Now, there are trainings and conferences throughout the world on all aspects of the subject.

One of Elisabeth Kübler-Ross's surveys of terminally ill patients in hospitals showed that 98% of them wanted to know they were dying; 60% of doctors did not want to tell them; and 80% of patients knew anyway. She found dying patients eager to talk about their impending death and relieved when they were allowed to unburden themselves and let her know how they felt about dying.

Telling the truth can be more controversial when it comes

to children, but Mother Frances Dominica of Helen House, a children's hospice in Oxford, wholeheartedly believes in the child's right to know – in whatever way is appropriate to their understanding. She has no rigid rules at Helen House – only that nobody ever lies to the children. She says children will never trust you again if you are caught out. She believes most children do know if they are dying, without ever apparently being told. One child wrote to her: 'I'm bored at home, and I'm fed up with my parents. Would you please book me into the Snoopy bedroom for the next week please, and they won't be coming with me.' He confided to her later, 'They don't know I know, and it is so hard to keep them from finding out that I do.'

Most people who are diagnosed as terminal guess the news from the changed attitude of people around them, but in recent years the percentage of doctors who tell people has gone up considerably. One of the problems now is that even people who would prefer not to know are often told. Generally, doctors who say patients don't want to face the truth can't face it themselves, and protect patients without asking. Terminally ill people and their families generally know with whom they can talk about death and dying and can sense the resistance in others. A dying person will let you know how much or what they want to know if you listen to them. Frank, my husband's best friend, died of a brain tumour which wasn't diagnosed until two months before his death. He had always led a very private life and rarely showed his feelings. When I visited him after his operation he said, 'One of these days I'll ask the surgeon what the score is.' This told me he didn't want to 'know' on a deeper level or discuss it. He was an intelligent man and by now bedridden, with his condition worsening. I asked him to tell me if he had any fears or concerns and we discussed general ones not associated with his condition. He died without discussing his condition again with the medical staff or family and friends.

Sometimes, people know they are dying but want to protect those closest to them. Then I might say something like, 'Don't you think they know anyway?' or, 'What do you think they know?' The dying person usually then realizes their family must know. The most painful example of family denial I have come across was Margaret. She was in her forties, an ex-teacher, married with two teenage daughters. She had had cancer for more than three years and now had secondaries. The word 'cancer' had never been used and her doctor, consultant and family colluded to ensure she wasn't told her prognosis. Her district nurse was worried about her and asked me to call. Margaret's husband opened the door when I visited and showed me into the living room where Margaret was on her own. He returned to the kitchen, where I heard him talking and laughing with a friend. It was immediately obvious that Margaret had only a short time left to live. She kept nervously saying, 'I'm not well, but I'm going to get better. The doctor and my husband say so.' She went on to say that her children complained about her keeping them awake at night with the awful rumbles her stomach made. I asked her what information she had been given about her 'illness'. She replied, 'No one will answer my questions. They keep telling me not to worry.' She was obviously very worried. I didn't feel able to break the collusion at this very late stage, so I taught her some relaxation exercises and did a guided visualization for her and gave her a hug. I stayed an hour and a half and explained I was away for a week, but would contact her when I got back. We then had another hug before I left. I was let out by the husband as silently as I had been let in. The next day Margaret rang me at work, and asked who she could talk to until I got back, as her family wouldn't communicate with her at all. All I could recommend was the Samaritans. When I rang on my return, I was told she had died. I offered to go and see the family, but they refused. I am haunted to this day by the unnecessary loneliness and fear surrounding Margaret as she died.

Of course, doctors can't always be a hundred per cent certain of their diagnosis, and it can be difficult for them to predict what time someone has left. You may have to put some pressure on medical staff to be open and honest in answering questions without using jargon, so you know what to expect. When my mother and I were told together by the consultant that she was dying, I asked if I could see someone to talk it over. The consultant looked at me in amazement and asked me why I needed to do this. I had to explain that I wasn't medically trained and didn't know the course her cancer would take; also that I had to see that she would be adequately looked after whilst I was at work. I finally saw a registrar who sat behind a desk and looked uncomfortable whilst I asked basic questions that I felt anyone in my position would need the answers to.

Taking control

One of the biggest causes of stress is not feeling in control of one's life. In terminal illness when a patient has less and less control over their body, it is really important that they feel their wishes are respected and they have choices in as many matters as possible. It is also important for relatives to be included in decisions that affect them.

In order to participate fully in decisions about care, it's important to learn as much as possible about the illness and about health-care options. Most people who are terminally ill would prefer to die at home. Modern methods of pain control, and the option of hospice care to give families a break from time to time, make this an increasingly realistic choice. Even if hospital or hospice care is the only practical alternative, patients and their families who are clear about what they want can feel an increasing measure of control over the kind of care provided.

Choosing when to die

We have more control over our own death than is commonly realized. Many people will keep themselves alive for a special event – the birth of a baby, or an anniversary. They may also choose to die on their own. Some New Zealand friends of mine told me their ninety-three-year-old mother was keen to meet her granddaughter's fiancé, whom she had met while staying in England. When they came home, she gave the couple a special engagement present and said, 'I won't be here for your wedding.' She wasn't. Even though she had no special illness, she died before it took place.

Fears of death

The four most common fears are being on your own; being a burden; being in pain; and what comes after death. Sogyal Rinpoche says, 'One of the tragedies of the Western world is that many die alone.' Unfortunately, even people with families often die feeling they are on their own. I've seen people literally turn their face to the wall when their questions are evaded, and their sense of connection is gone. Some patients are defensive and isolate themselves even when carers offer companionship.

Such isolation is also linked to many people's reluctance to be supported; their fear of being a burden. Thankfully, modern medical achievements mean many people with serious illnesses can take care of themselves to a large extent. My mother was very independent and feared being a burden on anyone. She also didn't like showing her body to people. She died of cancer of the liver and kept herself clean and changed and dealt with her own incontinency pads right up until the day she died.

The majority of people who are dying and expect to be in pain are cancer patients. Cicely Saunders, a pioneer of modern palliative care, says:

> Half the patients who die of cancer have no pain problem. If pain does come, it can be controlled while the patient remains active, alert and still themselves. And this can be done not only when they are in special units. Half our patients are in their own homes.[3]

There are still some people who unfortunately experience unnecessary pain, often as a result of a rigid hospital practice where they still do 'medicine rounds' at set times and expect patients' pain to fit in with them. This has been aptly described as a 'Chinese water torture', where patients are constantly dipped in and out of pain. Some GPs, also, are inexperienced in pain control, and you may have to insist on getting additional advice.

The fear of what comes after death is addressed in Chapter 12. Often this fear is greatly diminished if a person deals with any unfinished emotional business – see 'Handling the emotional pain', below.

Hospital care

There are now many specialist hospitals or wards for people who are dying. But the main emphasis in most hospitals is still on cure rather than care, and death is seen as a failure by many. When they are dying in hospitals, patients are often treated as socially dead before they are biologically dead. My mother was admitted to hospital for a week three months before she died of cancer. I lived fifty miles away and could only visit at weekends. She was on a surgical ward and said that apart from being given tablets and her meals, no one came near her. She was in a worse state at the end of the week than when she went in. She felt totally rejected and un-cared-for and had virtually stopped eating. None of the staff queried it when she left meals and there was no one to cajole her into eating them. She said she didn't feel the staff deliber-ately neglected her. They were just too busy doing practical things and didn't recognize her emotional needs.

In contrast, my husband's Uncle Ern went into hospital in a coma after a fall. The hospital doctor said it was obviously Ern's time to die, and asked his family how we would like it to happen. I explained he was an 'old soldier' and had been very independent, so it was important to let him die with dignity. Ern was put in a cot near the nurses' table in the ward and just given liquids. He died peacefully two days later, never coming out of the coma. I talked to him and said it was fine to let go and what a good job he had done. I re-assured him that I would see that his remaining sister-in-law, who had been sharing his house with him, was looked after.

Some professionals' 'cure at all costs' approach can rob patients of their dignity and choice about death. Rosemary, a Quaker friend of mine, was in her eighties and had Parkin-son's disease. Her nightmare was that she would develop senile dementia and become a burden. Unfortunately, she did become senile and realized it. She became too ill to be nursed at home and went into hospital. She had told us all that she was ready to die, but when she contracted pneumo-nia the hospital doctor, without asking her family, prescribed antibiotics. I found it agonizing to watch her spirit trapped inside a body that was obviously ready to go. It was some three weeks later that she finally died.

In response to such practices, the Natural Death Centre was founded in 1991 to help improve the quality of dying. One way they have done this is to popularize the idea of 'living wills'. These are documents in which you can indicate your wishes should the time come when you can no longer take part in decisions on your own future. Living wills do not ask doctors to do anything contrary to existing law, but should they be faced with a difficult decision on the pro-longation of life, they will know the considered opinion of the patient. In 1993 the media featured the story of a young man who was crushed in the Hillsbrorough disaster four years before and had been on a life-support machine ever since. His parents had to go to court to get permission for the machine to be switched off so he could die with dignity. They said afterwards what a relief it was.

For relatives, too, there can be problems. Joan was away on holiday with her husband when he had his final heart attack:

> We were trundled thirty miles over country roads to the nearest hospital. When we got there he was wheeled off and I was left sitting on my own. I asked to be with him but they refused. Two hours later they came out with his watch. I was then made to wait another few hours until a family member arrived to deal with all the business side.

Joan felt guilty and angry at not being with George when he died. They had been a very close couple who had shared everything and she had been with him during his previous heart attacks. She was given no opportunity to say goodbye. She is a capable person and would have preferred to be doing something after he died rather than being made to sit by herself and wait for relatives. She felt disempowered and helpless.

Relatives' difficulties in getting the care and compassion they need was highlighted in a report entitled 'Matters of Death and Life' by South Birmingham Community Health Council. One of the authors, Jennifer Cousins, wrote in the *Guardian*:[4]

> People complained bitterly about poor communication with hospital staff. It was crucially important that they knew as much as possible about the reasons for the death, but a disturbing number felt they never really got to the bottom of it and are still haunted by unanswered questions many years later. People were very distressed if for some reason they had failed to be with their relative when they died. But some people were not summoned in time, some were refused permission to stay, some were made to feel in the way, some sat bleakly in passageways outside cubicles.
>
> 'Only two of us were allowed in the room. We were not a very large family and we should have been around mum's bed, all together, to the end.'
>
> . . . We knew from the relatives who contacted us that post-

mortems can cause distress if permission is not sought first or if the results are not discussed afterwards. Yet only a third of health authorities routinely make the results available to relatives. Some hospitals, especially teaching centres, undertake post-mortems on all patients who die, regardless of clinical necessity.

I hope that hospitals will improve their response to dying patients and their families. Meanwhile, a determination to discover what your hospital's practice is, and to communicate your desires to staff, may result in a more flexible response. Such an effort will certainly help you to feel more in control of what happens.

Hospices

A patient is more likely to feel in control of his life in a hospice than in a hospital. Referral to a hospice is no longer seen as a one-way ticket. Patients are allowed home as much as possible, and families treat the place as an extension of their own home. Susan, a hospice nurse in New Zealand, told me her hospice aims to provide assessment, pain control, non-intrusive care, and to encourage the patient and those close to them to treat the hospice as home. But for her the most important aim is to encourage people to 'live until they die'. She said they encourage patients to set goals they would like to achieve, so they always have something to look forward to.

Hospices encourage families to participate in caring for their relative if they wish, and to join in with the activities and therapies. These can include art and music therapy and lots of laughter. I've often seen a jigsaw set up in hospices: it's a good meeting and talking place. Family and friends can visit at any time and in many cases bring in the family pet(s). Sometimes, though, families need permission to stay away and regain some normality in their lives. The family is seen as a unit of care, and concern extends beyond the patient's death into the bereavement phase.

When I asked Wyn Merrick of the Wellington, New Zealand, hospice what she thought was the fundamental difference between hospitals and hospices, she said she feels hospitals have a male energy and hospices a female one.

Dying at home

This is becoming more common again and is likely to give both patient and family the greatest opportunities for participation and being in control. As long as you and your family have adequate support and feel capable of caring for the dying person, having them at home is less likely to give rise to guilt and 'if onlys'. It will also help any children involved to accept death as a natural part of life, not something to be feared and hidden away. It is important to be able to get relief from caring, especially if the terminal illness is a lengthy one. For the dying person, being at home can be the best way to 'live until they die', provided the emotional atmosphere is open and accepting. A headmaster I knew who died at home of cancer was watching cricket and doing school work in the afternoon of the day he died.

Handling the emotional pain

The spiritual and emotional pain of dying can be more frightening to face even than physical pain. As Elisabeth Earnshaw-Smith points out,[5] close family members are also deeply affected by it:

> We have all felt the agony of watching a loved one mortally ill or hampered by handicap, and longed for release from our own anguish about it. Yet not to feel, and be seen to feel, that pain is unthinkable and a mockery of the relationship. Love, or a genuine concern, can be very costly. Could we ameliorate or obliterate this pain we would deny the importance of the occasion or diminish the value of the relationship which causes us to grieve.

As she says, emotional pain often cannot and should not be 'cured', but it must be understood and acknowledged. Often, the true cause of deep pain is in past experience. Many elderly people feel deeply alone when dying if they have lost their partner or others close to them. Some people feel their death has made all their deepest fears about themselves and life come true:

Mrs C. had for twenty-five years, and probably since child-hood, felt unlovable. Now terminally ill and in the hospice, although her physical condition was greatly improved, she was unable to accept friendship and reassurance from the staff or even from her husband and son. Believing that no-one cared for her or could alleviate her symptoms, she only wanted to die.

Severe physical pain brings with it, inevitably, emotional wounds.

In terminal illness the slow, relentless destruction of the body seems to threaten the destruction of the social and emotional life of the individual and the family; but when the deteriorating body is loved and cared for the emotional pain is often relieved and the family re-integrated and enabled to support one another.

The physical trauma and pain of a life-threatening illness will often change how a person reacts to others – their personality will alter. This is distressing for everyone close to them as well. It is important for family carers, in particular, to keep dealing with the feelings such changes bring up in them. The patient is sometimes so involved with their illness they may not be as aware of such side-effects. (See Chapter 4 for suggestions for dealing with negative feelings.)

How you can help

It is important to be aware that family carers are also likely to be going through an emotional and spiritual crisis. If you are a carer, it is vital to nurture yourself in this situation, to allow support in, and to take a break whenever possible.

The root of much emotional pain is spiritual despair or confusion. This is a good time to explore your beliefs – not through religion, necessarily, but possibly in music, poetry, art or nature. In *Where is God in all this?*[6] Rev. David Langford says,

The crisis of terminal illness is so great that it challenges the way in which many individuals view their life. It is these spiritual needs that we need to identify and then to assist these individuals in their search for meaning through this difficult time.

The suggestions below are based on his 'Principles of helping with spiritual pain':
- Provide a secure, caring environment: freedom, space and privacy; clean, fresh air, comfort, beauty; care for role and appearance.
- Listen: to questions; life stories; join patient's search for meaning; share emotional pain with sensitivity and compassion; enable expression of fear, anger, etc.
- Reassure: with respect for patient's integrity, worth and values; about concern for and provision for family/dependants; about physical care in illness and dying; with information (as desired and appropriate).
- Prepare for death: help with unfinished emotional business; help with reviewing of life (talk, look at personal photos); help them if possible to fulfil any last wishes; help family face their own feelings about the patient's death.
- Above all . . . *be there!*

Dealing with unfinished business

In *Maps to Ecstasy*, Gabrielle Roth suggests there are five cycles in life: birth, childhood, puberty, maturity, and the final cycle:

> If we arrive at the last cycle without having achieved the intimacy of maturity, our last years may be spent in pain, loneliness, and confusion. But if we do achieve intimacy, even if our life-partner dies before we do, we have the deep satisfaction in body, heart and mind that we lived fully to anchor our inward turning.

Most of us have unfinished business: things we wished we had said or done differently in our lives. Often, when the physical body is ready to let go, these things can stop us dying. One of the first questions I ask people who 'can't' die is, 'Is there anybody or anything you haven't forgiven?' Often what is troubling them is not some big dispute, but goes back to the loss or death of someone they didn't have a chance to 'complete' with before they lost them.

For many, the last few months being with someone they

are close to while dying can be the most fulfilling and rewarding time in their relationship. There is no longer any
time or need for pretence, and the barriers can come down.
One woman on a bereavement counselling course described
the night her husband died as being the happiest night of her
life. They had chosen to have him taken off the machines that
were keeping him alive. She said that as he slipped sway,
'We were able to talk lovingly and openly about our life together and my future without him.' In a similar vein, I heard
a fourteen-year-old say to her mother, 'Aren't we lucky
Daddy died of cancer? It gave us time to say what we wanted
to before he died.' Some dying parents I know have written
letters to their children to be opened at a certain age, and one
mother of teenagers recorded cassettes for her teenage
daughters in her last months in hospital.

For my mother, the last seven months of her life, from
when she had her terminal diagnosis in December to the following July when she died, were as she described them, 'the
best time of my life'. She moved into a flat she loved in Hove
in Sussex, gave teas for her friends, played the piano for a
nursery school and 'sorted out' the family. I went down
every weekend and shopped and prepared everything for
the following week. During those weekends we were able to
talk through and heal our earlier differences. The last few
months, when she was too weak to look after herself, were
spent with one of my nieces and her family in Oxford. As so
often happens, my niece had just had a new baby as my
mother was dying. A week before she died, my mother
asked my sister to take her home for the weekend. She saw
all her friends, gave away all the things she wanted to and
left everything in perfect order. She even said who she
would like at her cremation. She came back to my nieces on
the Tuesday of Wimbledon Tennis final week and watched
tennis on the Wednesday. (She had played herself until a
year earlier.) She took to her bed on Thursday and died on
Friday with her family around her.

There are suggestions in Chapters 2, 4, and 8 for healing
relationships. The following visualization is also a powerful
tool for a dying person completing any unfinished emotional
business:

Close your eyes, relax, and imagine a place that is special to
you. See any people who have been important to you around

you. Choose the person that feels the most important and tell them you are going to die. Watch their reaction. When you feel complete with this, tell them anything you have left unsaid, or anything you haven't done and feel you should have. Watch their response again. Now look at your future together to see how these future events will develop if you are no longer here. Think if there is anything you need to do before you go to influence these events. When you feel complete and at peace with this person, repeat the activity with the other individuals in the group.

Caring for a person who is dying

I know, you feel insecure, don't know what to say, don't know what to do. But please believe me, if you care, you can't go wrong. Just admit that you care. That is really for what we search. We may ask for why's and wherefores, but we don't really expect answers. Don't run away . . . wait . . . all I want to know is that there will be someone to hold my hand when I need it. I am afraid. . . . I have lots I wish we could talk about. . . . If only we could be honest, both admit of our fears, touch one another. If you really care, would you lose so much of your valuable professionalism if you even cried with me? Just person to person? Then, it might not be so hard to die.

This plea was written by a dying student nurse, and addressed to professional carers, but it goes to the heart of what all dying people need most: our presence and non-judgemental love. It is easy to feel inadequate to care for a dying person. Death has been hidden in hospitals behind sophisticated technology. This is a time, however, when simple care from the heart is the most valuable; and death itself is often surprisingly peaceful. A recent study of a hundred consecutive patients dying in a hospice confirmed that the final moments of life are likely to be peaceful, even for a group referred because of previous intractable physical, emotional or social problems. One of my clients, who was with her sister when she died, told me, 'I'd always imagined being at the bedside of someone who was dying would be horrific. It wasn't like that. I felt a great release.' At a recent conference I attended, a hospice nurse movingly described the night one of their patients was dying. She said all his family got into bed with him and stayed until he died, so he had the comfort of their touch.

Hans, a well-known sculptor, told me how he used his own artistic, creative process when he cared for his mother as she was dying of cancer. He focused on her to the exclusion of everything else. He was fifty-three years old then and she was eighty-three. They reversed roles in the last few months together. He bathed, spoon-fed, led and guided her into the spirit. He had started life as a Protestant, but had explored Buddhism, Hinduism, and other faiths as he travelled the world. When he thought she was ready, he prayed for help for her to leave her body. 'Greatest Creator, her temple is crumbling. Let her spirit return.' He prayed in this way several times before it happened. On the night she died, he slept next to her as usual. He held her hand and monitored her breathing.

> Her heart beat fast, whilst her breathing was slow and lengthy. I watched the separation of the mechanical part: as her pulse went; I could feel her spirit leaving her body. She was ready to die and had no fear to die. My mother was my great guide. I was able to give back to her what she had given me. Now I really appreciate life. Each day I am reborn and appreciate life. At night when I am ready to go to sleep, I die.

It is only recently in the West that we have become so isolated in our dying. On a recent trip to New Zealand I learned how the Maoris care for the dying. A member of the family stays with them day and night. No one sees themselves as alone. They are all part of the extended family. When the person dies, members of the family like to sit with them for several hours. They also wash and embalm the body ready for the lying-in-state at the *marae* (the original home of their family). This kind of care is practised by most societies in the world except ours.

Ian and Jane were inspired to practise a similar open-hearted approach when their young son Ben was given only a short time to live:

> We slowly and painfully realized that Ben was going to die. How could we ensure that his, and our last days together

were as good as they could be? How could we ensure that everyone remembered his short life in happiness, and celebrated his much-loved qualities?

As the death of a child is such a traumatic event to everyone – as to us – we had to help others come to terms with his death. Rather than hide Ben whilst he was dying, rather than mourn him alone in a darkened room even whilst he was alive, we opened our house to others. Children came first in ones and twos, friends of Ben's big brother Alistair. They were curious and concerned and far less afraid of death and dying than adults. Then their parents came, swept along by the children's enthusiasm, then others in the community came in a steady stream. They had all heard about Ben and us and how we wanted to make his last few weeks the best weeks of his life. The house seemed to be perpetually full of caring and laughing people, drawn like a magnet to Ben. He seemed to give them life, and make them less afraid of death, even as his own brief existence came to an end. It was then, and seems now, a truly remarkable time, when many people came to terms with that which they did not think they could bear. He died two months after his third birthday.

We still mourn. We cannot believe he is no longer alive even now, but the strangely happy memories of his dying weeks stay in our hearts, as they do in all those who were with him at that time.

Holistic care

There are many valuable non-medical ways to help care for a dying person. Each of the methods suggested below honours the whole being of a person, and this focus in itself (rather than looking at the illness) can be a great morale-booster.

- Massage and aromatherapy: often people find it difficult to like their bodies when they are dying, so massage and aromatherapy and the touch they bring can be very healing, as well as taking away aches and pains. Even if you are untrained, a gentle hand can soothe and reassure.
- Meditation and deep relaxation: I like the meditation I was taught by Joan Halifax, because it links with helping people to breathe well. She used it frequently when she was working with dying people – 'Breathing in / calm

mind and body. Breathing out / smile and release. In, out. Deep, slow. Calm, ease. Smile, release.' (See the Appendix for relaxation methods.)

- The visualization 'No fear to die' in the Appendix.
- Music: Theresa Schroeder-Sheker uses music to facilitate what she calls 'the unbinding of physical or spiritual pain'. Her work started as a result of working as a volunteer in a hospital to pay for her music training. She saw how patients literally had the door shut on them and were left to die on their own. She got into bed with one dying man and sat and held him in her arms and sang him opera arias. He died peacefully the next day. There are many tapes available now specifically composed to induce a sense of peace and relaxation.
- Laughter has traditionally been said to be a great tonic, and it is now recognized that endorphins are released when we laugh that really do make us feel better!
- Don't forget to make sure you yourself receive similar support as a carer.

After the death

In hospitals, bodies tend to be removed very fast after death. They are often covered and removed secretly, almost as if death was a contagious disease. In hospices, those close to the dead person are more likely to be able to stay and say their goodbyes, for several hours if necessary. It's not necessary to summon the undertaker immediately, either, if the death takes place at home. It takes time for the spirit to leave the body; some people say hours, others reckon about three days. Some friends whose mother died in hospital opened a nearby window, so her spirit could 'fly away'.

When a family have been looking after a dying person there is often a great vacuum left when they die. The family lose not only their relative, but all the social contacts they made with professional carers. Hospices generally have support groups where surviving relatives have a chance to share their experiences with others.

---

1 *May I Speak to You of Death*, cassette by Barry Long (available from the Barry Long Foundation, BCM, Box 876, London WC1N 3XX).
2 *On Death and Dying*, p.35 .

12

Beyond death

Death is nothing at all – I have only slipped away into the next room. I am I and you are you. Whatever we were to each other, that we still are. Call me by my old familiar name, speak to me in the easy way which you always used. Wear no forced area of solemnity or sorrow. Laugh as we always laughed at the little jokes we enjoyed together. Play, smile, think of me, pray for me. Let my name ever be the household word that it always was. Let it be spoken without effect, without the ghost of a shadow on it. Life means all that it ever meant. It is the same as it ever was. There is absolutely unbroken continuity. What is this death but a negligible accident? Why should I be out of mind because I am out of sight? I am waiting for you – for an interval – somewhere near just around the corner. All is well. (Canon Scott Holland)

I have become increasingly interested in near-death experiences, premonitions and dreams over the years as I have seen how they help many people over their fear of death and also throw light on the dying process. I remember meeting an American on one of my trips abroad who, although divorced, had gone back to nurse his wife when she was dying of cancer. He said he tried discussing all aspects of care and healing with her, but she didn't respond in any way. He finally bought her a copy of Elisabeth Kübler-Ross's book on near-death experiences and she died calmly and peacefully shortly after reading it.

Research into near-death experiences is relatively recent, even though extra-sensory experiences around death are now found to be common. Previously, many people who had such experiences kept them to themselves for fear of being thought abnormal, or even mad. It is still common practice for doctors to repress dying patients' visions with medication and then flee to the comfort of their other, less sick patients. Ironically, it is advances in medical science and the modern possibilities for resuscitation that have led to many more people having such experiences.

The *American Journal of Hospice Care* says:

> There appears to be no clear agreement among theorists on the nature and origin of paranormal experiences. What does emerge is that sensory-perceptual experiences can be a normal and expected component of the grief process.

David Lorimer, vice-chairman in the UK of the International Association of Near-death experiences, says that perhaps the most persuasive after-effect of such experiences lies in people's changed attitude to death and the possibility of an afterlife. People who have had near-death experiences tend to find they have an enhanced appreciation of beauty, silence, the present, and the small things of life. Their concern for others is greater and they have an increased sense of self-worth.

Such extra-sensory experiences are not merely peripheral phenomena of private interest, but evidence for a living universe with a spiritual role for humankind, where life and death and afterlife are all linked. A description of life and death I heard a long time ago and liked, is:

> A lifetime is like the waking time when our personality is in conscious existence – a state in which we can feel, touch, taste, smell, know and think, but are limited by space and time. Death is like our sleeping time when our 'innerself' or soul goes beyond space and time, but never ceases to be.

A historical perspective

From the East's belief in reincarnation and karma to Jesus Christ's resurrection, religion has always promised eternal life. It's interesting to look at historical accounts given of death and the afterlife in view of modern research into near-death experiences. Carol Zaleski, a Harvard theologian and author of *Otherworld Journeys*[1] has found accounts of near-death experiences in Greek, Roman, Egyptian, and Near Eastern myths and legends.

In the sixth century, Pope Gregory the Great collected such experiences as proof of life beyond. Some cultures see death as a journey whose final goal is the recovery of one's true nature. The Egyptian *Book of the Dead*, the Tibetan *Book of the Dead*, and the Aztec *Song of the Dead* all describe near-death experiences. All these cultures believed we leave our bodies and embark on a spiritual voyage when we die.

Premonitions

The Bible has hundreds of references to premonitions, visitations and dreams. In the case of major disasters, it's not uncommon for many people to experience a forewarning. There were hundreds of warnings from all over the world about the sinking of the *Titanic* and John F. Kennedy's assassination, documented before the tragedies occurred. Many researchers suggest premonitions are there to help brace us for the following tragic event.

Dr Melvin Morse and his research team have made a major contribution to our understanding of extra-sensory experiences around death. Dr Morse defines pre-death experiences as intensely real experiences that a dying person has while still conscious. Reality is not distorted or altered. The dying person often sees God, angels, dead relatives, or visions of heaven superimposed upon reality or actually present at the deathbed. The experiences are mystical and visionary.[2]

My friend Robbie's mother died in her nineties. In the week before she died, Robbie went into her bedroom to hear her say, 'Sit down, Willie, and wait – I'm coming.' She turned to Robbie and said, 'I've been thinking a lot about your father.' She then asked, 'Who is the young man who is sitting at the foot of your bed? He's wearing a grey suit.' She was describing Robbie's fiancé who had died more than thirty years earlier.

Aunt Nell, an elderly aunt of my husband's, dreamed frequently of her husband Paddy. For several months before her death she said she tried to reach out for him, but he was always just out of reach. Mike, father of a two-year-old, died suddenly in a drowning accident last year. He had said to his partner a few weeks earlier, 'Peri has had so much love that if anything should happen to either of us, she will be fine.' Everyone I have met who has experienced the sudden death of someone close to them has said that, looking back, there were signs of an inner knowing, not verbalized, that death would happen.

Near-death experiences

Dr Raymond Moody, who coined the term 'near-death experience' in his book *Life After Life*,[3] claimed that in any group of thirty people he could find someone who has had one or who knows someone who has. He described it as 'a mystical experience that happens to people who almost die. It is not to be confused with a drug-induced experience or hallucination.'

Nearly every experience of children and about a quarter of those of adults has in it an element of light. Those who experience the light say it is more than just light. There is a substance to it that 'wraps' them in a warmth and caring that they have never before felt.

Most near-death experiences include:

- Being out of your physical body and feeling peaceful and calm.
- Travelling up some sort of tunnel with a light at the end of it.
- Meeting with people who've died earlier, usually relatives.
- Seeing a 'being of light', commonly God, Jesus or the Buddha (depending on your religion or culture).
- Having a life review.
- Often consciously deciding to return to your body and life on earth.

In his article 'Heavenly Bodies',[4] Chris Stonor wrote about Mark Gagne, who was thirteen when he went into hospital for a routine operation to remove his tonsils:

After being given a general anaesthetic, instead of waking up in the hospital bed after a successful operation, his first conscious awareness was of floating near the ceiling, above the operating table, watching the doctors at work.

'I wondered who the person was on the table,' Mark said,

'and then realized it was me. I could see and hear everything going on in the room, even the clock that said eight-five a.m. Suddenly, I saw the anaesthetist tapping the dial and heard him say, 'I'm losing him, I'm losing him.'

Mark next saw a nurse turn on the heart machine, a doctor massage his chest and then his body go rigid, and jump, after being given an electric shock. Yet all the while, as Mark put it, 'I felt unafraid, just completely relaxed and at peace.' He next glanced at the clock at eight-thirty-six a.m., when he saw the doctor pull the sheet over his physical head and phone through to say, 'Send Gagne's file to the office – I'm afraid I've lost him. You had better notify his family.'

'The next thing I remember,' Mark said, 'was going through a tunnel at great speed and seeing a light at the end. As I moved into this light I felt an incredible feeling of love and then became aware of my aunt, who had died some months before, asking me if I wanted to come with her. I then judged my life – no one else judged me – with complete honesty. I looked at the good things I had done and the bad. I decided that I hadn't learned enough from my life. I decided to come back.'

Shirley, a colleague I run trainings for, told me about her near-death experience when giving birth some thirty years ago. She had never shared it with anyone else, not even her husband. She was seven months pregnant and moved as an emergency case from the local hospital to a maternity hospital. She heard the doctor saying he was fighting for her life and concerned about the baby. Shirley said she wanted to say, 'No you're not, I'm OK. I'll be back in a minute. It's all right, I'm not going to die.' She described the experience as like dropping down a hole. She experienced no fear. 'I wasn't concerned about myself. I had a deep knowing it was 'not my date'; it wasn't the right time. I realized I was on the edge of life and death and felt very peaceful. I realized I will know when it is my time to go.'

In one American study, eighty per cent of experiencers realized during their near-death experience that they regretted 'not having loved more', and ten per cent realized they had squandered their talents and became aware of their 'tremendous potential'. Not surprisingly, many people change after their near-death experience. Mark Gagne transformed from being a school bully, general troublemaker and lazy pupil to becoming a 'do-gooder and swot'. His headmaster was so worried about him that he was sent to a psychiatrist. 'Yet for the first time my life made sense. Things just fitted into place.'

Visions after death

Many relatives 'see' people just after they have died. One friend of mine, whose husband died of heart trouble in his fifties, said she woke up one morning feeling he was there making love to her!

About three of four days after Joti's grandfather died she had a vivid dream:

> The whole family was seated around the kitchen table. Most of us were weeping silently. Then my grandfather walked in, kissing each of us, and he told us that we should get on with our lives because time runs out so fast and that he was much better now. He looked completely relaxed and blissful. 'Everything is going to be fine,' he said softly. 'Goodbye.' Since that dream I haven't been so upset. I felt that I'd said goodbye and life had to carry on. Of course, I still grieved, but it wasn't with such despair and devastation.

A woman I met on holiday told me what happened to her when her father died in Germany. She was staying in a hotel in America when she received a phone call telling her of her father's death. Just then, the french windows in the room suddenly blew open with a strong gust of wind. Her husband said, 'Why don't you cry?' She replied, 'I don't need to: he is here with me.' She told me, 'My father spoke without speaking. I also felt him on the wing of the plane, as I flew back to Germany for the funeral.'

Molly's mother died at three o'clock in the afternoon in the living room of their house. The undertakers collected her the same day. That night, Molly woke to see her mother 'fluttering around the room, drawing curtains and so on. She told me she was concerned I was OK. I said to her, Don't worry, I'm all right. My mother then went away.'

Sandya's brother had been an alcoholic and had lost a leg in an accident as a result of his addiction. He had been unable to relate to his family and had not seen them for some years. They were rung by a hostel for down-and-outs to be told he had just died. A few weeks after the funeral Sandya was with a friend when she sensed her brother was with her. She was terrified he would look as he had come to look just before he died. Instead, she saw him as being whole and well and felt herself surrounded by a gold light. Her friend saw it too. Sandya's mother had exactly the same experience at the same time although in a different part of the country. Her son told her, 'I'm all right.' Both Sanda and her mother then felt completely at peace and could let him go.

1 Published by Oxford University Press, 1987.
2 *Closer to the Light: learning from children's near-death experiences* (Villard Books, New York, 1990).
3 Published by Bantam, 1983.
4 *Woman's Journal.*

Unexpected Deaths

Any man's death diminishes me, because I am involved in Mankind;
And therefore never send to know for whom the bell tolls; it tolls for thee.

(John Donne, *Devotions*)

13

Sudden death

Sorrow is not forever, love is. (Anon)

When someone dies completely unexpectedly, their family and friends are often left extremely shocked, with no opportunity to say goodbye, and much unfinished emotional business to resolve. Rita's husband was in his forties. One day he left for work in the usual way in the morning. That was the last Rita ever saw of him alive. He had a heart attack at Waterloo Station on his way home and was dead on arrival at hospital. They had never discussed what the other one would do in the event either of them died. Three years on, Rita has still not got over the shock.

It is not only the loss itself that is shocking but also, frequently, the threat to the griever's world-picture. Suddenly, nothing can be taken for granted and those involved are likely to feel extremely vulnerable. The extra element of fear can mean fewer people are willing to offer support and become involved themselves. Colin Murray-Parkes, in *Recovery from Bereavement*,[1] quotes research that shows how valuable preparation and prompt support can be in improving outcomes for those who are bereaved. Unfortunately, sudden death often occurs in the clinical environment of the resuscitation room or intensive care unit of a hospital, and there may not be adequate support for relative. Such deaths, therefore, may take longer to grieve and bring up more difficult feelings for the survivors.

In retrospect, it often seems as though those who die suddenly have 'known' on some level before it happens. Usually, no significance is given to such 'signs' at the time. For three months before my husband's death, he had a recurring nightmare about losing me. He'd wake up in a sweat and recount the same story of my disappearing from him, and trying to reach me and not being able to. I used to hold him and comfort and reassure him. In the lonely nights after his death I often felt quite bitter that it was me who'd 'lost' him and there was no one to comfort me.

The accident happened on our way back from holiday in Scotland. I was map-reading and missed the turning for the quiet B road we wanted to take: instead, we ended up on a busy main road. One moment we were in a queue of traffic stopping and starting and switching from one side of the dual carriageway to another. The next moment I experienced an enormous bang and momentarily blacked out. I came to to see blood dripping from my head on to the map on my lap below and to hear the words: 'He's had it. Get the girl out.' Some instinct stopped me from turning and looking at John. I undid my safety belt, undid the car door and stepped out and never looked back. I wasn't aware of who was around. I remember being led to another car and being sat down. A man who said he was a doctor had a quick look at me and said I'd be all right and that he'd be back when he'd seen to my husband.

I was then left sitting in the car by myself, with the blood still slowly dripping from my head. I was aware of people periodically coming and staring in at the window at me and making comments. I also heard the person who was driving the milk tanker that had hit us being told not to come and talk to me as it could affect him adversely if there was a court action.

Time seemed to have stopped. I don't know how long it was before the doctor, whose car I was sitting in, came back and drove me to the little cottage hospital in Moffat. I remember he told me my husband was in the ambulance behind. I didn't tell him I knew he was dead and he didn't tell me. I thought if I didn't say anything, it would prove to be a nightmare and that when I woke up John would be there.

At the hospital my cuts were seen to and a doctor told me John had died. I was left alone all night in a small room. I was wide awake and remember the words: 'I've just lost my husband' going over and over in my head. The wind howled non-stop outside and I thought of *Wuthering Heights*. At one stage a nurse came in and when she saw I was awake, brought me in some magazines. I tried to read, but the print blurred in front of my eyes. So I remember staring into space for what seemed like forever, completely numb and emotionless.

In the morning I was brought breakfast on a tray. The sense of unreality continued as the undertaker was brought in and I was asked to choose what wood I would like for John's coffin, and whether I wanted a cremation or burial. I remember hearing this voice coming from me giving answers which seemed to be completely disconnected. I remember choosing burial, although I knew John would have preferred cremation, but as I hadn't accepted he was dead, I couldn't bear the thought of his body being burnt.

Shortly after this my mother and stepfather arrived. They had travelled overnight from London. They were told I could leave hospital, so they booked in at a hotel in the main square in Moffat. I had to be taken to the coroner's office to make a statement. As with the funeral director, it all seemed unreal. After that we went and sat in the square. I remember people talking over me as if I wasn't there. My mother was relating the happenings to some locals. One woman replied, 'She's young, she'll get over it and marry again.' John hadn't been dead twenty-four hours at that stage.

Then John's body had to be identified. I was told it wasn't a good idea for me to see him, so my stepfather went. I was very angry when I was later told, after the funeral, that in fact his body and face were OK. The top of his head had been pushed in, but it was all neatly bandaged.

We stayed in Moffat another night and then got the train back to my flat outside London. Everything still seemed unreal. It had felt like summer when we left at the beginning of September; now, two weeks later, the leaves were falling. It felt as if the whole of nature was mourning for him too. I felt someone would pinch me, and I would wake up, and everything would be 'normal' again.

The simple funeral was arranged with the local vicar. I remember requesting that one of Rupert Brookes' poems that we both loved was read, but I was told it was not 'suitable', so Tennyson's 'Crossing the Bar' was read instead.

The sense of unreality was to stay with me for some six months. I remember feeling as if physically part of me was missing. I also felt as if everyone was staring at me, when I was in public places. I felt they could see part of me was missing.

The legal side dragged on and it wasn't until some two

years later, when a small settlement was made out of court, that I finally recognized that John wasn't going to come back and started grieving. Until then I'd felt if only they could prove it wasn't his fault, everything would be OK, and he would then come back.

What I wish had been different about the aftermath

- That I was left on my own in the first eighteen hours, so I had no one to talk to or share my feelings with. This made it difficult to open up later on.
- That I didn't see John's body and so accept the reality of his death. This was partly my fault, as John had told me how he hadn't wanted to see his parents dead, so he could remember them as they were when they were alive. I, with no other experience to go on, made the same decision about him. I have regretted ever since not having had the opportunity to touch him for the last time and to say good-bye.
- That those around me decided what I needed and felt without checking with me first. They were always wrong, which made me feel more impotent.
- That everything in it 'had' to be returned, even though the car was a write-off, including boxes of food left over from camping. I remember unpacking mouldy bananas on the living room floor some two months later and thinking, 'Is this all there is left of our marriage?'
- That there was no inquest to make sense of what happened. In Scotland an enquiry is held and a decision made without the people concerned being there. The accident was described as an 'act of God'. This made my own guilt feelings harder to resolve.
- That I didn't know about the grieving process, and was surrounded by people who did not support me in feeling my feelings. In keeping my tears and therefore my other feelings to myself, I lost touch with my good feelings about John.

The nature of John's death meant that guilt was a big issue for me. I couldn't stop asking myself what I had done that my husband had to die. If we had been on the right road would he still be alive? Was it my fault he was dead? Why was I still alive? (I certainly didn't want to be!) These feelings of guilt were with me for some years until I finally accepted that all John had ever wanted was for me to be happy and that he'd know I would never have deliberately taken the wrong route. So I gradually stopped punishing myself twice over. Firstly for his loss and secondly for the idea that I had caused it.

A common reaction, to try and 'make sense' of an accident, is the desire to know exactly what happened; to connect with the person who was killed. Susan, whose sister was killed in a car accident, describes how she and her mother reacted:

> It was like a film when the police arrived with three little bags marked A, B, and C for identification. We could not believe that none of Nicky's personal effects had survived the fire. We were not allowed to see her as all three girls had been destroyed beyond recognition. The police said it would be far too awful for us to see the car, but both of us felt almost driven to find the wreck. When we finally found the car my mother simply put her hand on the would-be floor (which had been searched by the police) and immediately pulled out one of Nicky's earrings. Later, I found her watch without the need for intensive searching.
>
> To this day, I believe Nicky must have seen the oncoming car, as she and I have always been terrible backseat drivers. I pray that she felt no terror or pain. On Christmas Day my mother and I went to see, and spoke with, the driver of the car in which Nicky had been killed to find out her last words.
>
> We know so much yet cannot bring her back, which just brings on more despair. You cannot replace someone who is irreplaceable.

My friend and colleague, Hilary, told me about her experience when her eldest son, Jonathon, died, aged twenty-eight, climbing Mont Blanc with his younger brother Dominic and a friend. Hilary said she lost not only a son but a best friend, as he had also been 'the man in her life' since her divorce, and protected her.

When she was first told she didn't take it in at all and felt no pain, but when it came to writing Jonathon's name, she couldn't spell it. Her GP, who was a great friend, arrived on the same day as the news was broken, when the family were together, eating their lunch. She remembers feeling guilty that they were sitting down and eating, when her eldest son was dead. The next day 'there was still an air of unreality and

I went and did a big cash-and-carry shop as normal for my job.'

Following the accident, her son Dominic had to pack up the car and drive back with their friend, who had been injured trying to save Jonathon. When he got home, they had to go and report Jonathon's death at the police station. 'We were made to shout the details across the desk to the policeman on duty. I felt as if I was reporting a lost dog, not the death of my son. I asked if we could go into a private room, but the policeman said, No, I'm making it as easy as possible for you. ' (It later turned out he had no training in helping people in loss situations.) Dominic was asked to describe Jonathan's injuries. He had not felt able to describe them to her earlier, so Hilary heard about them for the first time at the police station with the other people who were waiting listening in.

Hilary found it difficult that she could not see Jonathon's body – to say goodbye, and to see that he really was dead. The body didn't arrive home for over a week. No one described to her what state it was in, so she was worried it would be putrefied. She couldn't bear to see her beautiful son like that. Dominic had seen the body shortly after Jonathon fell and said about it, 'He wasn't there.'

> I still feel guilty that I shirked seeing the body. I didn't really want to see him dead.
>
> One of the strange things about my grief was that I felt almost high for a month after the funeral. My feelings were intensified, and my senses sharpened, but I felt guilty because it was uncommon. I could cope with my pain, but I found the children's difficult, especially Dominic's, who was with Jonathon when he died. It wasn't until Jonathon's birthday that Dominic and I were able to talk openly together about what had happened. We were both frightened of hurting each other. When we finally shared our grief, we were able to cry together and share our pain, and also our happy memories of Jonathon. Now I'm frightened to let go of that pain as I feel the pain is love.

I find for many people there is this fear of letting go of pain, in case they stop loving the person and forget them. We talked about fate: Hilary told me the family had an emergency call to London in the week prior to the boys' holiday, to see her daughter Nicola who was thought to have leukaemia, but happily didn't. It had been decided that if she had, Jonathon and Dominic wouldn't go on holiday. Only two days before he left for his holiday, Jonathon had gone to a launderette and asked to have his washing serviced instead of doing it himself, as usual. Two minutes after he walked out a bomb went off and all the people in the launderette were killed.

Like my husband, it was almost as if Jonathon had an inner knowing about his death. A couple of years earlier, he had told his brother, 'I've always thought I'd die in the mountains.' His mother received the following poem from him the day before she heard of his death:

> So what if I'm not there
> Just hold out your arms
> And feel us hug
> Feel my breath upon your cheeks
> The touch of my lips on yours.
> Smile and I'm looking into your eyes
> Cry and I will catch the tear
> And gently, so very gently
> Brush it back from whence it came.
> Look into the mirror, clearly unashamedly.
> Smile, let your eyes be filled with their natural gentleness.
> You are looking into my heart.

What helped Hilary after Jonathon's death

- Having Jonathon's coffin at home before the funeral. It was kept in the living room and draped with his favourite rug and the cat sat on it. Hilary slept in the same room and felt very peaceful.
- The moving funeral, which echoed Jonathon's life. She followed her gut feelings about what she should do and what was right for him, rather than the normal pattern of most funerals. The service and burial were in a little church on the moors which all the family knew well. A tape of Rachmaninov that Jonathon loved was played. The church was filled with wild flowers and his young friends came in bright clothes. Hilary wore a new flowered dress bought for her especially for the occasion by her daughters.

- Being in touch with another mother whose son, Andrew, also died on Mont Blanc a week later. Hilary read about his death in the newspaper and immediately wrote. 'It helped to compare notes and find we were plodding down the same path. Also, Dominic became tremendous friends with Andrew's brother.'
- The ceremony that happened the following year. Andrew's climbing group went back to the spot where he fell and left flowers for him and for Jonathon.
- Having the book *Lament to a Son*, written by a mother whose son had died, sent to her by another bereaved mother.
- Reading *Crossing the Void*, by a climber who described how he felt when he fell. He wrote that if he had died he didn't think he would have felt it.
- Giving a donation to Llanberis Mountain Rescue Operation, where Jonathon had often climbed, as a memorial.
- Joining the Compassionate Friends.
- Keeping a diary, written to Jonathon. It was started on Mother's Day after his death and Hilary kept writing in it for over six months.

Hilary has allowed me the privilege of reading her diary and of including the following excerpts:

Your death has made me totally unafraid of death. . . . Your death has been an all-consuming event for me. I feel very strong now. . . . The death of one of my children had always been the thing I dreaded most. The very thought of it happening made me sick with horror. It happened. I'm still here and still coping. . . .

I went to a party a few weeks ago – the first since your death, and everyone painfully avoided mentioning your name. That hurt so much. . . . (got through rolls of kitchen paper and my glasses keep steaming up writing this). . . . If I record my thoughts they will stop going round and round in my head and I can move on.

Friends are saying, 'I expect you are getting over it now.' How can they expect me to recover from losing you in six months, when you have been part of me for twenty-nine years? It's like losing a limb, only worse. Does one ever get used to hopping around on one leg or trying to cope with only one hand? Probably better than a mother getting over the death of a child.

In a way I dread the pain going. I'm getting used to it. I couldn't bear to be left with a nothingness.

I'm glad I sorted through your things. Your possessions are so important to me now. I've tried to face up to everything, even though it's been unbearably painful at times. For me that has been the best way. I was offered sleeping pills and tranquillizers, but I didn't want them. I wanted to feel everything. It's been almost like giving birth backwards – the pangs of returning you from whence you came.

I was able to use a guided visualization with Hilary where she met Jonathon again and left him with her father who died several years ago, and whom she was very close to. During this visualization, Jonathon gave her permission to let go of him and carry on living.

Murder

Surely murder is the most difficult death of all to accept. Like death in a disaster (see Chapter 14), it is untimely and violent, and grief reactions can be similar. In particular, the level of bitterness and anger will be higher than with other deaths and thus cause greater debilitation. Guilt can be heightened, particularly in the case of children, where the parents may feel they should have protected them more. Feelings of powerlessness and meaninglessness and a sense of being abnormal and freakish are common.

As Doug Magee points out in *What Murder Leaves Behind – The Victim's Family*,[2] grievers are likely to feel isolated and unsupported:

> The utter senselessness of one human being killing another scares us all and it is probably only normal that we go to unusual lengths to avoid hearing directly from victims' families. But such avoidance only prolongs our state of ignorance and increases our fear.
>
> The act of murder makes no sense and it is those closest to the victim who, in murder's aftermath, bear the brunt of the absurdity.

The most difficult circumstances of all must surely be when

the murder remains unsolved. How does one reach a resolution of grief then?

Research into murders showed that many male murderers struggle with deep inner guilt feelings about sex. Murderers show less anger, less fear, less aggression, less awareness of the event, rarely verbalize feelings, and maintain shallow or superficial interpersonal relationships. Seventy per cent of murderers have defective consciences, insensitive to the idea that violence is wrong; the importance of another person's life; and the importance of maintaining control and finding the right channels for expressing aggression. These factors are related to the murderer's lack of love and caring experiences.[3]

The murder of children is particularly hard to accept. The Compassionate Friends have started a support group called Parents of Murdered Children. Some areas of particular difficulty for relatives they have identified are:

- The caring professions and agencies do not automatically offer their services to families of murder/manslaughter victims and, if approached, are usually so daunted that they feel unqualified to help.
- The news media – reporters can be intrusive, inconsiderate and even unscrupulous whilst attempting to interview families of murder victims. Families can also be greatly distressed by publication of 'gory' details, and incorrect or distorted facts.
- The body becomes the property of the Crown until the coroner releases it for burial. This can sometimes take several weeks, or even months, particularly if the defence lawyers do not agree to the release.
- The legal process does not support the relatives. They may not be told the results of the post-mortem; be intimidated by police questioning; and are not given any consideration at the trial.

A mother, whose son was murdered, graphically expressed her feelings in the UK *Compassionate Friends Newsletter*:

My son Robert was stabbed to death in 1986, aged seventeen. He was the middle of my three children: Melanie was then twenty and John seven.

Many hours in those first few days after Robert's death are

forever lost to me in a sort of haze of horror that only another murdered child's parent could understand. In the hospital they tried to tell me Robert wouldn't live, explaining the size of his wounds and the damage done to all his major organs. I couldn't believe what they were saying until I actually put my arms around him after he came out of the theatre. When I kissed his icy forehead I knew, to all intents and purposes, he was gone.

After that you go through the motions like an automaton. I had to officially identify his body for the police, had to explain as gently as I could to his little brother that Robert wasn't here any longer, he'd gone to Heaven. Rightly or wrongly (I didn't know what to do for the best), I took John to see his brother in the mortuary so that he could say goodbye.

The Coroner's officer told me I couldn't bury my child; not to bother to arrange the funeral as it would be weeks, if not months, before they could release his body. It was actually six weeks.

Everything seemed unreal and I remember feeling so incredibly lonely. From the rush of sympathetic 'friends' and neighbours in the first couple of weeks, I was left with just my two genuinely caring friends. After that, you're pushed conveniently to the side: my murdered son, my family and myself were not important anymore. Everything was now geared to the 'offender', the reasons or, more accurately, the excuse for him doing what he did, the sympathy for this youngster. 'Well, he was only seventeen,' they'd say, forgetting that my son too was only seventeen and he didn't deserve his horrific death.

The system then takes over, the so-called wheels of justice: 'No questions, please – you don't understand the due process of law.' The 'offender' served less than fourteen months for the 'incident'. He is now walking free, back into the bosom of his family. He not only took my Robert's life, he destroyed mine and my daughter's and son's. Life does go on, I do know that. I now have two beautiful granddaughters, but the pain and anger is forever inside me; my world is incomplete.

Murder in the family

Dr Dora Black leads a team of three child psychiatrists at the Royal Free Hospital in London, the only centre in the country

to specialize in helping children who have had one parent
killed by the other. So far, they have seen a hundred children
with experience of such domestic violence. Dr Harris Hen-
dricks says:

> We know that rapid support after a tragic event helps tremen-
> dously. Yet in the cases of children who see a parent killed,
> help is nowhere near instant in the bulk of cases. By the time
> help is given, the child might have become introverted,
> aggressive and violent as a reaction to events. We need to
> hold their hands and help them, but there is no system or
> apparatus to reach many of them.
>
> The violence the children see is often horrifying: father stab-
> bing, strangling or shooting mother; and they may then be left
> with the corpse for some time before neighbours or police
> arrive. Then, as the only witnesses to the terrible crime, they
> are whisked off to the police station to make statements and
> probably not even allowed back for their favourite belongings
> such as a teddy bear or doll.

The children the team are helping have come to them by
word of mouth, by following up cases reported in newspapers, or referral some years later. Unfortunately, the
psychiatrists are often hindered in their work by well-mean-
ing relatives who believe that it is best for the child not to
relive their experience. Many children seen by the team have
never described what they witnessed to anyone apart from
the police. 'The emotions stay bottled up in them for many
months, maybe years, leading to psychological and psychiatric problems in later years.' Not only have they witnessed a
terrible event but they are also effectively orphaned by
(usually) the loss of their mother and imprisonment or hospi-
talization of their father. In addition, these children may
have to live with the stigma of being the child of a murderer.

Working through the feelings

A father whose two sons were murdered describe in a UK
Compassionate Friends Newsletter how he dealt with his feelings:

> Since the first screening of the *Everyman* programme 'As we

forgive them . . . ', I have been labelled as 'the man who for-
gave his children's murderer', which isn't strictly true. It
would be more accurate to say that I have conceived of the
possibility because, amongst other reasons, I don't wish to
carry that burden of hatred around with me any longer. My
two sons lived very full lives and I know they would want me
to continue mine by their example. If I allowed this tragedy to
beat me, to become engulfed in bitterness and hatred, that
would be letting them down. For many people bereaved by
violence, the label can simply be that of 'victim' or 'heart-
broken parent' – titles I would also prefer not to be associated
with because of their somewhat negative connotations. As far
as I am concerned, if I choose to take on the 'victim' label, I
will forever be the victim; if I accept being 'heart-broken', I
have given up the will to live. Sadly, this is a feeling many of
us have faced at some point.

Labels, however, can more often than not take the form of
expectation, judgement and disappointment of or from those
around us. So many families, already traumatized by a severe
loss, further tear themselves apart because, as individuals,
they have not been allowed to express their true feelings of
anger, fear, grief, or, at times, even joy, by those around
them, as much as they need to and *when* they need to. From
my own experience, all these emotions are very real and have
to be acknowledged and expressed in some way: they cannot
be buried, even with alcohol, tranquillizers or non-communi-
cation. And if we try to suppress them, they eventually erupt
in illness or strained and severed relationships. For example,
we might feel like saying to a loved one: 'I'm still angry/full of
pain, why aren't you?' But, more often than not, we avoid the
issue and either say nothing or say something we don't really
mean, as a cover-up; symbolically putting another nail in the
coffin. We might feel like speeding up our ultimate demise, to
be reunited with our lost children, but what about those we
would leave behind? Who is more important, the dead or the
family that are still alive?

I don't think we ever completely get over our losses. So
what, I ask myself, is the point in punishing those we love
when we could really be supporting each other through our
individual moments of crisis. It is so important to remember
that we are each responsible for our own emotions and no one
else's. In order to rebuild our lives successfully, we have to respect those emotions, not only in ourselves but in others too.

It can be a bit frightening at first but I have, during my own recovery, discovered that it's quite OK to be open.

For a long time, however, I also chose the path of silence. I compensated for it by writing down everything that came into my head: every memory – good, bad or suicidal – every moment of guilt, anger, pain; strength, or weakness; every trauma and triumph. Sometimes I worked through these difficult periods with the free expression found in drawing materials or clay, but whatever the selection, I (ostensibly) 'externalized' those feelings by getting them out of my system and pouring them into some inanimate object that couldn't be hurt by the explosion. I also found that, from the moment I began writing, I no longer needed the prescribed sleeping tablets at night. In effect, I faced my fears, because my greatest fear had been that of death itself and I lost that when Babs and the boys died. From then on, all the others seemed minor in comparison and I have been working through them, one by one, ever since.

Eventually, I came across the work of Elisabeth Kübler-Ross, a Swiss-American doctor who has spent over twenty years helping people worldwide to cope with death and dying. In the safe and loving environment of one of her 'Life, Death and Transition' workshops, I finally breached the dam of a reservoir of unshed tears, bottled up for over three years. In a later 'Follow-up Intensive' I began to get in touch with some of that 'killer rage' that we all have burning inside of us, especially when our families have been violated. That, in itself, is a very sobering and enlightening experience. Once you have touched that part of yourself – that dark, destructive side – or even witnessed it in somebody else, it is possible to conceive of anything, even 'forgiveness'. But it has to be worked through very, very carefully with somebody who knows exactly what they are doing. Only by honouring our feelings and emotions can we really begin to find healing.

---

1 Written with Robert Weiss and published by Basic Books, New York, 1983.

2 Published by Dodd, Mead & Co., USA, 1983.

3 Wille, Linde and Wolfgang in *The Human Side of Homicide*, edited by Bruce L. Danto, John Bruhns, and Austin Kutscher (Columbia University Press, New York, 1982).

14

Disasters

The only security in life is a reverence for it. (Anon)

The essential distinguishing feature of disasters is that they affect a group of people – from a family to a whole community – rather than private individuals. Many professionals used to traumatic deaths who work in the aftermath of a disaster say they feel it is the sheer size of the disaster, and the numbers of people involved, which they and the relatives find overwhelming.

William Yule, Professor of Applied Child Psychology at the University of London, recently carried out studies on several hundred child survivors of a shipping disaster.[1] Some of the most common reactions after the first few months were:

- Sleep disturbance, including fears of the dark and of being alone; bad dreams; and waking through the night.
- Separation difficulties: initially, most children wanted to be physically close to their surviving parents, often sleeping in the parental bed over the first few weeks.
- Concentration difficulties: when it was silent in the classroom, children were distracted by intrusive memories of what had happened to them.
- Memory problems, both in remembering new material, and some old skills, such as reading music.
- Intrusive thoughts: all were troubled by repetitive thoughts about the accident. These occurred at any time, although often triggered by reminders such as the sound of glass breaking or rushing water.
- Talking with parents: many did not want to talk about their feelings with their parents so as not to upset the adults. Thus, parents were often unaware of the details of

the children's suffering, although they could see they were in difficulty. There was often a great sense of frustration between parents and children.

- Talking with peers: at some points, survivors felt a great need to talk over their experiences with peers. Unfortunately, the timing was often wrong. Peers held back from asking in case they upset the survivor further; the survivor often felt rejected.
- Heightened alertness to dangers: most were wary of all forms of transport; not willing to put their safety into anyone else's hands. They were more aware of other dangers. They were affected by reports of other disasters.
- Foreshortened future: many felt they should live each day to the full and not plan far ahead. They lost trust in long-term planning, feeling their future was uncertain.
- Fears – Most had fears of travelling by sea and air, and of swimming. Most of the new fears were specifically related to their recent bad experiences rather than being just a general increase in fearfulness.

Similar reactions are also typical of adult survivors.

Immediate trauma

Denial is a common response to disasters: firstly because they are so sudden, and secondly because it can often be days or weeks before full information is available and/or bodies are found. In some cases the body is never recovered. Many of the deaths are untimely. Many killed are young. Janet Haddington of the National Association of Bereavement Services highlighted these problems when talking about the sinking of the pleasure cruiser MV *Marchioness* on the River Thames in August 1989 when fifty-one people, mainly under thirty, were drowned:

> The context in which the death occurred can increase the use of defensive shields to deny that the event has happened. The death of fifty-one party-goers in the middle of the capital city of England, with the banks of the Thames in sight, was shockingly unbelievable. Many families and friends were not aware, or were unsure, if their loved one had been on board. Many bodies were missing, and escape fantasies were rampant.

In the short-term, denial is a defence mechanism that protects grievers against the immediate full impact of loss, controls their exposure to painful levels of information, and facilitates gradual healthy adjustment.

In order to come to terms with the death, the bereaved need to know when, where, and how their loved one died. This need can be difficult to satisfy in the case of a major disaster. Some family members feel they have to visit the scene of the disaster, while others want to avoid it completely. The obvious advantages of viewing the body, a photograph, or the scene of the disaster, is that the potential to deny that the death has occurred is minimized. Pam Dix, whose brother died in the Lockerbie air disaster, told me how important it was for her to see and photograph the hole in the ground made where her brother's body fell. It was the last place he had been. She, her sister-in-law, and several members of the family visited the site of the crash on Christmas Day, only four days after the disaster. It was months before they were able to see the hole. The authorities often assert that relatives aren't in a fit state after a disaster to decide whether or not to see the body. Families can be left feeling powerless, but Pam discovered that (in the UK) once the body has been identified, the relatives have full control of viewing and funeral arrangements.

Disasters can give rise to other serious losses – home or physical ability, for instance. David Sturgeon, a consultant psychiatrist at University College Hospital London, said the King's Cross Underground fire and its aftermath deprived many of those severely hurt of good things in life such as the pleasure and fulfilment of playing a musical instrument, or experiencing the subtlety of touch, because of appalling injuries to their hands. Some also found that their friends' changed attitudes and reactions left them feeling isolated, and that their own ability to socialize and be involved in life became impaired.[2]

Disasters are so shocking that they create indelible memories. A teenager whose father died in a shipping disaster wrote:

For this article I did not need to use notes to help me plan it out, because all the information that I needed was still very vivid in my mind. . . . This March it will be three years since it happened, and I like to think that I am almost over the tragedy. My mother became anorexic afterwards, but with medical help and much support of friends and relatives, she has now almost recovered to her old self. We both still cry when the pictures come up on the television, and dearly wish that Anthony Graham Spink was still with us today.

Survivor guilt

It can be particularly hard for adult survivors to resolve their feelings of helplessness after a disaster. They may feel shame or irrational guilt. At Zeebrugge, in the *Herald of Free Enterprise* disaster, one man made himself into a human bridge to save others. A year later he felt guilty he had survived and others hadn't. He also felt guilty he hadn't helped more.[3]

Anger

Those involved in disasters are innocent victims, and survivors and relatives are often left with a deep well of anger they don't know how to deal with. This is particularly true of 'man-made' disasters which could have been prevented, where a faceless organization or authority is responsible. Some people channel their anger constructively by campaigning to ensure a similar disaster can't happen again.

For many, dealing with the authorities during and after the disaster can be an extremely frustrating experience. Mrs A.'s daughter drowned in the MV *Marchioness* disaster. Mrs A. felt she had been denied access to her daughter's body by male professionals who could not appreciate 'how mothers feel'. She was informed that her daughter's body, which had been recovered from the water four days after the accident, was badly deteriorated through swelling and heat. She believes newborn babies 'are crinkled and ugly, but when it is your own it is beautiful'. This is how she imagined her daughter in death, though the authorities' insistence gave her doubts, so that she was haunted by fantasies of how disfigured her daughter's body must be. When she did view the photographs eight months later, she recognized her daughter immediately. 'There was no mistaking her and she remained beautiful. How can a man tell me, her mother, that my child is no longer beautiful?' This breakthrough in her struggle in being allowed to see the pictures marked a turning point in her grief process. She has resolved her anger: 'You cannot go around blaming this Mr Authority all the time.'[4]

Lasting vulnerability

Survivors tend to avoid situations which could be reminiscent of the disaster, which in turn can lead to withdrawal and unresponsiveness. Richard Bates, a sub-editor on the *Guardian* who was caught in the fire on the King's Cross underground station, reveals the courage it takes to go back and face your fears:

Going back on the tube is harder to get used to. Shortly after coming home I went with my wife through King's Cross. The next time, I decided to get out and just stand inside the burned and blackened ticket hall. I stepped off that escalator and to my horror saw groups of policemen and firemen. All I could think of was getting out and went straight down to the platform. A train arrived and I sat there willing it to leave but it didn't. A policeman rushed on to the platform and shouted that no one was to get off.

Surely the horror couldn't be happening again? For the next few minutes I sat there rigid, holding my wife's hand and forcing myself to think of something, anything. Eventually we got going: I found out later that a workman's welding torch had started a small blaze among some rubbish near an escalator.

I have a strong sense of vulnerability. After all, an accident is no longer something that happens to other people. I avoid risks of any kind. Immediately after leaving hospital, I found myself hugging the inside of the pavements, keeping close to buildings. I do not dodge through traffic to cross the road; I wait for the green man to flash, aware of quizzical stares sometimes as I stand stubbornly alone on the pavement.

When I visit a restaurant, a cinema or concert hall, I make sure I know where the exit is. I try to sit on the end of the row. I remain uneasy in confined spaces such as aeroplanes from where there is no immediate way out.[5]

For relatives of the dead, there is the opportunity to reassess one's life, when faced with the fragility and uncertainty of it. In Pam Dix's case, she and her husband had often talked about having children, but were never able to decide. They decided 'when' the day after her brother's death at Lockerbie and now have two children.

The group experience

Emergency services and other carers, both voluntary and professional, can be seen as secondary casualties in a disaster. A stewardess in one air disaster worked from Sunday (when it happened) to Wednesday without a break. Her function was to see the relatives and take them to the different places to view the bodies. On the Wednesday she broke down in the staff rest room, in tears, and talked about her feelings of helplessness, anger and guilt.[6]

In families and other groups of survivors, relationships may become more strained as individuals grieve in different ways; the use of alcohol, tobacco and other drugs may increase; and accidents are more likely to occur. A.C. McFarlane, studying the effects of Australian bush fires, found how well parents adjusted had an important influence on their children's reaction. Equally, children's reaction to the fire affected the adjustment of the family. Eight months on, many families showed increased levels of conflict, irritability and withdrawal, and many mothers were over-protecting their children.[7]

As Derek Nuttall points out in 'Bereavement and After':[8]

The Aberfan disaster [when, in 1966, the coal waste from a giant tip above the village suddenly collapsed on the village school, killing 116 children] brought community grief. It was not just the sum of all the personal family bereavements, but a state of its own. All in the village, and its close neighbour Merthyr Vale, were affected. The scale of such a disaster, and the depth to which it touched people, meant that the community responded, as an individual responds, with shock, disbelief, numbness, anger, feelings of impotence. Help and understanding had to be made available for the community as well as individuals.

Many people feel there was a turning-point in the way the public and professionals in the UK view disasters after the Bradford football stadium fire of 1985, which millions of viewers witnessed on their TV screens. People were more easily able to identify with victims of the disaster and their families, and to recognize the long-term consequences of such an event. Oliver Leaman, a researcher at Liverpool Polytechnic, described one griever who seemed to have benefited from this wider awareness:

James was fourteen when his brother died in the Hillsborough disaster at Sheffield in 1989. James was at school in Liverpool, and his brother was both older than him and much respected by him, and there was no doubt that he was seriously upset by the loss. James's work at school and his relationships did not seem to be unduly affected by the event, though, and after an initial grieving period he seems to have settled down to being much the same person he was before, albeit undoubtedly marked by the experience of the tragedy. There was a well-devised structure of counselling both on a city and a school level. You cannot get into Liverpool without seeing directions to counselling centres, and Liverpool schools were very sensitive to the needs of grieving pupils, parents and teachers. Yet James went to none of these. He argued, persuasively, that the general atmosphere of a national disaster was very helpful to those who had suffered a personal loss on that occasion. It helped make sense of the event and many of the bereaved felt supported by the very number of those equally affected. The fact that the tragedy was not only an individual event but was also experienced by the entire city, and to a certain extent by the whole country, is a factor which James thinks is significant as part of the explanation for the apparently swift recovery which many of the bereaved seem to have made.[9]

Pam Dix told me how she felt about the publicity aspect of disasters after her experience with the Lockerbie crash:

The professionals kept the reporters away, but relatives often felt the stories printed bore no resemblance to what was really happening. The positive aspect is that the disaster remains in the news. The negative, both in the immediate aftermath and as time goes by and the search for the truth continues, is the showing of gruesome details. The *Independent*, for instance, published a picture of a body hanging over a house before it had been identified.

A doctor involved in Hillsborough said, 'I'd like to do physical damage to the person who took the photographs for the *Daily Mirror* and reserve a special act of aggression for the person who allowed them to be published.' As Pam says, there needs to be a balance between the media helping the world to see reality and not making disasters sensational. Relatives and survivors from the *Herald of Free Enterprise* disaster at Zeebrugge said how hard they found it to keep seeing pictures of the boat on its side some time after the event.

Because disasters affect many people at the same time, there can be more comfort and reassurance than usual as grievers share their experiences with others who have suffered a similar bereavement. Pam, who belongs to a support group called UK Families Flight 103, for relatives and friends of those killed in the Lockerbie disaster, says: 'It's the only group in the world who don't want you to change the subject and allow you to talk ceaselessly about it. It also brings together people who would not otherwise have met.'

John Shears, head teacher of the school that lost a pupil in the sinking of the cruise ship SS *Jupiter*, helped the surviving children to channel their emotions constructively through memorials and tree planting. At the request of Vivienne's parents, an evening of music and dance was held. Their daughter had been a keen singer. This enabled a lot of children and adults to be involved in a moving tribute, but one that emphasized the positive. This was followed some months later by a small service in the school, when Vivienne's class unveiled a plaque as their special tribute. They had raised the funds and they contributed readings to the occasion. John Shears says:

Vivienne lives on in our memory and despite the sadness of her loss, the care that has shone through the experience has made the school community a stronger one.

15

Suicide

> We can start from the assumption that no-one wants to be suicidal. Those who are, feel compelled to be so. (Norman Keir)

When death has been by suicide a whole new dimension of grief is involved. All the feelings of normal bereavement will be there, though anger and guilt are likely to be stronger. In addition, there may be a deep sense of rejection and of the impossibility of making sense of the loss. 'Longing' for the lost person takes on an entirely new meaning, since surviving relatives may feel now that they have never really known the person they now seek. Such feelings can last a lifetime.

When suicide occurs within a family, particularly if it involves a child, the shock is overwhelming. No one really expects the event, although the child may have talked of suicide and there may have been previous unsuccessful attempts, seen as cries for help; and parents may have been very fearful for the child. It can tear a family apart. Grieving sisters and brothers can retreat into themselves, their isolation causing further pain and fear to their parents. Often friends are at a loss to know what to say or to do, feeling helpless and inadequate.

The taboo of suicide

Killing yourself is a taboo – something forbidden – in our Christian-based culture. Until recently, the Church of England saw it as a mortal sin excluding the sinner from heaven, and the legal system punished those who attempted it as criminals. Suicide is no longer a criminal offence but, as

Alison Wertheimer points out in *A Special Scar*,[1] the term 'committing suicide' still suggests a criminal undertaking. We as a society give subtle hints of negative judgement in our language and attitude towards the survivors. If we gasp at the mention of suicide, it can be unhelpful, damaging, and prevent any real kind of communication. Relatives can feel stigmatized, and their religious beliefs can add to this feeling of shame.

There is a strong taboo in our society about talking of suicide. Relatives may be judged, ignored, or shunned; and they may feel that they are blamed for the suicide. Very subtly, they can be made to feel they have loved too little, or too much. But, says Adina Wrobleski, an American writer on suicide whose daughter died in this way, 'There are many bad parents whose children do not kill themselves. There are many good parents whose children do. Our society has too often fostered the belief that suicide occurs in bad families.'[2]

Lois, a member of the Compassionate Friends, wrote after the suicide of her son:

> The problem of feeling different is not helped by society's reaction to suicide. This is inevitable when one considers past attitudes, but it means that parents coping with this tragedy do not always receive the sympathy that is normally given to bereaved people. Not so long ago, I went through a period when I thought I could cope with Simon's death if I could tell people he had died of some natural cause. And this is where the problem lies. Suicide is unnatural, so survivors are treated differently. Yet I personally believe that, in many cases, suicide can be the end result of an illness in a similar way to other deaths.

Guilt and the search for meaning

The primary feeling after the shock of the actual suicide seems to be bewilderment and questioning – a search to answer the question, 'Why?' Why did he or she do it? Why did they not seek help? This is followed by such yearnings as, 'If only they had not acted on the impulse of the moment . . . had told me/someone how they were feeling . . . I had realized . . . had not left them alone that day.' The feeling of guilt that the survivor was not aware of the deceased's distress is very strong. It is a feeling of having failed; and seems especially fundamental if you are a parent. Sometimes this guilt can be 'real' in the sense that there has been a pattern of unawareness, or maybe there has been a recent quarrel. Sometimes there is imputed guilt such as, 'It all seemed to begin when his girlfriend left him'; or 'I can't stop blaming so-and-so'. The guilt can also be totally imaginary, but real agony to the sufferer nevertheless. People bereaved by suicide seem to take a long time to realize that there was very likely no 'one' cause, but far more probably a whole series of incidents, perceived failures, or unanswered questions. Jim Kuykendall, a clinical psychologist, says that if people really want to commit suicide and not just attempt to as a cry for help, they always will.

Suicide notes can provide some answers, but can sometimes also cause problems for those left behind, if they become a focus for minute and obsessive dissection of motives. Inquests are sometimes dreaded, sometimes looked forward to in the hope of finding 'an answer'. The process of grief can often be held up until they are over and 'the answer' is available.

I think at some time or other in our lives we have all wished to be dead. Sometimes the feeling can last a few minutes, sometimes days, sometimes months or years. Adolescents, in particular, are prone to such black moods. I felt like committing suicide for nearly a year after my husband's death, when there seemed to be nothing to live for. I don't think I was ever really serious, as I couldn't think of a way to do it which didn't involve someone else. As a friend of mine who is a Samaritan pointed out, when people are really suicidal they are inward-looking. They only see their own despair and are completely unaware of the effect of their behaviour on others.

Norman Keir, former Chairman of the Samaritans, said in the article he wrote for my *Good Grief (1)* teaching pack:

We can start from the assumption that no one wants to be suicidal. Those who are, feel compelled to be so. From the individual's point of view his or her suicide is never an irrational act. It has a purpose, which is to bring to an end some unendurable psychological pain. The journey towards suicide may be short or long. It is an ever-narrowing path strewn with discarded options. The victim eventually reaches a point at which there seems to be only one way forward and that is suicide. There may be little thought of death. The prime objective is not to be dead but rather to escape. Being dead may be nothing more than an unavoidable by-product. There may even be a kind of doublethink: 'I want to wake up dead' was how one man put it.

People seldom reach the end of the path for any one simple reason. More often than not there will be a multiplicity of reasons: bereavement, breakdown of an important relationship, loss of employment, financial problems, stress, poor health, terminal illness, and others. A common feature is a sense of isolation. This may have nothing to do with the absence of contacts – the victim may be surrounded by family, friends and colleagues. The problem lies more in the realm of communication. The victim feels unable to share his or her feelings with anyone. There may be a feeling that no one can help, or indeed should help. A common precursor to suicidal feelings is depression, which may result from some event in the victim's life or from some mental disturbance. It may be, as the writer William Styron described it, a failure of self-esteem.

A. Alvarez wrote:

Sociological theories woven around suicide are all to some extent true, some truer than others. Most are conflicting, partial and circular. We return constantly to an inner negation and hopelessness [of the individual] which social pressures may bring to the surface but which existed before those pressures and will probably continue even after they are removed.[3]

So what causes the inner feelings of hopelessness? Dorplat, Ripley and Robins, in a study in 1960,[4] concluded that ninety per cent of suicides were psychiatrically ill. The vast majority have major depression which is unrecognized and undiagnosed. The remainder have anxiety disorders, or a history of substance abuse; and there are a very few impulsive suicides, which occur after catastrophic loss or disaster. Due to a lack of knowledge about mental illness, symptoms are often not recognized by the person themselves or relatives and friends. In fact the ill person feels he ought to be able to control his feelings, because to display emotions that do not conform to society's is regarded as a weakness – a failure.

Eleanor 'Betsy' Ross says:

Some people, it seems, possess a special sensitivity to experiencing both the joys and pains of life to an intolerable edge. It has been said that, when one absorbs so much of the world, there is a tremendous need to express it. Some search for this expression – some choose escape. The suicide's silent cry rides the wind – and they cry out for so many![5]

I remember a consultant psychiatrist who was a kind and caring man, both at work and home. Two of his four children committed suicide in their late teens and early twenties, within a few years of each other. I had met them both and they seemed to have this special gentle, sensitive nature. Their close family ties, friends and interesting studies were not enough to compensate for the harshness of the world as they saw it around them.

For a depressed person, suicide can feel like a way to be autonomous. Suicide is often seen as going out of control, but in a way it is the ultimate in taking control. Many people, now more than ever, feel a lack of personal control in their lives with the rapid changes that are taking place in the world and the lack of security that follows them.

The following suicide note, written by David before he completed suicide on 12 May 1987, illustrates for me how one person felt he was taking control of his life. David, an amazingly astute twenty-two-year-old, was unusually well informed about his illness. His description of his feelings shatters myths and assumptions about suicide, and allows us an insight into his motivation to end his life. In granting permission for its use, it is the hope of David's family that the loved ones of other victims (who may not have left such complete and expressive messages) may find comfort in David's words.

Dear Mum, Dad and Stephany,
  First, some facts:
1. I LOVE YOU VERY MUCH.
2. I KNOW YOU LOVE ME VERY MUCH. If love alone could have made me better, I would be the most well-adjusted man

on earth. Please don't feel that you neglected to tell or show how much you loved me.

3. YOU WERE NOT TO BLAME FOR MY CONDITION. I believe my mental illness was the result of a chemical imbalance in the brain. A certain percentage of people, from all types of family situation, have a major mental illness. It was just the luck of a biological draw that I happened to be one of them. Whether it was Major Depressive Disorder, Schizoid Personality Disorder, Manic-Depressive Disorder or Schizophrenia, my mental illness made my life unlivable. But you are not to blame for that. So please don't let yourselves feel guilty.

4. I KNOW THAT YOU WILL MAKE IT THROUGH THIS. It won't be easy but you will have a lot of support from a lot of friends and relatives. Don't be like me, the ultimate schizoid loner. Count on the support of your friends and relatives.

If you only knew what goes on inside my head. I know you will say that I 'didn't try long enough or hard enough'. I have been emotionally disturbed since late childhood. I now have a major mental illness. I tried as long and as hard as I could.

I've had all sorts of suggestions, like, 'Repeat positive phrases over and over again. Don't eat foods with yeast. Take Haldol. Don't take Haldol. Accept Jesus as your personal saviour. Quit smoking. Get a girlfriend.' And the list goes on and on.

I know that the above suggestions were made with the best intentions but they lack an understanding of what mental illness is all about. That's why I found something in common with other people who are mentally ill. When they told me how being mentally ill affects their life, I understood, because my illness affected me in the same way.

If I were to tell Uncle Ray that I had bought a gun, that I felt suicidal, he would have no alternative but to call the hospital or the police. And, before you know it, I'd be back in the hospital.

I'd rather be dead.

It's not like I killed myself because I didn't get an A on an exam, or because I broke up with my girlfriend. Those are the kinds of depression that have a reason to happen. My depression came without any help from the outside. Nothing has happened to make me depressed except my depression.

It's not like I did this 'on a lark'. I've had over a year to think it over. But, I can hardly expect you to understand about something I myself don't understand. I don't know why I am the way I am. 'The man who didn't see it through.' That is what this is. If given a chance to choose between an eternity in Heaven, or another go-round as a human on earth, I'm certain I would choose the latter.

And now the business part of this suicide note:

Cremate and scatter me. (I don't care where.)

All my money goes to you, everything else too. Do with it what you will, but may I suggest sending a portion of my worldly goods to a mental-health research foundation of your choice.

As David requested, the family sent a donation in hopes that some day a cure will be found.

Anger

Strong feelings of anger in grievers are common in cases of suicide. This anger can be with yourself, the person who has died, God, other relatives, or outside agencies. Involved in this, is the stigma of the manner of death, and the feeling that the dead person has left you to 'pick up the pieces'.

I met one middle-aged couple whose eighteen-year-old son had committed suicide without warning two years earlier. He had appeared to be a normal teenager with good friends, a job he enjoyed, and a happy home life. He had never shown any signs of being depressed or unhappy. He left a note saying, 'I want you to know you have been the best parents you could have been, and that there was nothing you could have done to stop me.' When they told me I said, 'Didn't that make you angry?' They said, 'You're the first person who has said that to us. Yes, we felt if we were such 'good parents', then we should have been able to stop him.'

Joanna, now a trainee counsellor, vividly describes the anger and sense of betrayal she felt when her father committed suicide, and how she dealt with her feelings:

My dad hanged himself on Father's Day. He is dead and he left no note. This is the truth and will remain so. This is now my history and that of my family for ever. This fact will not change.

People ask me how I am, I say I am sad because my dad has just died. Were you expecting it or was it sudden, they ask? And there he is, hanging between us – him and the truth.

He killed himself the day before I left for a week's holiday, but the police didn't find him until I had gone. I found out on my return. My mum, from whom he was divorced, met me at the airport. She took me to a small office to tell me. How grateful I am for that.

I want you to know how I felt. I felt like my heart had been torn from me. I shook my head and laughed in disbelief. I wailed and cried with sadness. My always dad no longer existed and I'd had no warning. How could it be so?

His funeral was the next day and I travelled a great emotional and physical distance in those hours. The rest of my family had had a week to get used to this lack and the shock, while I was still reeling. I made him a card to connect with him somehow and to let him know how I wish he had stayed and how I had loved him. I picked roses from my garden for him and asked that both they and the card be buried with him.

The funeral was a paltry affair. There were members of his family from marriages one and two, an estranged friend, some work associates. He had no true friends to mourn his loss. The only thing the vicar could give thanks for in his life was the number of people he had helped pass their driving tests. I cried and still could not believe the box at the front held my dad. They burned him.

Afterwards, my mum, my brother and half-sister and I sat in a pub and told some truths about him. He had been a lying, cheating, womanizing, drunken, violent and very charming man. We called him all the names and laughed. And for a while I forgot my image of him hanging by his neck in a cellar and remembered him as the bugger he had been.

At home I got out my old photographs. At some I smiled, at others, of when he was a fine child and a handsome young man, I cried. I cried for what he had become and for how he had ended his life. And I cried for myself, my loss.

I wondered if there was something I could have done to make a difference in his life. And in truth I knew there was not. My dad's pain and anger began long before I knew him. A time when he had not been allowed to ask for help, to say he needed love, to be. Like many of us, his pain and anger were too old for words. And now he hangs for ever in the seedy basement of a rented house where he lived alone. A sad, bitter, frustrated and angry man.

I am telling you all this because I want you to know about him and about me. And how sorry I am that he did not stay. And so you can understand that although I loved him, I am also furious with him for what he has done. My dad hanged himself on Father's Day. He is dead and he left no note and I am furious with him for this.

He took away my right to tell him the things I wanted to say to him. My right to say I love you and a final goodbye. He also took away my right to hear the things he might have wanted to say to me. I am left with the feeling that his final message to me was Fuck You.

I have no illness to explain his death, no accident for which I can blame fate or mechanics or even a person. I have no idea how he felt or what he thought. And I never will have. All I have is the fact of him hanging. Too much, yet nothing at all. He took away my right to prepare for his death, for this very final separation. He left me brutally, aggressively, totally, and sometimes I find myself saying, how dare you do this to me? I feel an injustice has been done. I say, but I thought I was your favoured child. Why? Come back now. And still he hangs.

I know that although I now think of him often each day, there will come a time when I will not. When he will be someone I can talk about with fondness and humour and few tears. And until then I will keep feeling the things I feel and being true to myself and not to society's image of what is acceptable for those grieving. At the moment, therefore, I feel very sad and bloody angry and I wish he had stayed.

---

1 Published by Routledge, 1991.
2 *Suicide Questions and Answers* (Afterwards Publishers, USA, 1985).
3 *The Savage God: a study in suicide* (Penguin, 1987).
4 *A Study of Suicide in Seattle*, S3483T 1960.
5 Quoted in 'There Is No Stigma, There Is No Shame' by Laura Millest in UK *Compassionate Friends Newsletter*, Spring 1990.

The Farewell

Sorrow, like a river, must be given vent, lest it erode the bank.

(Mexican proverb)

16

Funerals and other rituals

I am learning to look at your life again
Instead of your death and departing. (Marjorie Pizer)

I came to realize the importance of ritual to those left behind
following my own devastating experience with my husband's funeral. This was attended by only twelve people: my
mother's logic was that as it was such a tragic death, the
funeral should be kept very simple and attended by as few
people as possible. I was persuaded that it would be inappropriate even to have a simple poem that was a favourite
of John's read, or to have people back after the service. I felt
as if I had no control over what was happening, and this
added to my sense of unreality. It was *my* husband who had
died, and yet I had no say over what happened – I felt impotent. Later, looking back, I felt angry that I'd had no
chance to say a proper goodbye and let him go. It would have
been the last thing I could have done for him, and I felt I had
failed him, myself, and his friends and family. I would have
liked to have celebrated his accomplishments: he had many.
Instead, the whole service was empty and meaningless to
me.

One of the greatest difficulties in the grieving process in
the Western world can be the lack of rituals and customs and
the chance to 'let go' after a death. It is now becoming common in some countries for the funeral service to take place in
the chapel of the funeral director. Once the service is completed the family, relatives and friends go home to
refreshments, whilst the dead person is taken off alone to the
cemetery or crematorium. In America it's now possible to
have no further contact with the body almost immediately
after the death. Specialist firms offer to take the body away,

and no family or friends are expected to attend any type of service or farewell.

This modern trend of dissociation contradicts folk wisdom all over the world. A funeral is an opportunity to share your personal loss with the community; to acknowledge that the death has really happened; to say goodbye; to mark the end of a life and the beginning of a period of mourning and readjustment; and to celebrate and give thanks for the life that has been. All these are important elements in the grief process and it's unwise to underestimate the powerful emotional effects of such rituals.

A variety of traditions

The rituals and customs surrounding a funeral reflect the beliefs of the person who has died, their family, and the society in which they live. The major world religions give hope – death is not seen as final but rather as a stage in the journey of life. People are naturally afraid of death and the way they will die, and about what sort of life, if any, there is after death. Religious beliefs incorporated into funeral services give the mourners hope and reassurance and help them to grieve and to look forward.

Hindu funerals aim to set the soul free for another incarnation. The body is cremated and the eldest son collects the ashes and scatters them in the nearest river. Christians and Muslims have traditionally preferred burial to cremation because of their belief in the physical resurrection of the body. A Christian funeral service will commend the dead person to God's care; proclaim the Christian belief in life after death; and remind the mourners of their own coming death and judgement before God. For Quakers, the whole service after the interment consists of tributes to the deceased, which are a great help in the letting-go process for those left behind.

The Catholic Christians of Mexico combine folk traditions with orthodox religious ritual. Following a death in rural Mexico, the family will usually hold a feast for the mourners who call to pay their last respects. All the relatives, neighbours and friends are informed so they can participate and help pay for the wake. In the case of a child's death, it is regarded as urgent to inform the godparents as they are expected to donate the child's clothing and coffin. When an adult dies, their friends will contribute the cross used during the nine days which the death ritual takes. (It is thought the soul does not withdraw until nine days have elapsed.) According to custom, the cross is formed exactly where the body was laid after death. Different powdered materials of various colours are spread over several rectangular layers of pressed sand. On the ninth day, the cross is taken up and any flowers decorating it are taken to the cemetery. There are different rituals depending on the age and sex of the deceased. For example, it is said when an adult dies that one goes into mourning, whereas children are buried with singing, dancing, and merrymaking and called 'little angels'. I think the Mexican tradition that friends and family help pay for the funeral is most helpful.

In Jewish tradition, the funeral takes place as soon as possible and is followed by seven days of mourning. Those in mourning sit on low chairs, and special prayers are said daily both at home and in the synagogue. Friends and relatives visit the family, to comfort them, every day. (Such traditions of support are common to most cultures.)

In the West we generally allow only one day to attend a funeral. Maoris in New Zealand, however, take the time to travel to their ancestral home, plus four days for the funeral. The coffin is left open for everyone to see the body unless it has been badly disfigured in an accident. Mourners have to follow protocol and are called on to pay homage. Maoris believe that if you don't let feelings – including rage – out, both physically and emotionally, you don't heal. Mourners, including children, speak to the dead person, offer appreciations, and clear up any unfinished emotional business.

I remember a few years ago driving through a small village in Sri Lanka and seeing the main street lined with people, standing quietly. A young man had been shot dead and the whole village had turned out to show their sympathy. Such community involvement is common in traditional rural cultures. If you were to visit a funeral ceremony of the Toraja people of Indonesia, you might think you had come upon a carnival rather than a funeral. The people who gather for the funeral are in very high spirits and they appear far from sad. Processions of people arrive at the funeral field with buffalo ready to be sacrificed in honour of the dead person. A large pavilion is built from bamboo and everyone awaits the procession which brings the body to the funeral. The dead must be given a good send-off. The dead person is about to become an ancestor. The dead depend on the living to per-form the death ceremony correctly so that they may rest peacefully. The living depend on the dead to link the family with the spiritual power which the ancestors possess. When the ceremony is performed correctly both the living and the dead are much happier.

Creating new rituals

Many of us no longer feel comfortable in any one particular religious or cultural tradition. People who have little or no faith may choose to have a non-religious service. The Humanist Association can help with this, and will lead the funeral if requested (in the UK there's a legal requirement to have an approved official to lead the service). David J. Williams of the British Humanist Association says:

> We are very happy to assist friends or members of the family to conduct the ceremony themselves, although most people don't have the courage to take it on. . . . Humanist funerals need not be terribly sad. If somebody has had a good life and is remembered with affection, there is no great cause for grief. The music can be cheerful and respectful at the same time. The words that are spoken might even cause the mourners to laugh. There is a proper place for a certain degree of ritual and the point of committal is to be marked with due respect.
>
> Finally, the occasion of the funeral allows us – society as a whole – to remind those of us still living that life is a good thing and we had better do something useful with it while we can. Some families ask for a non-religious funeral because it avoids awkward clashes of different religious faiths in a multi-cultural society. A Humanist funeral is not anti-religious: it celebrates the Human values we all share and cherish.

Many people don't realize that you can usually participate in the funeral service if you arrange this in advance with the officiating minister; or you can even arrange the whole funeral yourself. For some, the greatest way of showing their love, respect and grief is to have the ritual of an arranged funeral, and that is right for them, but for others perhaps the knowledge that one can arrange a funeral extremely simply, personally, and cheaply may be of benefit. It also may be of interest to people of other religions who would prefer to carry out their own funerals according to their customs or beliefs. Jane Warman wrote an article about doing it yourself for my *Good Grief (1)* teaching pack:

'I'd like to buy a coffin.'

'You mean, you'd like me to arrange a funeral?'

'No, I'd like to buy a coffin – five foot five and as plain as possible.'

'You don't want me to arrange a funeral?'

'*No*. I want to do it myself.'

'Well – I suppose it's all right.'

'Oh yes, I know it is – I've done it before.'

A close friend in his early thirties died of cancer. . . . His wife decided that we should do the funeral, and with the help of an outstanding and sympathetic GP this was arranged for the same day. We bought a coffin, did the minimum of preparation to his body, and took the coffin ourselves to the local crematorium in the back of an estate car. I felt privileged to have been part of this: it made a bond between the four of us who helped and I believe that knowing that we personally did everything we could has made it easier to grieve.

. . . For many people, the physical action of placing a loved person in the coffin and closing the lid is inconceivable, but there are usually others, perhaps friends and/or relations who could and would like to help. Also, many people think that there is a lot to be done in the preparation of the body – in fact, usually very little needs to be done and there is usually someone, perhaps a district nurse, who could help.

A service I was privileged to attend that moved me deeply was for Mike, who led men's groups, at Golder's Green Crematorium. It was a non-religious funeral service organized by Mike's partner and family. A member of the British Humanist Society was there in order to fulfil the legal requirements. The service was attended by more than two hundred people, including very small children, and lasted one and a half hours. In her introduction, Sarah, his partner, said, 'We want the service to reflect Mike's life. We don't want the children to be made to sit down, we want them to move around, as they would normally.' Mike had helped at his daughter Peri's nursery school.

The service included contributions from Mike's family and friends on all aspects of his life, including a Sufi dance. 'Death Is Nothing At All', by Canon Scott Holland, was sent out with the funeral details and read at the service. At the end many of us joined in a circle dance before leaving the chapel. A hundred people attended a gathering in the evening. This gave the opportunity for all Mike's friends, colleagues and family to meet for the first time.

Mike's father described what the ceremony meant to him:

It's difficult for me to think of the ceremony without making comparisons: though I've never experienced such a shock as Michael's death before, so any comparison must be futile. Yet I know that to have had to listen to some stranger (in a dog-collar) mouthing platitudes about someone of whose life he had no direct knowledge would have filled me with a negative emotion that I can't quite identify: not quite anger, not quite contempt; demeaning is as near as I can think at present. Yet I recognize the need to mourn together, and to celebrate together.

Part of my life has gone: the child, my companion; the teen-ager, strange and estranged; the student, with some echoes of myself; changing gradually into the thinking, searching, caring, loving son and father, from whom I could learn, and in whom I could confide, as to no one else. The succession of speakers and performers in the ceremony helped me to integrate all those elements, to recognize the continuity, the wholeness, the fullness and the achievement, to see how each stage was a necessary precursor of the next, and to mingle deep sorrow and despair with intense pride.

I heard about a service for a grandmother, where all the grandchildren were given balloons in memory of her. At the end of the service, as they floated off into the sky, the children called, 'Bye-bye, Grandma!' At a recent, thoughtful service for Dominic, who died of leukaemia aged twenty-eight, his mother said:

We asked you not to send flowers, because we knew that

Dominic would prefer any money to go towards helping others suffering from leukaemia. Nevertheless a single flower is a powerful image – so we have given one to each of you. We invite you now to bring your flower up and put it into one of the baskets as a personal gesture to Dominic. The baskets of flowers will then come with us to the cemetery to be strewn on top of the coffin.

It takes time to get the necessary information together and organize a funeral. Many people can find themselves organizing a funeral for the first time. In the case of sudden death, this can be a particular problem. Where a death is expected, the dying person often likes to be included in the arrangements. My mother planned who she wanted invited and personally asked them. If time is too short to plan a service, it is quite common to have a smaller funeral service for close friends and family and then a memorial service at a later date.

Children and funerals

I don't believe in forcing children to attend funerals or memorial services, but I do think they should always be given a choice. This often does not happen. Most adults I've met who weren't allowed to attend funerals as a child still regret it and/or feel angry or guilty about it. One man in his forties told me, 'Even though I was only three when my father died, I would have liked to have gone to the funeral.' Depending on their age, children will need to know the following to prevent the occasion being frightening or worrying:

- Why the service is being held and what will be included – prayers, a talk about the dead person, hymns, etc. Many children are happy to contribute if given the opportunity, even if it's only choosing the clothes they'd like to wear.
- Where and when the service will happen.
- What the coffin will look like, and what happens to it. At cremations, many children wonder where the ashes come from because they aren't told what happens to the coffin when it disappears at the end of the service.
- Who will be there, and who will be sitting next to them. It

is important there is an adult who is not too caught up in their own grief to care for the child. Younger children in particular will need physical contact; their hand held or sitting on the lap of someone they know well.

Children should similarly be prepared for the gathering afterwards. They can feel neglected, especially if small, so again it is important to make sure they have an adult nearby and/or other children to play with in another room.

If children choose not to go to the funeral, you can give them the opportunity to pay tribute in their own way, for example by writing a poem or planting a tree. Photographs or a video can be taken to show to them at a later stage.

Ideally, children should be given the opportunity to join in and plan the service. Mohamed is eight. He read the following letter from himself and Ali, his five-year-old brother, at the recent remembrance ceremony for his mother:

Dear Mum,

We miss you and love you. Many people care about us. Ali and I want you to know that, but still it is hard not to have you with us. I miss your cooking, Ali misses your hugs and we both miss your love. Dear Mum, we want you with us and sometimes it is very very sad. Angie says you are in heaven. Ali and I want you to be happy there. We'll always love you and remember you. Ali bought lovely pink and yellow flowers for you. I bought you nice flowers too.

Mum, Ali wants to say something to you.

Ali: We love you, Mum.

Alison, aged eight, sent this letter to arrive on the morning of the thanksgiving service for the life of her beloved grandfather:

Dear Grin-gran,

Do you remember this writing set? It's the one you gave me for Christmas.

The Target leaflet from church has St Paul say 'Help to carry one another's burdens.' It comes from the Good News Bible, Galatians 6.2. I think we are all trying to do that for each other.

I hope this notelet cheers you up. I like it because Care Bears are always cheerful. The sun is shining and there is a rainbow. Just two of them sitting there on the cloud makes me feel happy. I hope it does to you as well.

I hope we see you again soon.

Lots and lots of love.

The mourning period

Strict periods of mourning, with grievers wearing special clothes and restricting their social activities, have become less common in the West during this century. In Southern and Eastern Europe, however, it is still common to see women dressed in black or grey as an outward sign of their grief. Many cultures mark the end of the mourning period – often a year – with a service. In the Jewish tradition, for example, this is when the memorial stone is consecrated at the grave, and the Rabbi announces that the days of mourning are over. In the similar Maori tradition, it is the youngest and oldest members of the extended family who unveil the stone.

Remembrance

One of the biggest fears I find bereaved people have is forgetting the dead person. This is when a memorial can be helpful. Colin Murray-Parkes says:

> The bereaved need to create something very physical to fill the physical gap left by a dead person. A memorial is a physical symbol of an internal object, an outward and visible sign of a being who cannot be any more, a foot stamped into the naked concrete of eternity.[1]

Most people who choose to have a memorial find it helpful in their grief. Frances Clegg, who researched the subject for CRUSE, says:

> Many people described how, with the passage of time, the importance of this physical link gradually diminished and was gradually replaced by memories. Perhaps therefore for most of us a memorial provides us with a temporary link with the

deceased person during the extremely painful letting-go period.

I have experienced many people using the memorial as a tangible link, and focus of grief. Vera's son died of cystic fibrosis. For the first six months after his death, Vera regularly went to Phillip's grave and talked to him. A gay friend of mine's partner died more than ten years ago and was cremated. My friend gains comfort from visiting the place where the ashes were scattered on the anniversary of the death each year.

Suggestions for memorials

- Putting a plaque, seat, shrub, or tree in a favourite spot. Memorials by Artists has a register of artists throughout Britain who will make private or public memorials of any description, usually in stone.
- Giving a donation to a special charity.
- Combining donations with a memorial. The Woodland Trust have a 'Plant a Tree' scheme to remember loved ones, and commemorative groves.
- In the UK there is now a Memorial Advisory Bureau which campaigns to protect individual rights to erect memorials, and can advise you whether you have the right to do so (see Useful Addresses).

Remembrance rituals

Many crematoriums how hold annual memorial services which are becoming very popular. The services can include music, readings and addresses by different religious leaders as well as times of quiet. St Paul's Church, Walsall holds a Candle Memorial Service each December. The memorial candle lit by the family at the service is later taken home to be relit on Christmas morning.

Hospices, too, often hold anniversary services. Mary Potter Hospice in Wellington, New Zealand, for example, has a remembrance service every three months, for people who died three months or more earlier. People can attend more than once. People who were significant to the dead person are invited to bring a photo, light a candle, and name the person, as part of the service.

In New Zealand, too, there are Remembrance Trees at Christmas. Bereaved people can buy a light for the tree in remembrance; the money goes to charity.

In Mexico, the whole country joins in an extravagant celebration and remembrance of the dead on 1 and 2 November each year. Although Mexicans suffer sadness and anxiety in the face of death, the same as other human beings, they differ from many other cultures in that they turn death into something familiar and part of everyday life. It is referred to in the names of streets and avenues such as *Calzado del Hueso* (Bone Road) or *Barranca del Muerto* (Alley of the Dead). Popular songs are written about it.

Mexicans believe the dead return each year for a few brief hours of earthly enjoyment with the living. The previous day, 31 October, is a market day when families purchase their supply of flowers, candles, vigil lamps, food, and other necessities to set up the family and community altars. On 1 and 2 November the dead traditionally return from the hereafter to visit their relatives who have been left behind in the world; so the living await their loved ones joyfully, with music and everything the departed enjoyed in life. In some communities cemeteries are cleaned, weeded and the tombstones painted. Relatives then put their offerings, which consist of new hats, cigarettes, bandannas, and bowls of food, on the graves. Other graves are decorated with new crosses and clusters of burning candles. A path is strewn with petals of fresh flowers from the cemetery to each home, enabling the souls to find their way to the family altar, where they will feed on the odours given off by the offerings. After 2 November, friends and relatives are invited to 'raise the dead' and consume the food. In the UK, the Natural Death Society is organizing its first 'Day of the Dead' in 1993.

---

1 Editorial in ECRUSEE *Bereavement Care*.

Appendix

Sorrow that has no vent in tears makes other organs weep. (Anon)

Relaxation techniques

Remember, it takes many years to build up tension, so it can take a long time to lose it completely. Relaxation, like all skills, takes time to learn, so don't give up too easily. It's common to find yourself yawning frequently, and having stomach rumbles and watering eyes to start with. As part of your learning, become aware of the things that make you tense and the changes that then happen in your body. Learn to take action to relieve tension before it becomes built-in.

Basic technique

A simple method is to sit in a comfortable chair (one with armrests will be best) with your feet on the floor, slightly apart, your bottom well back in the seat and your hands loosely in your lap, one on top of the other. Close your eyes. Check right through your body, starting with the top of your head. Feel yourself relaxing each part before you move on to the next. When you feel ready, open your eyes again. Have a good stretch.

Breathing

When you are tense you will tend to breathe too quickly and shallowly. This exercise will encourage you to breathe more deeply and relax your abdominal muscles, where a lot of tension can be held.

Sit well back in a comfortable chair. Put one hand on the upper part of your chest and feel your breathing slow down under it. Put your other hand on top of your abdomen and feel yourself breathing into this hand. When you're into a good rhythm, drop both hands gently into your lap. When you feel ready, open your eyes and have a good stretch.

Relieving headaches or migraine

Follow the basic relaxation technique above, then picture warmth moving *very slowly* down from your head, across your shoulders, down your arms, into your hands, and then to the tips of your fingers and thumbs. When you feel ready, open your eyes and have a good stretch.

Acute stress – emergency technique

Stop. Breathe out, unclench your teeth, drop your shoulders, unclench your fists. Relax and breathe in slowly. Move around more slowly. Lower your voice and speak more slowly. If possible, think about or do something else – for instance, go into the garden, or another room.

Deep relaxation

I regret there's no room here to include instructions for this, but I strongly recommend Jane Madders' tape, *Relax: techniques of relaxation for migraine, fatigue and general tension*, and her book, *Stress and Relaxation*. Both are available from the Midlands Migraine Association, c/o Mrs K.M. Hay, 5 Temple Road, Dorridge, Solihull, West Midlands B98 8LE. Alternatively, *Simple Relaxation: the Mitchell method for easing tension*, by Laura Mitchell, published by John Murray.

Visualizations

The first few times you do a particular visualization, it's helpful to record it on cassette tape or get a friend to read it to you, slowly. (Don't forget to read the basic relaxation technique to begin each one.)

Your special place

Sit or lie in a comfortable place and relax, using the basic technique above. Imagine yourself in your own special place. It could be on a warm beach; somewhere in the country; or your own armchair. It's your own special place. There is nothing you have to do, nowhere you have to go and nothing you have to be. When you have found your place, just luxuriate in the peace and stay as long as you want before stretching and coming back to the room. (Even a minute doing this can have an amazingly relaxing effect.)

The temple of silence[1]

Sit or lie and relax, as in the basic technique above. Imagine a hill covered with greenery. A path leads to the top, where you can see the temple of silence. It is a spring morning, sunny and pleasantly warm. Notice how you are dressed. Become conscious of your body ascending the path, and feel the contact of your feet with the ground. Feel the breeze on your cheeks. Look about you at the trees and the bushes, the grass, and the wild flowers as you go up. You are now approaching the top of the hill. Ageless stillness pervades the atmosphere of the temple of silence. No word has ever been uttered here. You are close to its big wooden portals: see your hands on them and feel the wood. Before opening the doors, know that when you do so, you will be surrounded by silence.

You enter the temple. You feel the atmosphere of stillness and peace all around you. Now you walk forward into the silence, looking about you as you go. You see a big, luminous dome. Its luminosity not only comes from the rays of the sun, but also seems to spring from within and to be concentrated in an area of radiance just in front of you.

You enter this luminous silence and feel absorbed by it. Beams of beneficent, warm, powerful light are enveloping you. Let this luminous silence pervade you. Feel it flowing through your veins and permeating every cell in your body. Remain in this luminous silence for two or three minutes, composed and alert. During this time, listen to the silence. Silence is a living quality, not just the mere absence of sounds.

Slowly leave the area of radiance; walk back through the

temple and out the portals. Outside, open yourself to the impact of the spring, feel its gentle breeze once more on your cheek, and listen to the singing of the birds. Slowly walk back down the hill to where you started your walk. Rest there a moment before opening your eyes. You may like to ground the experience by drawing or writing about it in your journal.

The wise person

Sit or lie comfortably and follow the basic relaxation technique above. Imagine yourself in a meadow, on a warm sunny morning. Gradually become aware of your environment. See or sense the trees and flowers, smell the scents, feel the grass under your feet, hear the sounds – birds, water, insects. Be aware of what you are wearing.

As you look around, see a mountain near the meadow and feel a sense of exhilaration as you decide to climb it. At the edge of the meadow see a gate. Go through it and take the path up the mountain. Stop and look at the views on the way. Notice how the air is getting purer and the silence deepens. When you reach the top there is a vast plateau with a shaft of sunlight shining down on you. Feel the sun shining right through every part of you. Far off you notice someone coming towards you. They could be male or female, someone you know, or have never met before. This person is wise, loving and full of compassion. They have all the answers you need to know. As they walk towards you, greet them in any way that seems appropriate. Feel the strength and warmth of your wise person as you share with them your feelings. You can talk about any problem or ask any question you want. Take all the time you need to hear their response and then ask for a quality to bring back with you. (Examples of qualities are love, compassion, strength, joy, or laughter.) Imagine what your life would be like with this quality.

When you feel ready, and remembering you can visit your wise person any time you want, say goodbye in whatever way is best for you and slowly go back down the mountain to the meadow; then open your eyes. You may like to ground the experience by drawing or writing about it in your journal.

A woman who had had an abortion did this visualization with me. She took the foetus to her wise person, who turned out to be her grandfather. The grandfather said he would look after the foetus for her, and gave her the quality of forgiveness.

No fear to die[2]

This visualization is great for anyone who's feeling alienated, as well as those who are afraid of dying.

Close your eyes and picture in detail the room in which you are sitting now. In your imagination, move up and away from the room and form a clear picture of the building that contains it. See the building getting smaller as you rise higher and higher. From above, the whole area in which you live lies below you: houses, streets, parks, countryside, shops. People and cars are barely visible in the streets. Think how each person is the centre of their own world, with their own thoughts and hopes, their own problems and projects. Imagine them in their homes too.

Continue your ascent. Your view expands, enabling you to see other towns and cities in the area, green fields, lakes, and sea. As you rise higher, you can glimpse oceans and other countries as well as banks of clouds.

Now you have the whole planet Earth before you, blue and white, slowly rotating in empty space. From this immense height you can no longer see people or even guess their existence: but you can think of them, four and a half billion people, each one living on that same planet, breathing the same air. Four and a half billion hearts of people of many different races are beating down there. Think about this for a while, as you continue to visualize the planet Earth.

Now, as you move away from it, you see the Earth becoming smaller and smaller as different planets come into view.

The Earth has now vanished, the sun is but a tiny point of light among innumerable stars, and you have lost all trace of it. Billions of stars are all around you, below, above, on all sides. There is no more 'down', no more 'up'.

All those billions of stars constitute but one galaxy in the universe. It is one among an unknown number of other galaxies reaching out in every direction to infinity.

At this point, think of the infinity of time. Here there is no 'tomorrow' and no 'yesterday'. No haste, no pressure. Everything is scintillating peace and wonder.

When you feel ready, open your eyes again and bring back with you this sense of expansion. You may like to ground the experience by drawing or writing about it in your journal.

Recommended reading

Bach, Richard: *Jonathon Livingstone Seagull* (Pan Books, 1972). This was the start of my acceptance of being 'different' to my family, and building my new spiritual family. I realized that all the support we need is there for us in life, but not necessarily where we expect it to be.

Illusions (Pan books 1978). This includes the story of the reluctant Messiah: 'You don't have to suffer to be a Christian, just be happy and in that way you make others happy too!' What a weight that lifted from my shoulders: I felt free for the first time to be myself and not what others wanted.

Bluebond-Langer, Myra: *The Private Worlds of Dying Children* (Princeton University Press, 1977).

Burton, Lindy: *Care of the Child Facing Death* (Routledge, 1974).

Capacchione, Lucia: *Recovery of Your Inner Child* (Simon & Schuster, New York, 1991). This book suggests practical ways to get to know and understand the needs of your hurt inner child, so you can nurture him/her instead of letting them control your life.

Cleese, John, and Robin Skinner: *Families and How to Survive Them* (Methuen, 1988). This gave me a new insight into what makes families 'tick'. It also helped me to recognize that we are always drawn to people with similar experiences. We can then use these relationships to either free ourselves and grow, or to block off.

Collick, Elizabeth: *Through Grief: the bereavement journey* (Darton, Longman, Todd/CRUSE, 1986).

Daily Word religious meditations are available from Silent Unity, 11 Boyn Hill Avenue, Maidenhead, Berkshire SL6 4ET

Disasters: planning for a caring response (HMSO, 1991).

Dominica, Mother Frances: *The Illness and Death of a Child* (The Church Literature Association, 1988).

Dyregrov, Åtle: *Grief in Children* (Jessica Kingsley, 1990).

Fabian, Ailsa: *The Daniel Diary* (Grafton Books, 1988).

Ferrucci, Piero: *What We May Be: the visions and techniques of psychosynthesis* (Turnstone, 1985). Outlines a specific programme of easy-to-perform exercises that form the basis of a total system for psychological and spiritual growth. I used psychosynthesis training as the foundation of my healing and integration.

Furman, Elna: *The Child's Parent Dies* (Yale University Press, 1974).

Goldstein, Sol: *Divorce Parenting: how to make it work* (Methuen, 1987).

Grant, Brian: *Conciliation and Divorce: a father's letter to his children* (Barry Rose).

Hay, Louise H.: *You Can Heal Your Life* (Eden Grove Publications, 1987). Louise suggests exercises, affirmations and valuable steps into becoming a whole, healthy, happy individual. I have found her book invaluable in releasing old hurts and fears.

Hesse, Herman: *Siddhartha* (Pan Books, 1974). This traces the search of a wealthy prince (the Buddha) for the meaning of life. He finally finds it sitting and watching a river.

Jewett, Claudia: *Helping Children Cope with Separation and Loss* (Batsford, 1984).

Krementz, Jill: *How It Feels When a Parent Dies* (Gollancz, 1983).

Krystal, Phyliss: *Cutting the Ties that Bind* (Sawbridge Enterprises, 1986). She introduced me to my 'cosmic parents' who later became my own, and was the start of my healing my relationship with them.

Kübler-Ross, Elisabeth: *On Death and Dying* (Tavistock/Routledge, 1970).

Living with Death and Dying (Souvenir, 1982).

On Children and Death (Macmillan, 1985).

Kushner, Harold: *When Bad Things Happen to Good People* (Pan Books, 1982). This confirmed what I already knew in my head: that we aren't being deliberately singled out or punished when bad things happen to us.

Levine, Stephen: *Who Dies?* (Gateway Books, 1986).

Lewis, C.S.: *A Grief Observed* (Faber, 1961).

Linn, Eric: *150 Facts About Grieving Children* (available from The Publishers Mark, Inchie Village, Nevada 89450, USA).

Lorimer, David: *Body, Mind and Death in the Light of Psychic Experience* (Routledge & Kegan Paul, 1984).

Millman, Dan: *The Way of the Peaceful Warrior*, and *The Sacred Journey of the Peaceful Warrior* (H.J. Kramer, USA, 1984 & 1991). We have all we need inside us. All we have to do is trust and use our abilities. Also, we choose our life experiences in order to develop and master what we have come into this life to learn. I've been constantly pushed into situations that have made me 'own my power': the latest being Tessa Strickland asking me to write this book!

Moody, Raymond: *Life After Life* (Bantam Books, 1983).

Morgan, John D. (ed): *The Dying and Bereaved Teenager* (Charles Press, 1990).

Murray-Parkes, Colin, and Robert Weiss: *Recovery from Bereavement* (Basic Books, New York, 1983).

Neuberger, Rabbi Julia: *Caring for Dying People of Different Faiths* (Austin Cornish, 1990).

Parents Are Forever (Relate, 1985)

Peck, Scott: *The Road Less Travelled* (Arrow books, 1990). The natural law of life is to have 'problems', once we accept that we can go ahead and deal with them.

Pietroni, Dr Patrick: *Holistic Living: a guide to self-care* (Dent, 1987).

Pincus, Lily: *Death and the Family* (Faber, 1961).

Pringle, Mia Kellmer: *The Needs of Children* (Hutchinson, 1987).

Randall, Neville: *Life After Death* (Corgi Books, 1980).

Rinpoche, Sogyal: *The Tibetan Book of Living and Dying* (Rider, 1992). This book presents simple but powerful spiritual practices that anyone, whatever their religion or culture, can use to transform their lives, prepare for death, and help the dying.

Roth, Garbrielle: *Maps to Ecstasy* (Mandala, 1990).

Schiff, H. Sharnoff: *The Bereaved Parent* (Souvenir Press, 1977).

Siegal, S. Bernie (MD): *Love, Medicine and Miracles* (Arrow books, 1989). This inspiring book shows how 'terminal' patients in his care have taken control of their illness. Through the healing power of love, they have changed, enriched and prolonged their lives far beyond medical expectation.

Speck, Peter: *Loss and Grief in Medicine* (Bailliere & Tindall, 1978).

Tatelbaum, Judy: *The Courage to Grieve* (Heinemann, 1981).

Taylor, Liz McNeil: *Living with Loss* (Fontana, 1983).

Tompkins, Susan E.: *Is Death the End?* (Christian Education Movement, 1979).

Walbank, Susan: *Facing Grief: bereavement and the young adult* (Lutterworth Press, 1991).

Ward, Barbara and associates: *Good Grief (1): exploring feelings, loss and death with over 11s and adults*

Good Grief (2): exploring feelings, loss and death with under 11s (teaching packs and details of training courses available from Good Grief, 19 Bawtree Road, Uxbridge, Middlesex UB8 1PT).

Wass, Helena, and Charles A. Cott: *Childhood and Death* (Hemisphere, New York, 1985).

Wells, Rosemary: *Helping Children Cope with Divorce* (Sheldon, 1989).

Wertheimer, Alison: *A Special Star: the experiences of people bereaved by suicide* (Routledge, 1991).

Whitaker, Agnes (ed): *All in the End Is Harvest: an anthology for those who grieve* (Darton, Longman, Todd/CRUSE, 1984).

Worden, William: *Grief Counselling and Grief Therapy* (Tavistock, 1983).

Useful addresses

There are bereavement services and support groups in many towns now: contact your local library or Citizens' Advice Bureau for more information. If you want to explore your emotions in more depth, 'alternative' and personal growth magazines such as *Human Potential*, *Kindred Spirit* and *Caduceus* carry advertisements for trainings and support groups.

ACT (Action for the care of families whose Children have life-threatening and Terminal conditions), The Institute of Child Health, Royal Hospital for Sick Children, Bristol BS2 8BJ (0272 221556).

BACUP (Cancer), 121-3 Charterhouse Street, London EC1M 6AA. (071 608 1661; 0800 181199 from outside London).

British Association for Counselling (BAC; can recommend counsellors nationwide), 37a Sheep Street, Rugby, Warwickshire CV21 3BX (0788 78328/9)

British Humanist Association, 14 Lambs Conduit Passage, London WC1R 4RH (071 430 0908).

British Organ Donor Society (BODY), Balsham, Cambridge CB1 6DL (0223 893636).

British Society for Music Therapy, 69 Avondale Avenue, East Barnet, Hertfordshire EN4 8NB (081 368 8879).

Cancer Link, 17 Britannia Street, London WC1X 9JN (071 833 2451).

Compassionate Friends (international organization to support bereaved parents), 53 North Street, Bristol BS3 1EN (0272 539639 – helpline; 0272 665202 – admin.). There are also branches in the USA, New Zealand and Australia.

Contact a Family (support with special needs), 16 Strutton Ground, London SW1P 2HP (071 222 2695).

CRUSE (originally to support widows; now provides counselling service for all bereaved people), Cruse House, 126 Sheen Road, Richmond, Surrey TW9 1UR (081 940 4818/9042).

Disaster Action (a charity whose members have all been bereaved or survived a disaster. Their purpose is to share their common experience and provide support and guidance to those affected by disaster), 11 Lamb Street, London E1 6EA (071 377 6691).

Foundation for Black Bereaved Families, 11 Kingston Square, Salters Hill, London SE19 1DZ (081 761 7228).

Foundation for the Study of Infant Deaths, 15 Belgrave Square, London SW1X 8PS (071 235 1721).

Gay Bereavement Project, Unitarian Rooms, Hoop Lane, London NW11 8BS (081 455 8894).

Gingerbread (for single and divorced parents), 35 Wellington Street, London WC2 (081 240 0953).

Hospice Information, St Christopher's Hospice, 51-59 Lawrie Park Road, London SE26 6DZ (081 778 9252).

Jewish Bereavement Counselling Service, Kings Fund Centre for Health Service Development, 126 Albert Street, London NW1 1NF (071 267 6111).

Memorial Advisory Bureau, 139 Kensington High Street, London W8 6SX (071 937 0052).

Memorials by Artists, Harriet Frazer, Snape Priory, Saxmundham, Suffolk IP17 1SA (0728 888934).

Miscarriage Association, PO Box 24, Ossett, West Yorkshire (09248 30515).

National Association of Bereavement Services (NABS), 20 Norton Folgate, Bishopsgate, London E1 6DB (071 247 1080 – referrals; 071 242 1010 – admin).

National Association of Victim Support Schemes (NAVSS; support for families of murder victims), 17a Electric Lane, London SW9 8LA (081 326 1084).

National HIV Prevention Service, 82-6 Seymour Place, London W1H 5DB (071 724 7993).

Natural Death Centre, 20 Heber Road, London NW2 6AA (081 208 2853).

Parents of Murdered Children Support Group (part of the Compassionate Friends), 92 Corbets Tey Road, Upminster, Essex RM14 2BA (0708 640400).

Relate (formerly Marriage Guidance), Herbert Gray College, Little Church Street, Rugby CV21 3AP (0788 73241).

Samaritans, 10 The Grove, Slough, Berkshire SL1 1QP (0753 532713).

SANDS (Stillbirth & Neonatal Death Society), 28 Portland Place, London W1N 3DE (071 436 5881).

Twins and Multiple Births Association, 54 Parkway, Exeter, Devon EX2 9NF (0392 431605).

Voluntary Euthanasia Society, 13 Prince of Wales Terrace, London W8 5PG (071 937 7770).

Woodland Trust (plant-a-tree scheme to remember loved ones; also commemorative groves), Autumn Park, Dysart Road, Grantham, Lincolnshire NG31 6LL (0476 4297).